CU00749896

FROM REFORMATION TO IMPROVEMENT

FROM REFORMATION
TO IMPROVEMENT

*Public Welfare in
Early Modern England*

The Ford Lectures
Delivered in the University of Oxford
1994–1995

PAUL SLACK

CLARENDON PRESS · OXFORD
1999

Oxford University Press, Great Clarendon Street, Oxford ox2 6DP
Oxford New York
Athens Auckland Bangkok Bogotá Buenos Aires
Calcutta Cape Town Chennai Dar es Salaam Delhi Florence Hong Kong Istanbul
Karachi Kuala Lumpur Madras Madrid Melbourne Mexico City Mumbai
Nairobi Paris São Paulo Singapore Taipei Tokyo Toronto Warsaw
and associated companies in
Berlin Ibadan

Oxford is a trade mark of Oxford University Press

Published in the United States
by Oxford University Press Inc., New York

©Paul Slack 1999

The moral rights of the author have been asserted

All rights reserved. No part of this publication may be reproduced,
stored in a retrieval system, or transmitted, in any form or by any means,
without the prior permission in writing of Oxford University Press.
Within the UK, exceptions are allowed in respect of any fair dealing
for the purpose of research or private study, or criticism or review, as permitted
under the Copyright, Designs and Patents Act, 1988, or in the case of
reprographic reproduction in accordance with the terms of licences
issued by the Copyright Licensing Agency. Enquiries concerning
reproduction outside these terms and in other countries should be
sent to the Rights Department, Oxford University Press,
at the address above.

British Library Cataloguing in Publication Data
Data Available

Library of Congress Cataloging in Publication Data
Slack, Paul.
From Reformation to improvement: public welfare in early modern
England / Paul Slack.
p. cm.
"The Ford lectures delivered in the University of Oxford,
1994–1995."
Includes bibliographical references and index.
1. Public Welfare—England—History. 2. Social problems—England—
History. 3. Almshouses—England—History. 4. Workhouses-England—
History. 5. England—Social policy. 6. England—Social
conditions—16th century. 7. England—Social conditions—17th
century. 1. Title.
HV249.E89S55 1998
362.5´0942—dc21 98-13517
CIP
IBSN 0-19-820661-5

1 3 5 7 9 10 8 6 4 2

Typeset by Vera A. Keep, Cheltenham
Printed in Great Britain
on acid-free paper by
Bookcraft Ltd., Midsomer-Norton
Nr. Bath, Somerset

PREFACE

The text of this book is, in large part, the Ford Lectures as they were delivered in the University of Oxford in Hilary Term 1995. I have added a brief introduction and a final, concluding chapter, but resisted the temptation to expand the lectures further. Though based at various points on original research, their aim was to try to make sense of themes extending over a long period and to explore their interrelationship. A more detailed treatment would certainly have been possible, but it seemed to me that it might impede, if not altogether obscure, the flow of the argument. One consequence is the retention of some rhetorical echoes of the original oral delivery, but I have tried in the footnotes to substantiate my arguments and to indicate some of the areas where there is room for debate and further research.

I am greatly indebted to the Ford Electors for inviting me to give the lectures, an honour for any historian of Britain and one I especially value since it comes from my own University; and I owe them thanks for their hospitality and help in various ways. Many other colleagues and friends have given me advice in the course of preparing and delivering the lectures, especially Barbara Harvey, Paul Langford, Joan Thirsk and David Underdown, themselves Ford's Lecturers, and Gerald Aylmer, Marilyn Butler, Ronald Hutton, Joanna Innes, Martin Ingram, the late Jennifer Loach, and David Vaisey. I owe a particular debt to John Maddicott for his encouragement and example, extending now over more years than either of us cares to remember. A grant from the British Academy enabled me to gather material from local archives.

I have left out of the text which follows the references to the Reverend James Ford which opened and concluded the lectures. These were more than the customary expressions of piety. In the 1830s and 1840s, as Vicar of Navestock, Essex, Ford illustrated the later development of my theme. The parish records, now in the Essex Record Office, show that he was a conscientious chairman of the vestry, much involved in public and parochial welfare. He extended the schoolhouse, arranged for the repair of roads, and restored, under new trustees, the charities of his parish. One of his chief concerns was the workhouse which had originally been founded in 1741, in pursuance of the Workhouse Test Act of 1723 which has a place in Chapter 6 below; and he was as sceptical about the centralizing New Poor Law authorities of 1834 as any later defender of local and civil societies might have been. I like to think that my theme might have caught his interest, and that my final chapters comply in some measure with his intention, to fund lectures on 'the history of England from the Revolution [of 1688] to the present time'.

Parts of the lectures were drafted, where this preface is written, in what was once another parish workhouse set up under the auspices of the 1723 Act, at Kirkby Stephen in Westmorland. Reminders of the efforts of early modern Englishmen to reform and improve public welfare are all around us.

The Old Poorhouse   P.A.S.
Kirkby Stephen
August 1997

CONTENTS

LIST OF ABBREVIATIONS

Place of publication, or location of source, here and in the footnotes, is London, unless otherwise stated.

AO	Archives Office
APC	*Acts of the Privy Council*
BL	British Library
Bodl.	Bodleian Library, Oxford
Cal. SP Dom.	*Calendar of State Papers, Domestic*
DNB	*Dictionary of National Biography*
Econ. Hist. Rev.	*Economic History Review*
EETS	Early English Text Society
Eng. Hist. Rev.	*English Historical Review*
HMC	Historical Manuscripts Commission, Reports
OED	*Oxford English Dictionary*
P&P	*Past and Present*
PRO	Public Record Office
RO	Record Office
RP	*Rotuli Parliamentorum* (6 vols., 1783)
SR	M. Luders et al. (eds.), *Statutes of the Realm* (11 vols., 1810–28)
STC	*A Short-Title Catalogue of Books . . .1475–1640* (first compiled by A. W. Pollard and G. R. Redgrave; 2nd edn., 1976–91)
Thomason	*Catalogue of the Pamphlets . . . Collected by George Thomason, 1640–1661* (1908)
Trans. Roy. Hist. Soc.	*Transactions of the Royal Historical Society*
VCH	*Victoria County History*
Wing	D. Wing, *Short-Title Catalogue of Books . . . 1641–1700* (2nd edn., 1972–8)

INTRODUCTION

The subject of this book is public action for the public good in England between the early sixteenth and the early eighteenth centuries, the shapes that it assumed, and the reasons why it took the forms that it did. It is partly, therefore, a book about concepts, about the slogans and assumptions which justified and endorsed civil activity, many of them derived—like 'the public good' itself—from the notion of *bonum publicum*. The first such term to gain wide currency in English was 'the common weal', which determines my starting-point and is the subject of the first chapter. Another, established by the end of the seventeenth century, was 'public welfare', which gives this book its subtitle.[1]

Terminological innovation did not stop, of course, in the 1730s, which I have taken as my finishing-point. 'Social welfare', for example, appears to have been a coinage of the Victorian age.[2] Much of what follows will necessarily be concerned with all that that term now implies. Social welfare, however, has boundaries narrower than those of the common weal and the public welfare, and it is important to my theme that that attenuation should not be antedated. In the period with which I am concerned, welfare had not yet been separated out as a definite subset of concerns for governments and citizens, and at the beginning of the period its connotations were almost boundless. In much of Renaissance thought, as in the Middle Ages, there was no clear distinction between, on the one hand, the purposes of political and civic activity—the common good or public good—and, on the other, the political structures which might deliver it—the 'commonwealth' in its other sense. *Respublica*, another Latin origin of the common weal and the public good, encompassed both of these;[3] and the titles of my chapters are intended to indicate that the nature of political authority and the functions it served continued to be intimately related. I hope, therefore, that my pursuit of public welfare may throw some light on broader topics which are of particular interest to historians of the early modern period: perceptions of civil order, for example, and of the

---

[1] For these and equivalent terms, see below, pp. 6, 65, 75, 79, 83, 88, 100.
[2] Prof. Jose Harris informs me that John Ruskin may have been the first to use the term in something like its modern sense.
[3] Q. Skinner, *The Foundations of Modern Political Thought* (2 vols., Cambridge, 1978), vol. i, p. xxiii; J. H. Burns, *Lordship, Kingship and Empire: The Idea of Monarchy 1400-1525* (Oxford, 1992), 150-1.

boundaries of the public realm and the body politic, and hence the nature and extent of 'civic consciousness'.[4]

It follows that this book is as much about the agents who translated concepts into activity as it is about the terminology they employed. Some of those agents were corporate bodies, councils and corporations; others were individuals, from monarchs to magistrates and projectors. All of them found one formulation of the public good or another congenial, turned it to their own purposes, and in doing so determined the practical outcome. Sometimes the aim was reformation, with the implication of radical, comprehensive, once-for-all innovation (or restoration). Sometimes it was improvement, implying gradual, piecemeal change, not necessarily determined by any overarching theory or ambition. There would, I think, be little dispute that, in broad terms, the second became more prominent than the first in the course of the period, as my main title indicates. That too reflects a process in which the implications of welfare came to be more precisely and also more narrowly defined. I want to explore some of the reasons for the shift, and hope to justify my finishing date of 1740 by showing that it was by then fully completed.

Finally, the book pays some attention to the practical consequences: the various kinds of public provision for public welfare in early modern England, as well as the intellectual and political circumstances which determined their quality and quantity. They took many forms—from the poor law to the regulation of public health, from the reformation of manners to urban planning. Institutions—almshouses, hospitals, and workhouses—play a particularly prominent part in my story because they seem to me most effectively to exemplify its main contours. But my intention is to show that its diverse elements have some coherence, and in doing so to illuminate the English side of another theme which has interested historians of early modern Europe, and about which there is still a good deal to be said: the ways in which European states came to provide those manifold public services for the welfare of their citizens which have been held to be one of the more distinctive features of their history.[5]

The sorts of activity and attitude I have in mind can be illustrated by some remarks of Robert Burton, writing in the 1620s, in the middle of my period. Setting out 'an Utopia of mine own, a new Atlantis', he included among much else the following requirements:

cities . . . with fair broad and straight streets, houses uniform, built of brick and stone, like Bruges, Brussels . . . few or no suburbs . . . public halls for all societies,

---

[4] Cf. P. Collinson, *De Republica Anglorum, Or, History with the Politics Put Back* (Cambridge, 1990), 20-3; J. G. A. Pocock, *The Machiavellian Moment: Florentine Political Thought and the Atlantic Republican Tradition* (Princeton, NJ, 1975), ch. 10.

[5] E. L. Jones, *The European Miracle* (Cambridge, 1981), ch. 7. Cf. below, p. 160.

bourses, meeting-places, armouries, in which shall be kept engines for quenching of fire, . . . hospitals of all kinds, for children, orphans, old folks, sick men, madmen, soldiers, pest-houses etc. . . . conduits of sweet and good water, aptly disposed in each town, common granaries, as at Dresden . . . Stettin . . . Nuremberg etc.

That these were practical propositions and not mere Utopian fantasies is evident from the references to foreign cities; and Burton's attention was not confined to towns. In the countryside he would have 'some supervisors, that shall be appointed . . . to see what reformation ought to be had in all places, what is amiss, how to help it'. The supervisors would instruct landowners who either 'know not how to improve' their property, 'or else wholly respect their own, and not public good'.[6] Here are notions of reformation for the public good—and even of limited improvement to the same end—whose origins and development I wish to pursue.

It would be possible to examine in turn each of the topics, or groups of topics, on Burton's agenda. Rather than divide the subject according to modern government departments, however—as it might be, health, housing, education, and so on—I have chosen to follow the broad theme of welfare in its various guises through the period, noting the ways in which it could encompass different reforming purposes and strategies at different times, and concentrating on episodes of particular creativity or activity. At any particular moment, public welfare or one of its synonyms carried along with it a diverse baggage train of more or less essential bits of supporting equipment from Burton's list. In pursuing its itinerary through time, as bits of impedimenta were acquired or jettisoned, polished up or forgotten, it seemed to me most useful not to look at each individual piece of baggage, but to examine the lines along which the welfare train ran; and if it is objected that the train metaphor implies the kind of Whiggish teleology which Geoffrey Finlayson has criticized with respect to a later period,[7] I hasten to say that not all of the railway lines were parallel, and that some of them led to dead ends.

Nevertheless, there was a chronological sequence. The lines of development which I shall examine in successive chapters fell in roughly chronological order, though they overlapped, sometimes competed, and often intersected. And together they had a cumulative impact which helps to explain why English men and women were in some respects more confident about their collective capacity to improve their welfare in 1740 than they had been in 1500, and why they set about it in the ways that they did.

[6] Robert Burton, *The Anatomy of Melancholy*, ed. H. Jackson (Everyman edn., 1932), i. 97-101.
[7] G. Finlayson, *Citizen, State, and Social Welfare in Britain 1830-1990* (Oxford, 1994), 3.

THE COMMON WEAL

The fact that I begin in the early sixteenth century is not meant to imply that there had not earlier been policies and activity to advance the public welfare in a multitude of directions. Any such presumption would obviously be false. Religious institutions, both lay and clerical, had for centuries been involved in pious works, which were defined to include the maintenance of such public services as hospitals, roads, and bridges, as well as almsgiving; and public attitudes towards charity had been shifting with some deliberation since (and arguably in part in response to) the demographic and economic crises of the mid-fourteenth century.[1] Central government, council and parliament, had long been concerned with economic and social regulation, exemplified again since the Black Death in labour and sumptuary legislation. The institutions of local government also, in towns, manors, and parishes, were—from the 1460s if not before—increasingly involved in what might be termed social control: in regulating alehouses, vagrants, illicit sexual behaviour, and unruly pastimes.[2] The topics which will occupy this book all have a prehistory which will be referred to in what follows and drawn on for comparative purposes in the concluding chapter.

It nevertheless makes sense to start in 1500, and to consider the period up to the 1560s as a single entity. Over that period, projects, policies, and civic activity for welfare purposes all came together for the first time under a single banner—that of the common weal—and it was carried forward by combined (and sometimes contending) forces of unusual variety and determination. It was recognizably the first of a number of similarly con-

---

[1] G. Jones, *History of the Law of Charity 1532–1827* (Cambridge, 1969), 3–4; B. Tierney, *Medieval Poor Law* (Berkeley, Calif., 1959); B. Harvey, *Living and Dying in England 1100–1540: The Monastic Experience* (Oxford, 1993), ch. 1; M. Rubin, *Charity and Community in Medieval Cambridge* (Cambridge, 1987).

[2] S. J. Gunn, *Early Tudor Government, 1485–1558* (1995), 175–7; M. K. McIntosh, 'Local Responses to the Poor in Late Medieval and Tudor England', *Continuity and Change*, 3 (1988), 209–25; M. K. McIntosh, *Autonomy and Community: The Royal Manor of Havering, 1200–1500* (Cambridge, 1986), 255–61; M. Ingram, 'Reformation of Manners in Early Modern England', in P. Griffiths, A. Fox, and S. Hindle (eds.), *The Experience of Authority in Early Modern England* (1996), 58–9, 61; C. Dyer, 'The English Medieval Village Community and Its Decline', *Journal of British Studies*, 33 (1994), 407–29.

stituted cycles of innovation and diffusion which can be identified in the evolution of welfare policy and practice, and which will be considered in successive chapters. In the case of the common weal, I shall look first at what the banner may have signified for its several carriers, and then at how they employed it to practical effect.

I

It has always been easier to say what the common weal was not than to define what it was. It was not a programme, still less a manifesto for a party, not even a strategy. Well before the 1540s it was a rhetorical slogan conferring legitimacy on almost any public activity; and it was in origin simply a translation of a commonplace aspiration: an Englishing of the *comen profit*, *comen bien*, or *bien publique* to which fifteenth-century statutes had appealed.[3]

There were alternatives, as in Fortescue's 'the good publique' and 'the good universal profit'.[4] But 'weal' or 'wealth', meaning well-being, was preferred to 'profit' or 'good' for the noun, and 'common' to 'public' as the adjective. This latter preference, with its echo of 'the commonalty' and *communitas*, may not be fortuitous, for there are grounds for thinking that the common weal may have begun its rhetorical life as a Yorkist rallying cry.[5] It achieved something like respectability in the Acts of Resumption of 1467 and 1473, and then in other statutes and proclamations of 1482 and 1483.[6] In 1483 also it was being used locally, as by the Glovers of York and the Bakers of Exeter as well as the London Goldsmiths in their ordinances.[7]

---

[3] *SR* ii. 477, 509, 499. On the importance of the concept of *bonum commune*, the common good, in late medieval political thought more generally, see Q. Skinner, *The Foundations of Modern Political Thought* (2 vols., Cambridge, 1978), i. 58–9; A. Black, *Political Thought in Europe, 1250–1450* (Cambridge, 1992), 22–34.

[4] Sir John Fortescue, *The Governance of England*, ed. C. Plummer (Oxford, 1926), 350.

[5] D. Starkey, 'Which Age of Reform?', in C. Coleman and D. Starkey (eds.), *Revolution Reassessed: Revisions in the History of Tudor Government and Administration* (Oxford, 1986), 19–21. Prof. Elton, however, had some doubts about Dr Starkey's arguments: *Historical Journal*, 30 (1987), 715–16.

[6] *RP* v. 572; vi. 71, 219 (for Exeter), 244 (against traitors); T. Rymer, *Foedera* (3rd edn, 10 vols., 1739–45), vol. v, pt. 3, p. 138; L. C. Attreed (ed.), *The York House Books 1461–90* (2 vols., Stroud, 1991), ii. 714. For 'wele' and 'welfare' in a 1464 proclamation, see A. Allan, 'Royal Propaganda and the Proclamations of Edward IV', *Bulletin of the Institute of Historical Research*, 59 (1986), 152.

[7] A. Raine (ed.), *York Civic Records* (8 vols., Yorkshire Archaeological Society, Record Ser., 1939–53), iii. 183; L. T. Smith (ed.), *English Gilds: The Original Ordinances of More than One Hundred Early English Gilds* (EETS, 1870), 337; T. F. Reddaway and L. E. M. Walker, *The Early History of the Goldsmiths' Company 1327–1509* (1975), 211. The Goldsmiths had earlier used such terms as 'common profit' and 'common welfare': ibid. 212, 258. It is possible that the common weal caught on particularly early in the south-west: see, with respect to Exeter in 1498, I. S. Leadam (ed.), *Select Cases in the Court of Requests A.D. 1497–1569* (Selden Society, 12, 1898), 4, and an early statute reference, to the common weal of Devon, in *SR* iii. 53 (4 Henry VIII, c. 8).

It occurs in early Tudor legislation, notably on enclosure in 1489,[8] and in proclamations from 1490, including a clutch of six, between 1514 and 1516, on foreign as well as domestic policy, which may be said to have firmly established the term in public discourse.[9]

By then the common weal was sometimes dropping its usual attribution—'the common weal of the realm' or locally 'of the city'—and standing alone as an almost abstract though undefined ideal: the general well-being. That was what it meant in Edmund Dudley's *The Tree of Commonwealth* of 1510.[10] The fact that 'commonwealth' was also the usual term for a body politic or what we would call a state causes some difficulty for the historian. It is not easy to tell, for instance, whether such 'enemies of the common-wealth' as enclosers, engrossers, and vagrants were regarded as inimical to the state or to the general welfare.[11] It is likely that both were intended, for there was as yet no clear appreciation of the state in its modern abstract sense, and even if there had been, confusion between politics and welfare was too useful to be entirely abandoned. Thomas Starkey, struggling to define 'the true common weal' around 1530, thought that it 'rested in' a healthy 'political body', by which he meant 'the multitude of people, the number of citizens'; and the soul and heart of the body were 'civil order and politic law administered by officers and rulers', however constituted accord-ing to the particular 'governance of the comminalty and politic state'.[12] Systems of government were hence different from both the body politic and the common welfare, which could themselves perhaps be distinguished.[13] But it was much more important to Starkey, and to his less clear-minded contemporaries, that without the proper functioning of the first—govern-ment—there could be no perfect state of the second and the third—body politic and common welfare; and the perfect state of the second and the third, the common weal in each of its senses, amounted to the same thing.

In contexts relating to reformation, therefore, what Starkey elsewhere termed 'the common weal and politic order' were generally conflated in a

    [8] Ibid. ii. 542. 6 Henry VIII, c. 5, and 7 Henry VIII, c. 1, also on enclosure, followed suit (ibid. iii. 127, 176). In their Acts of Resumption, however, the early Tudors preferred 'universal weal' to the Yorkists' common weal: *RP* vi. 336; *SR* iii. 153.

    [9] P. L. Hughes and J. F. Larkin, *Tudor Royal Proclamations* (3 vols., New Haven, Conn., 1964–9), iii. 263 (coinage); i. 27 (grain exports), 57 (foreign affairs), 60 (coinage), 63 (Calais), 72 (coinage), 80 (pardon), 86 (Statute of Winchester) (1490–1511), 122 (enclosure), 123 (truce with France), 124 (livery), 126 (French peace); iii. 267 (retaining), 269 (apparel) (1514–16).

    [10] Edmund Dudley, *The Tree of Commonwealth*, ed. D. M. Brodie (Cambridge, 1948); N. Wood, *Foundations of Political Economy: Some Early Tudor Views on State and Society* (Berkeley, Calif., 1994), 78–9.

    [11] R. W. Heinze, *Proclamations of the Tudor Kings* (Cambridge, 1976), 95; *SR* iv(i). 5.

    [12] T. F. Mayer (ed.), *Thomas Starkey: A Dialogue between Pole and Lupset* (Camden Society, 4th ser., 37, 1989), 31, 33.

    [13] Starkey is not entirely consistent on this latter point: see T. F. Mayer, *Thomas Starkey and the Commonweal: Humanist Politics and Religion in the Reign of Henry VIII* (Cam-bridge, 1989), 115.

single ideal, what Clement Armstrong called 'the right order of common weal'.[14] Order does not, however, take us very far in understanding the modes of thought which sheltered under the common-weal umbrella. As resonant and more revealing is the concept of 'decay', the process which produced the antithesis of order. That at least implied that right order lay in the past, and needed only to be restored or re-formed. It also identified a range of targets for reform, both physical and moral, linked and bound together by the chains of metaphor and verbal association which were characteristic of contemporary rhetoric.

It may have been decayed rents in urban account rolls, as Professor Dobson suggests, which gave birth to those many complaints, beginning again under the Yorkists and pronounced in the 1480s, of towns in 'decay and . . . great poverty', in 'desolation, decay, ruin . . . without a reformation'.[15] But the image was soon extended: to husbandry and population, brought down by enclosure, and then to the whole common weal, 'long time . . . in sore decay', according to Dudley in 1510.[16] And decay bred corruption, and corruption disease, in an association which was as familiar in the analogy of the body politic as it was evident in the 'foul noyous and uneasy' streets of towns, 'replenished with much uncleanness and filth', according to paving and rebuilding statutes from the 1470s to the 1540s.[17] Fear of contamination—from the stench of plague, from pox and the sweat—cries out from early Tudor by-laws and proclamations, against 'all filthy and stinking things, ordures, corrupt airs and evil savours', against beggars with 'great sores or maladies tedious loathsome or abhorrible to be looked upon', and against prostitutes and brothels, closed in Southwark in 1546 because they spread 'corruption among the people'.[18]

Whether or not this language gained some of its power from real circumstances of rampant disease and visible urban dilapidation (and the case seems to me persuasive),[19] it was a mode of discourse which acquired

---

[14] S. J. Herrtage (ed.), *England in the Reign of Henry VIII*, pt. 1 (EETS, extra ser., 32, 1878), p. lv; S. T. Bindoff, 'Clement Armstrong and His Treatise of the Commonweal', *Econ. Hist. Rev.*, 14 (1944), 67, 71.

[15] R. B. Dobson, 'Urban Decline in Late Medieval England', *Trans. Roy. Hist. Soc.*, 5th ser., 27 (1977), 11–13; Attreed, *York House Books*, ii. 729; HMC, *14th Report*, app. viii, *Lincoln . . .* (1895), 263.

[16] 4 Henry VII, cc. 19, 16; Dudley, *Tree of Commonwealth*, 22. Later references are legion: see e.g. Herrtage, *England in the Reign of Henry VIII*, p. xcviii; F. J. Furnivall and J. M. Cowper (eds.), *Four Supplications 1529–1553* (EETS, extra ser., 13, 1871), 102.

[17] *RP* vi. 177; *SR* iii. 768. On the late 15th-c. paving statutes, see p. 162 below, and on the Henrician statutes for rebuilding 101 towns, see R. Tittler, 'For the "Re-edification of Towns": The Rebuilding Statutes of Henry VIII', *Albion*, 22 (1990), 591–605.

[18] London Corporation RO, Journal 11, fos. 348, 338; Hughes and Larkin, *Tudor Royal Proclamations*, i, no. 265, p. 365.

[19] P. Slack, 'Social Policy and the Constraints of Government, 1547–58', in J. Loach and R. Tittler (eds.), *The Mid-Tudor Polity c. 1540–1560* (1980), 95–6. Urban disease is easier to

a life of its own between the reigns of Edward IV and Edward VI. It was resilient because it could identify shortcomings in the environment, in society, and in the individual, and interpret them as part of a whole. By the 1540s the many 'faults' of the realm which needed to 'be amended' could be translated—as they were in one of Edward VI's schoolboy exercises—into 'sores' that must 'be cured'.[20] All kinds of mischief, heresy, and error were 'pestilent', and the laws against them 'medicines'; and most of the kingdom's moral failings could be subsumed under the headings of idleness and covetousness, the old deadly sins of sloth and avarice decked out in new clothes. These were now much trumpeted as afflictions of a whole society, the first the 'mother of all vices', the second a 'dropsy' which corrupted the body of the common weal.[21]

Just as it could readily take on board and refurbish the mental furniture of the past, moreover, so the diagnostic rhetoric which sustained the common weal could absorb new, foreign imports and evolve with them. It would not otherwise have persisted for so long. First humanism and then religious reform obviously had a profound effect. Apart from anything else, they provided models of ideal or nearly ideal commonwealths which lay in the European present, not the English past: Starkey's Flemish and French cities, for example—'so goodly, so well builded and so clean kept'[22]—and those godly citadels whose impact on England will occupy our attention in the next chapter. We shall see at many points in this book that there was a European reservoir of ideas and projects, accessible and often drawn upon by intellectuals and politicians, anxious that England should keep up with its neighbours. It is not at all obvious, however, that such novelties brought radical change at the difficult-to-plumb level of modes of public consciousness and frames of mind, at any rate before the 1560s. New images were added to the vocabulary and new or neglected targets identified, but they did not destroy the whole framework.

Thus the political 'corruption' diagnosed by civic humanists merely added a welcome extension to the old link between the processes of physical and

---

identify than decayed property. The latter must have been widespread after the dissolutions, but the extent of urban decay before then is controversial: see Dobson, 'Urban Decline' and, for a measured summary of the whole issue, A. Dyer, *Decline and Growth in English Towns 1400–1640* (1991).

[20] W. K. Jordan (ed.), *The Chronicle and Political Papers of King Edward VI* (1966), 165.

[21] Dudley, *Tree of Commonwealth*, 40; Hughes and Larkin, *Tudor Royal Proclamations*, i. 89, 154, 191; BL, Lansdowne MS 238, fo. 309ᵛ; W. R. D. Jones, *William Turner: Tudor Naturalist, Physician and Divine* (1988), 133, 188. For avarice and sloth in late medieval sermons, see G. R. Owst, *Literature and Pulpit in Medieval England* (Cambridge, 1933), ch. 6; S. Wenzel, *The Sin of Sloth: Acedia in Medieval Thought and Literature* (Chapel Hill, NC, 1967). A statute of 1463 had linked the 'decline, desolation and ruin' of towns to 'ociosite', idleness: 3 Edw. IV, c. 1.

[22] Mayer, *Starkey: A Dialogue*, 62.

moral decay. Humanist debate about the opposite poles of *negotium* and *otium* gave an intellectual edge to the hackneyed attack on *ociosite*, idleness.[23] The influence of Renaissance medicine, which extends from Linacre to several of the Edwardian reformers,[24] likewise reinvigorated familiar images of the body politic. Classical texts on husbandry, newly available in print in the years around 1500, conferred similar intellectual respectability on that concern with the plough which might otherwise seem a native English growth from an indigenous literature of complaint.[25] As for civic virtue, that could be added quite simply to the definition of the ideal common weal, as in Starkey's version: 'the prosperous and most perfect state of a multitude assembled together in any country, city or town, governed virtuously in civil life'.[26]

The language of Protestant godliness might seem very different from that of humanist civility, even when the latter had been transposed, as it was by Starkey, into a decidedly 'Christian civility'.[27] Godly reform was certainly more pessimistic: deeply sceptical of what rational civil policy might achieve, and dismissive of 'things that be only in *Utopia*', to quote the translator of Bucer's *De regno Christi*.[28] Drawing even more than Henrician humanists on earlier complaint literature, Edwardian preachers were less inclined to prescribe particular remedies for the ills of the commonwealth than to assert the imminence of God's punishments and the need for a general reformation.[29] Yet the social sins they identified were familiar ones, and the novelty

[23] Q. Skinner, 'Sir Thomas More's *Utopia* and the Language of Renaissance Humanism', in A. Pagden (ed.), *The Languages of Political Theory in Early Modern Europe* (1987), 128–9, 143–5, and Pagden's introduction, 8–9.

[24] e.g. John Hales translated Plutarch on 'the preservation of good health': STC 20062. See also below, p. 17. For Starkey and Sir Thomas Smith, see Mayer, *Starkey and the Commonweal*, 74–5; J. Strype, *The Life of the learned Sir Thomas Smith* (Oxford, 1820), 159–60.

[25] J. Thirsk, 'Making a Fresh Start: Sixteenth-Century Agriculture and the Classical Inspiration', in M. Leslie and T. Raylor (eds.), *Culture and Cultivation in Early Modern England: Writing and the Land* (Leicester, 1992), 18–19, 21.

[26] Mayer, *Starkey: A Dialogue*, 38. For a conciliar reference to civility in the context of public-health policy, see P. Slack, *The Impact of Plague in Tudor and Stuart England* (1985), 203.

[27] Mayer, *Starkey and the Commonweal*, 217–19.

[28] [Martin Bucer,] *A Treatise How by the Worde of God, Christian mens Almose ought to be distributed* (n.p., ?1557), 26. The translator was probably John Ponet: his additions can be identified by comparison with Bucer, *De Regno Christi* (Basle, 1557).

[29] When it comes to identifying the intellectual roots of early Tudor social policies, humanist and Protestant (and indeed older) strands seem to me so closely intertwined in their public rhetoric, and so similar in their implications for policy, as to be impossible to disentangle, though much ink has been spilled on the subject. The issue is considered in somewhat different ways by M. Todd, *Christian Humanism and the Puritan Social Order* (Cambridge, 1987) and P. A. Fideler, 'Poverty, Policy and Providence: The Tudors and the Poor', in Fideler and T. F. Mayer (eds.), *Political Thought and the Tudor Commonwealth* (1992), 198–9. Both would agree, however, that humanist and Protestant strands pointed to similar short-term goals. A later, Elizabethan shift of attention from social sins to individual ones might arguably be attributed to Protestantism alone, but even that had other roots, in a literary revival of classical satire: P. Collinson, *The Birthpangs of Protestant England* (1986),

of their evangelical insistence on correction and reformation can easily be exaggerated. The correction and reformation of manners, to take that vital touchstone of Reform, goes back, as Dr Ingram has reminded us, to the formulae of the ecclesiastical courts. Bishop Longland of Lincoln, no less, could be praised for his 'fervent zeal for reformation . . . as well of heretical doctrines as of misbehaviour in manners'—just as he could be a warm advocate of action 'for the commonweal' and an enclosure commissioner in 1526.[30]

It is of course the case that Longland would scarcely have sounded exactly like John Hales, exhorting people on his enclosure commissions twenty years later to 'godly and honest' reforms lest 'sword, famine and pestilence' overtake them. There was a new style, and it had plainly been audible to Roger Edgeworth, preaching in Marian Bristol, when he mocked the 'goodly preambles' of Edwardian statutes and those who claimed to set forth 'goodly and godly matters as . . . for a common wealth'.[31] Even so, the change of tone from goodly to godly was harmonious enough to make the transition relatively smooth, and to blur, for the moment, a shift in the rhetoric of reform which had radical implications for the future.

Much the same mixture of scarcely differentiated noises came back from the localities. 'The wretched life of ociositie or idleness . . . the root of all vice' was the target of Henry Gee, the great reforming mayor of Chester in 1539, taking his surveys of the poor, and attacking popular games, extravagant churchings, and women's fashions. He had plainly been reading proclamations; and so no doubt had his Marian successor, John Webster, who tried to ban Christmas Day breakfasts in 1557 because they encouraged people to spend the whole day 'idly in vice and wantonness'.[32] In the great dearth of 1556, the public provision of corn in Worcester could still be

18–19; A. McRae, *God Speed the Plough: The Representation of Agrarian England, 1500–1660* (Cambridge, 1996), ch. 3.

[30] Ingram, 'Reformation of Manners', 54; J. J. Scarisbrick, 'Cardinal Wolsey and the Common Weal', in E. W. Ives, R. J. Knecht, and J. J. Scarisbrick (eds.), *Wealth and Power in Tudor England: Essays Presented to S. T. Bindoff* (1978), 67; P. Gwyn, *The King's Cardinal: The Rise and Fall of Thomas Wolsey* (1990), 414.

[31] BL, Lansdowne MS 238, fo. 311ᵛ; J. Wilson (ed.), *Sermons very fruitfull, godly and learned by Roger Edgeworth* (Woodbridge, Suffolk, 1993), 362–3. In 1547 statutes on vagrancy and chantries had 'godly'and 'good and godly' purposes: *SR* iv(i). 5, 24, and others followed; but it is worth noting that in 1477 a statute banned 'ungodly and not commendable plays': *RP* vi. 188.

[32] R. H. Morris, *Chester in the Plantagenet and Tudor Reigns* (Chester, n.d.), 340, 336; BL, Harleian MS 2150, fos. 62ᵛ, 128ᵛ. On Gee, see J. Kermode, 'New Brooms in Early Tudor Chester?', in J. C. Appleby and P. Dalton (eds.), *Government, Religion and Society in Northern England 1000–1700* (Stroud, Glos., 1997), 144–58; A. D. Mills, 'Chester Ceremonial: Re-creation and Recreation in an English "Medieval" Town', *Urban History Yearbook*, 18 (1991), 5. 'Idleness and ociositie' occurs in a statute of 1533, encouraging the growing of hemp: *SR* iii. 421.

greeted as 'a godly purpose and a godly motion', despite Edgeworth's ful-
minations down the road in Bristol. Over in Norwich, even regulations for
street-cleaning had been 'good and godly' in 1552. When the supplicants for
the London hospitals in the same year proposed to remove 'our old sore of
idleness' from its 'filthy puddle' in the streets into the 'fresh field' of 'godly
exercise', they were drawing on a deep-seated tradition of instructively
mixed metaphors, as well as adding to a long agenda for reform.[33]

Given the flexible imagery and multifarious ends which could be attached
to the common weal, it is hardly surprising that it was popular, a tool so
widely used that it has left ample room for historical debate about whose
grip on it was first or firmest.[34] In fact, it could be employed with equal
conviction by Wolsey and his critics such as Skelton, by Cromwellian projectors and Edwardian moralists, by Northumberland (at least in his proclamations) as well as by Somerset, and by town councillors and jurors in
local courts leet into the reign of Mary and beyond. That wide appeal tells us
more, however, than that the rhetoric of the common weal was a flexible, all-
purpose tool. It shows also that it carried with it no implication about who
was authorized to use it, about who could rightly claim to be 'good commonwealthsmen'.[35] Consequently it left unresolved a fundamental issue
which will recur more than once in this book: the problem of agency. In
whose hands did the initiative for reform properly lie? And to whom should
projectors and moralists address their proposals?

Far from giving a clear answer to those questions, the rhetoric of the
common weal muddied the waters by never quite throwing off its par-
ticipatory and hence potentially subversive associations. That was why
Sir Thomas Elyot preferred 'public weal' to common weal as a translation of
res publica; the common weal was *res plebeia*.[36] Perhaps Elyot knew something of the political world of the City of London where, until the 1530s,
there were occasional committees for the common weal: sometimes meet-

[33] Worcs. RO, Worcester Chamber Order Book 1, 1540–1601, fo. 66ᵛ; W. Hudson and
J. C. Tingey, *The Records of the City of Norwich* (2 vols., 1910), ii. 127; W. Lempriere (ed.),
John Howes' MS. 1582 (1904), 47–8.
[34] Besides Starkey, 'Which Age of Reform?' and Elton in *Historical Journal*, 30 (1987),
715–17, see B. Bradshaw, 'The Tudor Commonwealth: Reform and Revision', *Historical
Journal*, 22 (1979), 455–76; J. A. Guy, 'The Tudor Commonwealth: Revising Thomas Crom-
well', *Historical Journal*, 23 (1980), 681–7; G. R. Elton, 'Reform and the "Commonwealth-
Men" of Edward VI's Reign', in P. Clark, A. G. R. Smith, and N. Tyacke (eds.), *The English
Commonwealth 1547–1640* (Leicester, 1979), 23–38; G. R. Elton, *Reform and Renewal:
Thomas Cromwell and the Common Weal* (Cambridge, 1973); and most recently
C. S. L. Davies, 'The Cromwellian Decade: Authority and Consent', *Trans. Roy. Hist. Soc.*,
6th ser., 7 (1997), 178–80.
[35] For some diverse later uses of the term, see S. L. Collins, *From Divine Cosmos to
Sovereign State* (Oxford, 1989), 79; A. McRae, 'Husbandry Manuals and the Language of
Agrarian Improvement', in Leslie and Raylor, *Culture and Cultivation*, 50; below, p. 27,
n. 98.
[36] Sir Thomas Elyot, *The Book named the Governor* (Everyman edn., 1962), 2.

ing daily, as representatives of the major companies did in 1527, debating 'matters concerning the common weal of the city', compiling agendas for 'reformation of many things' from weights and measures to tippling, bawdry, and vagabonds, and demanding more regular consultation between aldermen and the Common Council.[37] There could be little mileage in such reminders of medieval urban *communitas*, once there had been a 'Pilgrimage of Grace for the commonwealth', however, not to mention 'men called common wealths' agitating in 1549.[38] John Ponet's argument in 1556 that the commonwealth in both its senses was superior to the king similarly had no immediate future. By the 1560s there were evident risks in public discussion of what Sir Thomas Smith called 'feigned common wealths', Utopias 'such as never was nor never shall be'.[39] Like the publisher of Smith's own *Discourse* in 1581, Elizabethan advocates of the common weal had to disclaim anything that might seem 'prejudicial to any public authority'.[40]

Yet that still left open the question of where precisely, in the contested public territory of Professor Collinson's 'monarchical republic', public authority, and hence responsibility for the common weal, lay. It was in part the old problem of 'counsel' which Fortescue had addressed in the context of his *dominium politicum et regale*, and in part the new problem faced by intellectuals trying to import civic humanism into a kingdom without the clearly defined public and political arenas of city states where 'civil life' could be fully pursued.[41] When would-be reformers in the 1530s envisaged 'conservators', 'justices', or 'centeners' as guardians of the common weal, they necessarily had some difficulty defining their role: were they mere

[37] London Corporation RO, Letter Book O, fos. 47–52; I. W. Archer, *The Pursuit of Stability: Social Relations in Elizabethan London* (Cambridge, 1991), 30–1. For other instances, see BL, Add. MS 48019, fos. 225ᵛ–230 (n.d.) (also in [Richard Arnold,] *The Customs of London, otherwise called Arnold's Chronicle* (1811), 80–9); London Corporation RO, Journal 13, fo. 435ʳ (1535).

[38] M. L. Bush, ' "Up for the Commonweal" ', *Eng. Hist. Rev.*, 106 (1991), 299; F. W. Russell, *Kett's Rebellion in Norfolk* (1859), 202. Cf. John Twyne of Canterbury on the activities of *reipublicae consultores*, councillors of the commonwealth, in 1549: Corpus Christi College, Oxford, MS 256, fo. 154ᵛ; and a popular party 'for the common wealth' in Warwick in 1564: T. Kemp (ed.), *The Black Book of Warwick* (Warwick, 1898), 13.

[39] J. H. Burns, *Lordship, Kingship and Empire: The Idea of Monarchy 1400–1525* (Oxford, 1992), 152 n. 13; Sir Thomas Smith, *De Republica Anglorum*, ed. M. Dewar (Cambridge, 1982), 144. Cf. Morison's attack on 'imagined' commonwealths after the Pilgrimage: Fideler and Mayer, *Political Thought and the Tudor Commonwealth*, 203.

[40] E. A. Lamond (ed.), *A Discourse of the Common Weal of this Realm of England* (Cambridge, 1893), 146.

[41] P. Collinson, 'The Elizabethan Exclusion Crisis and the Elizabethan Polity', *Proceedings of the British Academy*, 84 (1994), 60–1, 71–5; Burns, *Lordship, Kingship and Empire*, 63–4; A. Fox and J. Guy, *Reassessing the Henrician Age* (Oxford, 1986), chs. 6, 7. Cf. the difficulties William Marshall had when translating Marsilius of Padua into language applicable to English circumstances: S. Lockwood, 'Marsilius of Padua and the Case of the Royal Ecclesiastical Supremacy', *Trans. Roy. Hist. Soc.*, 6th ser., 1 (1991), 89–119; and on this theme after 1570, see M. Peltonen, *Classical Humanism and Republicanism: English Political Thought 1570–1640* (Cambridge, 1995).

counsellors of the king, or his provincial military agents not unlike major-generals, or civilian executors of parliamentary statutes?[42] Clement Armstrong implied that cooperation would be necessary between the king, his lords, and 'the governors and rulers of his rich towns' if the common weal were to be reformed, but he thought also that the king should impose a 'discreet counsellor' on London to reform abuses directly.[43]

In the mixed polity of early and mid-Tudor England, the common weal was bound to be a vehicle which lacked a single agreed driver as much as it lacked a clear destination. Capacious and pliable, without any of the momentum which historians commonly attribute to coherent ideologies, if it was to move at all it needed a push — either from the pressure of circumstances or from the impetus of political will. When we look at what movement there was in the early sixteenth century, it appears that both kinds of stimulus were generally needed, whoever was in the driving seat — whether king and council, parliament, or the governors of Armstrong's rich towns. I want now briefly to consider the contribution of each of these.

II

No one could have more political will than that epitome of central authority, Thomas Wolsey; and few politicians ever faced quite the same circumstantial pressures, including those of famine, pestilence, and war. It would, I hope, be generally recognized that the cardinal presided over a period of creativity in social policy unparalleled since the mid-fourteenth century. It opened with the 'common weal' proclamations of 1514–16, and its most conspicuous innovations were indeed directed to the management of crises: the beginning of the public effort to control plague in 1518; the first commissions for grain searches and market provision in the dearth of 1527;[44] the great enclosure commission of 1517 sparked off by 'commotions' and riots in Hampshire.[45]

---

[42] Mayer, *Starkey and the Commonweal*, 115–16; T. F. T. Plucknett, 'Some Proposed Legislation of Henry VIII', *Trans. Roy. Hist. Soc.*, 4th ser., 19 (1936), 136; G. R. Elton, *Studies in Tudor and Stuart Politics and Government* (4 vols., Cambridge, 1974–92), ii. 72–3; C. Phythian-Adams, *Desolation of a City: Coventry and the Urban Crisis of the Late Middle Ages* (Cambridge, 1979), 277.

[43] R. H. Tawney and E. Power, *Tudor Economic Documents* (3 vols., 1924), iii. 122, 112.

[44] Slack, *Impact of Plague*, 201–2; P. Slack, 'Dearth and Social Policy in Early Modern England', *Social History of Medicine*, 5 (1992), 3–4. For Wolsey's activism in matters of common weal, see also P. Gwyn, *The King's Cardinal: The Rise and Fall of Thomas Wolsey* (1990), ch. 10.

[45] Scarisbrick, 'Wolsey and the Common Weal'; *Letters and Papers, Foreign and Domestic, of the Reign of Henry VIII* (38 vols., 1862–1932), *Addenda*, pt. i, pp. 50–1; A. L. Merson (ed.), *The Third Book of Remembrance of Southampton, 1514–1602* (3 vols., Southampton Record Ser., 1952–65), i. 20–2, 25. The enclosures attacked outside Southampton had, ironically, been made 'for a common weal' (p. 22). Similar disturbances about enclosure of town lands in Coventry (1509), Nottingham (1512), Gloucester (1513), and London (1514) had provoked the 1515 enclosure statute: Phythian-Adams, *Desolation of a City*, 183; W. H. Stevenson et al. (eds.), *Records of the Borough of Nottingham* (6 vols., 1882–1914), iii. 340;

Repeated as they were, however, for another century, what were initially
emergency measures became part of that Tudor armoury of social paternal-
ism of which Wolsey must be acknowledged the founder.

What has not, perhaps, been sufficiently appreciated is the extent of the
local impact of the cardinal's energy in matters of common weal. It is
particularly notable in the five years after 1517, when several towns were
badging their poor, taking surveys of grain, or setting up their first corn
stocks.[46] Wolsey's interference in London after Evil May Day 1517 is well
known. In the next twelve months there were orders tightening up the
watch, expelling vagrants, badging beggars, controlling food prices, and
cleaning the streets 'for the avoiding of contagious infections', some of them
'at the commandment of the lords of the king's most honourable council',
others for 'good furtherance . . . of the common weal'.[47] But the authorities
of York and Lincoln, Wolsey's sees, were also cleaning ditches and streets
and dealing with beggars and vagrants at the same time.[48] The cardinal's visit
to Norwich in 1517 coincided with orders for the conservation of river
banks, for a canal-raker, and for collecting muck 'in the ways'; and his visit
to King's Lynn in 1520 with regulations 'for reformation of pulling . . . down
of houses', for nightly watches and lanterns in the streets.[49] When one
finds the court leet of Coventry in 1517 and 1518 making by-laws against
vagrants, unlawful games, suspect alehouses, for 'cleaning . . . and sweeping
of the streets . . . also to see the pavements well paved', all 'for the wealth of
the city', and then in 1520 taking a 'view' of the number of people and the
amount of corn in each ward, one suspects that Wolsey was interfering there
too, cleansing the common weal from top to bottom.[50]

Gloucestershire RO, GBR B2/1, fos. 118ᵛ–19; Tawney and Power, *Tudor Economic Documents*, iii. 17–18.

[46] For other examples besides those cited below, see P. Slack, *Poverty and Policy in Tudor
and Stuart England* (1988), 116; Slack, 'Dearth and Social Policy', 4.

[47] London Corporation RO, Journal 11, fos. 277ʳ, 286ᵛ–287, 289ᵛ, 305ʳ, 319, 323ᵛ–324,
337–8, 348; Repertory 3, fos. 164, 166ʳ, 168ᵛ, 189ᵛ, 190, 192ᵛ, 194ʳ; Heinze, *Proclamations of
the Tudor Kings*, 17.

[48] Raine, *York Civic Records*, iii. 59, 66; HMC, *Lincoln*, 27. For Wolsey's relations with
these towns, see D. M. Palliser, *Tudor York* (Oxford, 1979), 46–7; J. W. F. Hill, *Tudor and
Stuart Lincoln* (Cambridge, 1956), 23–5.

[49] Hudson and Tingey, *Records of Norwich*, vol. ii, pp. cxxxviii, 109–10; King's Lynn
Borough Archives, Hall Book 5, fos. 219ᵛ–220ʳ, 224, 227ʳ, 232ᵛ. The mayor of Lynn at the end
of 1520 was Thomas Miller, whom Wolsey put into the town as governor when its liberties
were suspended in 1521–4, and who was MP when Lynn and Norwich together promoted the
first Henrician rebuilding Acts of 1534: S. T. Bindoff, *The History of Parliament: The House
of Commons 1509–1558* (3 vols., 1982), ii. 605–6.

[50] M. D. Harris (ed.), *The Coventry Leet Book* (4 vols., EETS 134, 135, 138, 146, 1907–13),
iii. 652–3, 656, 658, 662, 674–5. Wolsey's links with Coventry are uncertain, but one of his
agents in his dealings with London was Roger Wigston, whose family had Coventry ties and
who became Recorder of the town in 1529: London Corporation RO, Repertory 3, fo. 192ᵛ;
Phythian-Adams, *Desolation of a City*, 350.

Taken one by one, many of these regulations naturally had precedents. York had badged beggars in 1515, and had been trying to keep its streets clean for generations; in Coventry, aldermen had been told to search their wards for examples of 'misrule' in 1510.[51] What is striking, however, is the near-coincidence of all these different kinds of activity in towns scattered across the country between 1517 and 1522. It is a distinctive concentration, a cluster of related episodes of the kind we shall see at many other points in this book. Wolsey's cluster may not have been the first. The 1480s would probably repay attention, since central government interest in the common weal and urban decay was then matched by local by-laws like those in Leicester for 'the good police' of the town and 'a very due reformation, remedy and correction' of nuisances from vagabonds and bawds to unpaved streets.[52] But Wolsey's commissions, his exemplary punishments in Star Chamber, his efforts to enforce sumptuary and labour laws which attracted the derision of John Skelton, and his 1526 articles to justices of the peace, all imparted a new drive to local government, just as surely as his patronage of the new learning introduced a device as 'very good for the common wealth' as the College of Physicians.[53] The cardinal's style of central command was one mode of responding to the social and intellectual stimuli which made reform of public welfare necessary and fashionable all over western Europe between the 1520s and the 1540s.

A second, more distinctively English mode of response to the same stimuli was the legislative one, though it had some of the same ingredients as central command. There is no need to repeat Sir Geoffrey Elton's reconstruction of the crucial role played by Thomas Cromwell in managing parliamentary (and other) projects for reform of the common weal; and I have no wish to question the importance of the foundations for the Elizabethan poor law which were laid in Parliament between the 1530s and the 1550s. A per-

[51] Raine, *York Civic Records*, iii. 166, i. 113, ii. 165; *Coventry Leet Book*, iii. 629.

[52] M. Bateson et al. (eds.), *Records of the Borough of Leicester* (7 vols., Cambridge and Leicester, 1899–1974), ii. 305–9, 317, 324. Cf. *VCH Wiltshire*, vi (1962), 100; Attreed, *York House Books*, i. 258, 394–5; Raine, *York Civic Records*, i. 58, 113; Stevenson et al., *Records of Nottingham*, ii. 325, 347–9; F. J. Furnivall (ed.), *The Gild of St Mary, Lichfield* (EETS, extra ser., 114, 1920), 11–13.

[53] Gunn, *Early Tudor Government*, 177; J. A. Guy, *The Cardinal's Court: The Impact of Thomas Wolsey in Star Chamber* (Hassocks, Sussex, 1977), 30–3, 120; G. Walker, *John Skelton and the Politics of the 1520s* (Cambridge, 1988), 157; Hughes and Larkin, *Tudor Royal Proclamations*, i. 153–4; 14 & 15 Henry VIII, c. 5. For Wolsey's relations with the localities, see also H. Garrett-Goodyear, 'The Tudor Revival of Quo Warranto and Local Contributions to State Building', in M. S. Arnold, T. A. Green, S. A. Scully, and S. D. White (eds.), *On the Laws and Customs of England: Essays in Honor of Samuel E. Thorne* (Chapel Hill, NC, 1981), 231–95; and for the financial and foreign-policy pressures which inspired his domestic policies, see S. J. Gunn, 'Wolsey's Foreign Policy and the Domestic Crisis of 1527–8', in S. J. Gunn and P. G. Lindley (eds.), *Cardinal Wolsey: Church, State and Art* (Cambridge, 1991), 174–5; S. J. Gunn, 'The Act of Resumption in 1515', in D. Williams (ed.), *Early Tudor England: Proceedings of the 1987 Harlaxton Symposium* (Woodbridge, Suffolk, 1989), 90–2.

manent welfare apparatus was being forged out of disparate local and legislative efforts to cleanse the physical and moral environment still further, by
employing the idle, supporting the deserving, listing and supervising devi-
ants and unfortunates of all kinds.[54] It must be admitted, however, that
historians of the poor law, including the present writer, have sometimes been
mesmerized by its local antecedents and its later development, and have
been tempted to overstate both its insularity and the smooth inevitability of
its legislative evolution.

The innovatory draft bill for the poor of 1535, for example, which became
in much reduced form the 1536 statute and so started the whole process, was
a very mixed bag. Its first part, with proposals for public works, certainly
seems to rest as firmly on English experience as it did on the 'common
wealth' project by Christopher St German, which Professor Guy has identified.[55] Much of the second part of the 1535 draft owes more to foreign
models, however, particularly in its description of the duties of search and
supervision of two 'censors or overseers of poverty and correctors of idleness' in each parish. 'Overseers' is William Marshall's word for very similar
officers in Ypres, whose regulations for the poor he had translated; while the
'censors' come from that most famous of all humanist tracts on welfare, the
De Subventione Pauperum of 1526, written for the magistrates of Bruges by
Juan Luis Vives, the friend of More and client of Wolsey.[56]

Though less easy to document, such influences continued. How could
they not when parliaments contained, alongside dyed-in-the-wool representatives of the provinces, men whose education or experience gave them
some inkling of European horizons? The House of Commons of 1547, for
example, had in it the king's teachers, Cheke and Cooke, Thomas Phaer,
humanist lawyer and physician, and others whom Phaer would have termed
'learned men having a zeal to the common wealth': Richard Morison and
William Turner, for example, who had studied in Italy, and Thomas Smith,
the civilian and ex-student at Padua, who might, Mr Davies suspected, have
influenced the Vagrancy Act which this House rushed through all its stages
in a week.[57] That experiment in forced labour, the unworkable 'Slavery

[54] Elton, *Reform and Renewal*; Slack, *Poverty and Policy*, 114–24; E. M. Leonard, *The Early History of English Poor Relief* (Cambridge, 1900), chs. 3, 4.
[55] G. R. Elton, 'An Early Tudor Poor Law', in *Studies in Tudor and Stuart Politics and Government*, ii. 137–54; J. A. Guy, *Christopher St German on Chancery and Statute* (Selden Society, supplementary ser., 6, 1985), 25–31, 127–35.
[56] Elton, *Studies in Tudor and Stuart Politics and Government*, ii. 145; F. R. Salter (ed.), *Some Early Tracts on Poor Relief* (1926), 51, 19; Guy, *St German on Chancery*, p. 30 n. Neither censors nor overseers survived into the 1536 statute, but the latter reappeared in 1572: see below, p. 38.
[57] C. S. L. Davies, 'Slavery and Protector Somerset: The Vagrancy Act of 1547', *Econ. Hist. Rev.*, 2nd ser., 19 (1966), 543–4; biographies of those named in Bindoff, *House of Commons 1509–1558*; Thomas Phaire, *The Boke of Chyldren* (1955), 15. It is tempting to add to the list William Thomas, who wrote a history of Italy in 1549 praising its hospitals, but he may not

Statute', would have been cheered on by many other Members too: by William Stumpe, the industrial entrepreneur of Malmesbury who was involved in plans for employment at Osney Abbey, Oxford, by Thomas Bell, who had a similar project on foot in Gloucester, and by representatives of towns currently embarked on schemes for poor relief, like King's Lynn, Coventry, and London.[58] This latter group of Members must have been influential when the same House had first to repeal the Vagrancy Act and then in 1552 to replace it with something more practicable. Parliament was thus well suited to fashion what Dr Loach accurately called 'a peculiarly English and concrete form of "civic humanism" '.[59] But Parliament was not acting in splendid isolation; and neither could it do its job quickly. Ten years later, in 1563, an element of 'coercion' was at last put behind charitable collections in a new poor relief Act, probably at the instigation of Members from Exeter;[60] but even then the task of producing that unique English achievement, a uniform statutory system of parish rates, was only half begun.

In some ways more productive before the 1570s than the legislative option was a third mode of innovation, which might be called the local option: the process of evolution and emulation, generally within and between towns, which produced devices such as surveys and assessments for the poor before they had statutory backing. It also produced the various expedients which enabled urban authorities to cling onto some of the welfare resources threatened by the dissolutions, provided that they were willing to appeal to the same propaganda in favour of 'deeds of charity and common wealth' as the central government.[61] Professor Scarisbrick has shown how towns managed in the 1540s and 1550s to remodel, and so retain, a portion of the institutions and endowments which had supported charitable and public works. Schools have received particular attention, without the last word

have entered the House until 1552: E. P. Chaney, 'Philanthropy in Italy: English Observations on Italian Hospitals, 1545–1789', in T. Riis (ed.), *Aspects of Poverty in Early Modern Europe* (Florence, 1981), 192.

[58] Bindoff, *House of Commons 1509–1558*, iii. 404; ii. 413; King's Lynn Borough Archives, Hall Book 6, fos. 69ᵛ, 75ʳ, 89ᵛ; Phythian-Adams, *Desolation of a City*, 220.

[59] J. Loach, 'Parliament: A "New Air"?', in Coleman and Starkey, *Revolution Reassessed*, 117.

[60] 5 Eliz. I, c. 3; D. Dean, 'Locality and Parliament: The Legislative Activities of Devon's MPs during the Reign of Elizabeth', in T. Gray, M. Rowe, and A. Erskine (eds.), *Tudor and Stuart Devon: The Common Estate and Government. Essays presented to Joyce Youings* (Exeter, 1992), 83, 84–5.

[61] 2 & 3 Edw. VI, c. 5. Such deeds included 'repairing of walls, bridges, setting poor people on work'. Cf. *Cal. Patent Rolls 1553*, 503; J. J. Scarisbrick, 'Henry VIII and the Dissolution of the Secular Colleges', in C. Cross, D. Loades, and J. J. Scarisbrick (eds.), *Law and Government under the Tudors: Essays Presented to Sir Geoffrey Elton* (Cambridge, 1988), 64–5.

having been written on the subject.[62] More instructive in the context of this book, however, both because of their continuing importance for English welfare and because they can be set in an international context, are hospitals.

English hospitals had not been isolated from Renaissance ideas about their function and shape before the Reformation. In the early fifteenth century, for example, there were abortive moves to impose 'correction and reformation' on institutions which seemed 'for the most part decayed'.[63] The English stock of 600 or so hospitals and almshouses[64] was nevertheless still being added to by pious donors in 1505, when Henry VII founded the Savoy. Designed 'to receive and lodge nightly one hundred poor folks', the Savoy was in some respects traditional in purpose, a refuge and hospice rather than a reformatory. But its constitution was based on the statutes of Santa Maria Nuova in Florence, which the king examined, and its cruciform shape looked back to the Great Hospital in Milan. It introduced a breath of fresh air from the movement for hospital reform in Italy. Under construction while More was writing about the hospitals of *Utopia*, and intended to be matched by similar huge foundations in Coventry and York, the Savoy Hospital might well have set a fashion.[65] Moreover, we have only to look ahead—to Cardinal Pole's and Bishop Bonner's encouragement of such works of charity—to see that English towns might have taken part in the new philanthropy of the Counter-Reformation, and added to the great hospitals a host of lesser institutions and confraternities intimately involved with reclaiming and redeeming the undeserving, abject poor.[66]

Religious reformation stopped, or rather distorted that. With fraternities disbanded and charitable endowments in lay hands, if hospitals were to

[62] J. J. Scarisbrick, *The Reformation and the English People* (Oxford, 1984), 67–8, 114–26. On schools, see N. Orme, *English Schools in the Middle Ages* (1973), ch. 10, and the work of Joan Simon, most recently 'The State and Schooling at the Reformation and After: From Pious Causes to Charitable Uses', *History of Education*, 23 (1994), 157–69. How towns managed to afford the investment necessary in former guild and monastic property remains something of a puzzle, but for some welcome light on the subject, see R. Tittler, *The Reformation and the Towns: Politics and Political Culture in England c.1540–1640* (Oxford, 1998).

[63] R. M. Clay, *The Medieval Hospitals of England* (1909), 212, 222, 229; 2 Henry V, c. 1.

[64] McIntosh, 'Local Responses to the Poor', 220–3. On the difficulty of counting surviving institutions, see C. Rawcliffe, *The Hospitals of Medieval Norwich* (Norwich, 1995), 149.

[65] H. M. Colvin (ed.), *The History of the King's Works*, iii *1485–1660 (Part I)* (1975), 196–206; K. Park and J. Henderson, ' "The First Hospital Among Christians": The Ospedale di Santa Maria Nuova in Early Sixteenth-Century Florence', *Medical History*, 35 (1991), 164–88; J. Henderson, 'The Hospitals of Late-Medieval and Renaissance Florence: A Preliminary Survey', in L. Granshaw and R. Porter (eds.), *The Hospital in History* (1989), 74–5; Johannes J. Gilinus, . . . *del hospitale grande de Milano* (?Milan, 1508), ch. 8.

[66] E. Duffy, *The Stripping of the Altars: Traditional Religion in England 1400–1580* (1992), 552; B. Pullan, 'Support and Redeem: Charity and Poor Relief in Italian Cities from the Fourteenth to the Seventeenth Century', *Continuity and Change*, 3 (1988), 193–202.

survive at all their purposes had to be redefined—and redefined by secular and civic governors. That too, however, was a European phenomenon, as the Merchant Adventurers among the London aldermen trying to reconstruct their own welfare facilities must have been well aware. In 1538 they petitioned for the re-establishment of St Bartholomew's and St Thomas's, not, they hastened to say, for 'priests, canons and monks carnally living', but for 'the miserable poor lying in every street, offending every clean person passing by the way, with their filthy and nasty savours'. Bishop Ridley could add an evangelical voice: Christ himself was to be taken up from the streets, cleaned and given succour in what became the five carefully differentiated hospitals, for the sick, the old, orphans and foundlings, lunatics, and the idle. But it was the governors of the City, working away in committee on 'plats' and models, who perfected a scheme designed to reform and rehabilitate the poor and remove poverty from view, if not eliminate it altogether. By the time Edward VI gave them the lands of the Savoy and Bridewell, once his father's palace, they had ready what they called 'a perfect platform of a common wealth'.[67] In its fusion of civic opportunism, Christian charity, and educated patrician self-interest, it was not unlike the blueprints for centralized welfare institutions in several continental Reformed cities.

One part of the London apparatus was unusual, however, possibly even unique: Bridewell, 'the house of labour and occupations' of 1552 where the poor were to be set to work in 'sciences profitable to the common weal'.[68] A hospital specifically and solely for employment appears to have no parallel in the many published welfare projects, from Flanders to Poland, which often stressed the need for labour but visualized its place outside institutions.[69] So far as I am aware, it had no precise precedent in reality in other European cities or states, which could generally either banish idle beggars or find work for them in the galleys. The closest parallel, and a possible model, was the Trinity Hospital of Paris, set up by the Parlement in 1545 to provide religious exercises, education, and work, chiefly for children. One of its purposes was certainly to train its inmates in a variety of trades, and it may have been known to some of the Londoners, like Richard Grafton, who had Parisian connections.[70] But it was in effect a combination of Christ's Hospital

---

[67] *Memoranda, References, and Documents relating to the Royal Hospitals of the City of London* (1836), appendix, pp. 1–4; Tawney and Power, *Tudor Economic Documents*, ii. 312; Lempriere, *John Howes' MS. 1582*, 17; Slack, 'Social Policy and the Constraints of Government', 108–13.

[68] Tawney and Power, *Tudor Economic Documents*, ii. 311; *Memoranda*, p. 57.

[69] Salter, *Early Tracts*, 14–15, 91; Andreas Fricius Modrevius [Modrzewski], *Commentariorum de Republica emendanda* (2nd edn., Basle, 1559), 63. Cf. N. Z. Davis, *Society and Culture in Early Modern France* (1975), 42–3, for provision of work outside institutions in Lyon.

[70] H. Heller, *Labour, Science and Technology in France 1500–1620* (Cambridge, 1996), 39–40. On innovation in Paris, see also B. Geremek, *Poverty: A History* (Oxford, 1994), 128–30, 146.

and Bridewell, and it never acquired the local prominence or international renown of the latter.

If Paris may have provided one inspiration, Bridewell also had roots closer to home. One was no doubt the recent failure of an alternative means of setting the poor to work, the forced labour promised by the 1547 Slavery Act. It sprang also from an older English interest in labour productivity, which had been given fresh point by the peculiar economic conditions of the 1540s, and by the new economic thinking stimulated by debasement and inflation. Bridewell's founders were aware of the need for import substitutes, for example, promising metalworking found nowhere else in the realm, and the production of caps—a direct echo of the *Discourse*—as good as those made in France.[71] But whatever its origins, Bridewell brought something new to European experiments with remodelled institutions, and spawned offspring in cities across the continent.[72] England's first contribution to European welfare strategies was not the national poor rate (though that was the second); its first contribution was the workhouse.

Not surprisingly, Bridewell and the other London hospitals were even more influential in the English provinces. Other towns adopted part—or even, in miniature, the whole—of the London system in buildings they had rescued from the debris of the dissolution. Several towns borrowed the name of Christ's Hospital, and some copied its intended function as the central manager of the whole of civic poor relief: St John's Hospital, Winchester, Bablake Hospital, Coventry, and St Bartholomew's Hospital, Gloucester are examples.[73] In early Elizabethan Ipswich, Christ's Hospital in the old Blackfriars supplemented Henry Tooley's great foundation of almshouses by providing space for orphans, the sick, and a bridewell and its founders obtained copies of the London orders as a model. Bablake Hospital Coventry incorporated Bond's Hospital, founded for the old in 1506, a new hospital for boys modelled on Christ's, and finally, in the 1570s, a bridewell, all of them round a single quadrangle. Somewhat similar arrangements seem to have been intended in Canterbury, and also in Oxford, where the earl of Huntingdon gave the city the dissolved College of St Mary in New Inn Hall Street in 1562 as a hospital for the poor sick, for the education of ten poor children, and to set ten poor adults to work.[74] It was

---

[71] J. Thirsk, *Economic Policy and Projects* (Oxford, 1978), 14–18, 24–9; Tawney and Power, *Tudor Economic Documents*, ii. 308; Lamond, *Discourse*, 63, 126–7.

[72] P. Spierenburg, *The Prison Experience: Disciplinary Institutions and Their Inmates in Early Modern Europe* (New Brunswick, NJ, 1991), 25–6, ch. 3; C. Lis and H. Soly, *Poverty and Capitalism in Pre-Industrial Europe* (Hassocks, Sussex, 1979), 118–20.

[73] A. Rosen, 'Winchester in Transition, 1580–1700' in P. Clark (ed.), *Country Towns in Pre-industrial England* (Leicester, 1981), 158; 14 Eliz. I, c. 5, ss. xxx, xxxi.

[74] J. Webb (ed.), *Poor Relief in Elizabethan Ipswich* (Suffolk Records Society, 9, 1966), 12, 14; J. Webb, *Great Tooley of Ipswich* (Ipswich, 1962), 150; *VCH Warwickshire*, viii (1969), 135, 137, 139, 275; ii (1908), 329; E. Hasted, *The History and Topographical Survey of the County of Kent* (12 vols., 1797–1801), xi. 189; *VCH Oxfordshire*, iv (1979), 344.

never much more than a paper scheme, but it was another attempt to create a perfect miniature commonwealth: a model house of learning and labour, correction and reformation.

The three modes of development of social policy, whose intersecting trajectories I have tried to sketch out, were, of course, connected with one another, and connected by more than chronology and a roughly common subject-matter. It is possible to piece together parts of what must have been an elaborate network of links of family and interest binding them together. If we start with Wolsey's enclosure commission of 1517, for example, Roger Wigston one of its members, was brother of William, founder of the famous hospital at Leicester in 1513, and he was later Recorder of Coventry. The John Hales added to the enclosure commission in 1518 was related and perhaps known to the later John Hales, of Coventry and the 1548–9 commissions.[75] The insistent Coventry connection—even St German had contacts there—might lead us to one of its mayors, Julian Nethermill, probable instigator of the great census of 1523, who married his daughter to William Garrard, haberdasher of London; and Garrard sat on a 1545 committee considering London's hospital scheme, alongside John Royse, who endowed Abingdon School in the 1560s.[76] The founders of the London hospitals naturally point us in all directions, as in the case of Richard Gresham, client of Wolsey and Cromwell, friend of Henry Tooley of Ipswich, patron of Armagil Waad—which takes the chain forward to Cecil's Elizabethan commonwealth—and a member of the Mercers Company—which takes the chain back to Linacre and Thomas More.[77]

Such links could be multiplied. I illustrate them not in order to show that there was anything like a 'commonwealth party': quite the contrary. They show what one might expect: that shared institutions, cultural backgrounds, and commercial associations gave the English élite—provincial as well as metropolitan—similar experiences of public action and similar public attitudes.[78] The people I have mentioned also spanned three political

---

[75] Bindoff, *House of Commons 1509–1558*, iii. 612; J. C. Wedgwood and A. D. Holt, *History of Parliament: Biographies 1439–1509* (1936), 948–9. The genealogy of the Hales family is difficult to unravel, but John II was trained in the household of Christopher Hales, cousin of John I: Bindoff, *House of Commons 1509–1558*, ii. 274–7.

[76] Guy, *St German on Chancery*, 6–7; P. W. Hasler, *The History of Parliament: The House of Commons 1558–1603* (3 vols., 1981), iii. 120–1; Bindoff, *House of Commons 1509–1558*, ii. 191; Phythian-Adams, *Desolation of a City*, 71, 260; London Corporation RO, Journal 15, fo. 213; A. E. Preston, *The Church and Parish of St. Nicholas, Abingdon* (Oxford Historical Society, 99, 1935), 297–8. Richard Grafton, another member of the London connection, also had Coventry links and was MP for the town in 1563: *VCH Warwickshire*, viii. 249; Hasler, *House of Commons 1558–1603*, ii. 210–11.

[77] Bindoff, *House of Commons 1509–1558*, ii. 249–50, iii. 531; Webb, *Great Tooley*, 11, 68.

[78] For some of the intricacies of links across the early Tudor political system, see S. Gunn, 'The Structures of Politics in Early Tudor England', *Trans. Roy. Hist. Soc.*, 6th ser., 5 (1995), 77–8.

generations, in which opportunities for action changed more quickly than the modes of thought which justified it. The dissolution created a middle generation of men who could plunder the common weal while also claiming to preserve and promote it, like Sir John Mason, trying to take over Abingdon while protecting its hospital, or Sir Nicholas Arnold who got his hands on Llanthony but also helped to secure St Bartholomew's Hospital for Gloucester.[79]

Yet I want also to stress continuities across these three different generations. The first enclosure commissioner of 1517 was Bishop Veysey of Exeter, benefactor of Sutton Coldfield, where he tried to introduce the kersey industry from Devon and which he had incorporated, paved, and endowed with the school which Robert Burton attended. His perception of the needs of the common weal was not very different from that of John Fisher, town clerk of Warwick under Elizabeth, organizer of poor relief, and, along with yet another Wigston, one of the supporters of the earl of Leicester's hospital in the town.[80] The link between Veysey and Fisher, and the representative of the generation which separated them, was Fisher's elder brother, Thomas, who had bought some of Veysey's Warwickshire property. Secretary to Somerset and an encloser, MP in 1547 and would-be private resident of the Warwick guildhall which became Leicester's Hospital, he must have known that equally characteristic figure among Edwardian predators, John Hales, 'Hales the hottest', preaching the Christian commonwealth and founding a grammar school in St John's Hospital Coventry while building himself a mansion in the remains of the Whitefriars.[81]

III

It is not easy to summarize what these three generations of good, and not so good, commonwealthsmen had achieved. Their various enterprises had given the drive to reform the common weal no clearer a sense of direction in the 1560s than it had in 1510. The many projects considered and embarked upon in the early years of Elizabeth's reign show that the steam had not gone out of the effort. It may even have been given new urgency by the great mortality crisis of the later 1550s, though whether that was more important than the determination of a new regime to prove its commonweal credentials is uncertain. Statutes on wages and corn exports, poor relief,

---

[79] Bindoff, *House of Commons 1509–1558*, i. 32, ii. 582–4; Hasler, *House of Commons 1558–1603*, i. 350.

[80] *VCH Warwickshire*, iv (1947), 234; W. Dugdale, *The Antiquities of Warwickshire* (1730), 913–14; [G. Bracken,] *History of the Forest and Chase of Sutton Coldfield* (1860), 59–64; A. L. Beier, 'The Social Problems of an Elizabethan Country Town: Warwick, 1580–90', in Clark, *Country Towns*, 51; Bindoff, *House of Commons 1509–1558*, iii. 613–14.

[81] *Sutton Coldfield*, 59–60; Bindoff, *House of Commons 1509–1558*, i. 212, ii. 136–8, 276–7; Hasler, *House of Commons 1558–1603*, ii. 238–9; *VCH Warwickshire*, viii. 72, 139, 398.

and enclosure in 1563, and an ecclesiastical census in the same year, all seem to suggest purposeful reforming intent. But the strategy is less obvious than the impression of a government firing simultaneously at several targets.[82] The Statute of Artificers is a familiar example, with its different purposes which have been the subject of divergent interpretations;[83] and another statute of 1563, introducing Cecil's pet project of Wednesday fish-days, pointed in as many directions as any earlier common-weal device, 'restoring' as it promised to do frugality and fishing, piety and ports.[84]

In that case, Cecil typically defended himself from the charge of 'innovation' by pointing to Thomas Cromwell's new legislation, which had been conservative in purpose; and most of the common-weal devices adopted in the 1560s were in effect backward-looking. There were no radical new solutions to old issues. The evils of covetousness could not have been clearer following the age of plunder, but there was no answer to the question posed by the *Discourse* of whether it should be suppressed, or harnessed to the needs of the common weal. New searches for corn in 1562 and a further enclosure commission in 1565 suggested suppression; projects of foreign origin for pawnshops, merchants' exchanges, and lotteries (with the profits going to the improvement of harbours and public works) might seem to hint at accommodation.[85] The ambiguities of the Usury Act of 1571, and Cecil's own qualms of conscience about it, proved that there was confusion.[86]

There could be no clearer focus in the response to idleness, since that tried vainly to harmonize economic, moral, and police dimensions. Something of the consequent tension was nicely expressed in the project Cecil considered

---

[82] Some of the uncertainty about policy in these years arises from a gap in the Privy Council register between 1559 and 1562. On mortality and its possible consequences, see F. J. Fisher, 'Influenza and Inflation in Tudor England', *Econ. Hist. Rev.*, 2nd ser., 18 (1965), 128–9; J. S. Moore, 'Jack Fisher's 'Flu: A Visitation Revisited', *Econ. Hist. Rev.*, 46 (1993), 280–307. The ecclesiastical census of 1563 counted households rather than (as might have been expected) communicants, which may suggest some intent to reform the structure of parishes or dioceses. (I owe this point to Dr Alan Dyer, who, with Prof. David Palliser, is preparing an edition of the census.)

[83] S. T. Bindoff, 'The Making of the Statute of Artificers', in S. T. Bindoff, J. Hurstfield, and C. H. Williams (eds.), *Elizabethan Government and Society: Essays Presented to Sir John Neale* (1961), 56–94; G. R. Elton, *The Parliament of England 1559–1581* (Cambridge, 1986), 71–2, 262–7; D. Woodward, *Men at Work: Labourers and Building Craftsmen in the Towns of Northern England, 1450–1750* (Cambridge, 1995), 183–4, 193–5; D. Woodward, 'The Background to the Statute of Artificers: The Genesis of Labour Policy, 1558–63', *Econ. Hist. Rev.*, 2nd ser., 33 (1980), 32–44.

[84] 5 Eliz. I, c. 5, s. 11; PRO, SP 12/27/71.

[85] F. A. Youngs, *The Proclamations of the Tudor Queens* (Cambridge, 1976), 114; J. Thirsk (ed.), *The Agrarian History of England and Wales*, iv: *1500–1640* (Cambridge, 1967), 227; N. Jones, *God and the Moneylenders: Usury and Law in Early Modern England* (Oxford, 1989), 50–1; Elton, *Reform and Renewal*, 120; C. L'Estrange Ewen, *Lotteries and Sweepstakes* (1932), 29, 36–40.

[86] Jones, *God and the Moneylenders*, 34–65.

for the erection in Westminster of 'a house of occupations,—or rather an house of correction'—a term with a distinguished future ahead of it now that correction had moved beyond the jurisdiction of the church courts.[87] Bridewell itself was torn from the beginning between its functions of employing the unemployed and of punishing 'sin', especially sexual immorality, which some of its founders had had particularly in their sights. Its provincial copies increasingly became those punitive houses of correction which had to be physically separated from the new workhouses of the seventeenth century, if only by a dividing wall.[88]

At the same time, other hospitals were moving in the contrary direction, and shifting towards more respectable targets. William Wigston had founded his hospital at Leicester for the 'blind, lame, decrepit, paralytic or maimed in their limbs and idiots wanting their natural senses, so that they be peaceable'; but its Elizabethan patron, the earl of Huntingdon, was much more exclusive in his 1576 statutes, banning more than twenty different kinds of offenders, 'taletellers, brawlers . . . common beggars, dicers' and the like, and insisting that those admitted should 'live godly'.[89] Professor Jordan's statistics demonstrate that private benefactors of all kinds gave their money neither for houses of correction nor for hospitals for the sick, but to endow almshouses for respectable, gowned, Trollopian worthies: places like Cecil's own foundation at Stamford, which excluded lepers, lunatics, and victims of the French pox or other infectious diseases.[90] There was an increasing fastidiousness here, well caught in an early seventeenth-century description of Christ's Hospital, Abingdon, which praised its gardens, with their herbs, flowers, 'borders with fruit trees', and 'fair sweet water', where before there had been 'nothing but stinking ditches and filthy dunghills, very unwholesome and noisome to the poor'.[91] Yet that too was the language of the common weal. Its capacious intellectual confines could accommodate all these diverse missions, as modern jargon would term them, and leave ample room for future development.

The common weal also left, at the end of its first half-century, one prominent set of political beneficiaries: not so much the Crown or Parliament,

[87] S. A. Peyton, 'The Houses of Correction at Maidstone and Westminster', *Eng. Hist. Rev.*, 42 (1927), 258; BL, Lansdowne MS 7, fo. 45.

[88] Archer, *Pursuit of Stability*, 238–43, 250–6; Tawney and Power, *Tudor Economic Documents*, iii. 441–2. Cf. J. Innes, 'Prisons for the Poor: English Bridewells 1555–1800', in F. Snyder and D. Hay (eds.), *Labour, Law and Crime: An Historical Perspective* (1987), 58–63.

[89] G. Cowie, *The History of Wyggeston's Hospital* (Leicester, 1893), 12; A. H. Thompson, *A Calendar of Charters and other Documents Belonging to the Hospital of William Wyggeston at Leicester* (Leicester, 1933), 69, 77.

[90] W. K. Jordan, *Philanthropy in England 1480–1660* (1959), 257–74; *Ordinances made by Sir William Cecil . . . for the order and governement of xiij poore men, whereof one to be the warden of the Hospitall at Stanford Baron* (1597).

[91] Francis Little, *A Monument of Christian Munificence*, ed. C. D. Cobham (Oxford, 1871), 93. Cf. E. Prescott, *The English Medieval Hospital 1050–1640* (1992), 99–100.

though each gained something from trying to appropriate it, but inter-
mediate bodies, most of them corporations, which were created by royal
patent for the management of public welfare. At first sight that may
seem a surprising conclusion, given central suspicion of participation in the
common weal, even in the modest and authorized shape of those 'incorporations' whose very name was anathema to both Henry VIII and Elizabeth.
'There is no one thing that more continueth a daily hurt to the realm than
corporations', wrote Sir John Mason, opposing the Edwardian incorporation
of Abingdon, and plainly expecting conciliar sympathy. Ten years later,
Nicholas Bacon agreed that there were too many of them: 'men of wisdom
and understanding' were unanimous that it was neither 'meet nor convenient' to increase their number further.[92]

Yet these bodies 'corporate and politic' proliferated; and they multiplied
because Crown and council had no alternative when they needed to fill the
vacuum left by the dissolution of religious orders and fraternities. Quite
apart from the councils of the fifty-one monastic and other boroughs,
including Abingdon, which were incorporated between 1540 and 1570, there
were the governing boards of forty-one grammar schools, incorporated by
letters patent in the same period, the various bodies running seventy-five
new or restored hospitals and almshouses established in the same three
decades, and hence a whole miscellany of groups of governors and trustees
managing charitable resources, public activities, and sometimes in consequence whole towns: Crediton and Loughborough, Bury St Edmunds,
and Abingdon before incorporation.[93] Here was a multitude of little common weals as susceptible to the ideals of civic humanism as the corporation
of London itself.

They did not introduce anything radically new. From one point of view,
they were simply inadequate, attenuated substitutes for the many subsidiary
associations which had enriched the late medieval common weal. The Crown
needed some body or other to manage public works and facilities, just as it
needed someone to take over the decayed urban properties of religious

[92] *Letters and Papers, Henry VIII*, iv(i). 978; BL, Lansdowne MS 7, fo. 50; P. F. Tytler,
England under the Reigns of Edward VI and Mary (2 vols., 1839), i. 362; D. MacCulloch,
Suffolk and the Tudors: Politics and Religion in an English County 1500–1600 (Oxford,
1986), 329. Cf. BL, Lansdowne MS 19, fos. 6ʳ, 144ʳ, for doubts about the incorporation of
Wells in 1574–5.
[93] Calculations of numbers from R. Tittler, 'The Incorporation of Boroughs, 1540–1558',
History, 62 (1977), 41–2; *Calendars of Patent Rolls*; McIntosh, 'Responses to the Poor', 222–
3. On the towns mentioned, see *Calendar of Patent Rolls 1558–60*, 417–18 (Crediton);
J. Simon, 'Town Estates and Schools in the 16th and 17th Centuries', in B. Simon (ed.),
Education in Leicestershire 1540–1940 (Leicester, 1968), 10 (Loughborough); MacCulloch,
Suffolk and the Tudors, 329 (Bury); *VCH Berkshire*, iv (1924), 439–40 (Abingdon). For
similar instances, see Simon, 'State and Schooling', 167 (Louth); D. Hey, *The Fiery Blades of
Hallamshire: Sheffield and Its Neighbourhood, 1660–1740* (Leicester, 1991), 202–4.

orders and guilds which it did not have the resources to maintain.[94] When benefactions for hospitals and houses of correction seemed sluggish, Elizabethan statutes tried to encourage the process by making their incorporation easier, not more difficult; there was no alternative.[95] Central government might be speaking with two voices, but it had to face the reality of its own incapacity.

Adopting a longer historical perspective, it might also be said that the mid-Tudor incorporations represented no more than the acceleration of a process of legal definition of corporate entities which had begun in the fourteenth century, if not earlier, and been given new momentum by the Reformation and the need for a reformed 'politic order'. We will return to the question of continuity in the final chapter, but its importance should not be underrated. The long-term significance of corporate identities, before and after 1500, was underlined by the second and greatest of Ford's lecturers, Maitland. He wished the future urban historian, neglecting 'neither English life nor Italian thought', to explain 'the transition from rural to urban habits, and the evolution . . . of that kind and that degree of unity which are corporateness and personality'.[96] Though the history of English corporate bodies remains to be written, their survival and formal evolution were essential ingredients in the dissemination of civic and civil consciousness in the sixteenth century.

They also provided an answer to the vexed question of where, in practice, responsibility for the common weal lay. It lay with them. The answer went largely unrecognized by contemporaries, because there were more vociferous candidates claiming that distinction. Writing to Cecil on the 'distresses of the common weal' in 1558, Armagil Waad looked still, as some earlier projectors had done, to a council which sought consensus through counsel. The Privy Council should set up a working party containing a divine, a common lawyer, a civilian, and a merchant, 'to devise, travail and study upon all manner of means whereby the commonweal may be reformed, benefited and kept in good order'.[97] That was the authentic common-weal tradition which had sanctioned relatively open debate and tracts like the *Discourse*. When it withered away after the 1560s, its legacy was claimed by the agents of godly or monarchical rule, sometimes proud to be thought 'good commonwealthsmen',[98] but consistent advocates nevertheless of the

[94] Cf. Palliser, *Tudor York*, 278; R. W. Hoyle (ed.), *The Estates of the English Crown 1558–1640* (Cambridge, 1992), 39.

[95] 14 Eliz. I, c. 14; 39 Eliz. I, c. 5. Cf. 18 Eliz. I, c. 3, s. ix; 35 Eliz. I, c. 7, s. xxvii.

[96] F. W. Maitland, *Township and Borough* (Cambridge, 1898), p. vi. For the early medieval background, see S. Reynolds, 'The Idea of the Corporation in Western Christendom before 1300', in J. A. Guy and H. G. Beale (eds.), *Law and Social Change in British History* (1984), 27–33, and cf. below, pp. 161–3.

[97] PRO, SP 12/1, fo. 154.

[98] As Henry Sherfield, godly magistrate of Salisbury, and the Restoration Duke of

different kinds of absolute authority considered in the next two chapters.

As late as 1659, therefore, the duke of Newcastle could be as hostile to corporations as Mason and Bacon a century before, warning Charles II that there were far too many of them, that each was 'a petty free state against monarchy'. In actuality, that continuing lament was an unconscious tribute to the true legatees of the common weal. William Sheppard's study *Of Corporations*, also published in 1659, was more appreciative and more accurate. Surveying the many bodies which governed towns and parishes, hospitals and crafts, he saw a host of corporations, every one of them transforming a community—a 'comminalty'—into something which was 'in a sort immortal'.[99]

Newcastle were: P. Slack, 'The Public Conscience of Henry Sherfield', in J. Morrill, P. Slack, and D. Woolf (eds.), *Public Duty and Private Conscience in Seventeenth-Century England: Essays Presented to G. E. Aylmer* (Oxford, 1993), 164; Margaret Cavendish, *The Life of William Cavendish Duke of Newcastle*, ed. C. H. Firth (1886), 327.

[99] T. Slaughter, *Ideology and Politics on the Eve of the Restoration: Newcastle's Advice to Charles II* (American Philosophical Society, Philadelphia, 1984), 40–1; William Sheppard, *Of Corporations, Fraternities and Guilds* (1659), sig. A3ᵛ, pp. 3–4, 24–6.

2

GODLY CITIES

Looking for bright spots in an otherwise diseased commonwealth in 1585, William Cecil identified 'good towns' with their 'discreet preachers, very zealous towards God', and watchful 'for her Majesty's safety'.[1] It was perhaps less the queen's than the town's safety which most concerned the more zealous of these preachers, several of whom were masters of the civic hospitals considered in the last chapter: Thomas Sampson at Wigston's, Leicester, for example, or Thomas Cartwright at Leicester's Hospital, Warwick, or Arthur Wake at St John's, Northampton. In 1630 one of the last of the line, Robert Jenison, master of Mary Magdalene Hospital and lecturer in Newcastle upon Tyne, discussed *The Citie's Safetie* at some length. Protection from divine punishment—from plague, famine and the sword, from fire and flood—belonged, he asserted, 'peculiarly to godly cities, even to such as God will take and acknowledge for his own, and to godly persons in them. Over such cities God will in special manner watch for good, and will establish them in safety.' Jenison's confidence was unqualified: 'Doubtless, we belonging to godly cities, and being for our parts members thereof, shall escape . . . many dangers, and remain a quiet habitation.'[2]

In reality, godly cities were for the most part the most unquiet habitations, as we know from the work of Patrick Collinson, David Underdown, and other historians who have told us a good deal about such places: cities 'set on a hill', like Colchester and Dorchester, 'second Genevas' like Coventry and Stratford-upon-Avon.[3] Despite the attention already given to them, however, they demand some prolonged consideration here. In efforts to reform manners, repress idleness, and employ and relieve the poor, their magistrates and ministers proclaimed a very deliberate and influential vision of the public welfare. Godly cities, according to Jenison, were those purged by 'a

---

[1] PRO, SP 12/184/50.

[2] Robert Jenison, *The Cities Safetie* (1630), 11, 29. On Jenison, see R. Howell, *Newcastle upon Tyne and the Puritan Revolution* (Oxford, 1967), 85–6.

[3] P. Collinson, *The Birthpangs of Protestant England* (1986), 30; D. Underdown, *Fire from Heaven: Life in an English Town in the Seventeenth Century* (1992), p. ix; A. Hughes, *Politics, Society and Civil War in Warwickshire 1620–60* (Cambridge, 1987), 80; *VCH Warwickshire*, iii (1945), 280–1.

thorough reformation', and marked by 'their impartial uprightness in executing justice and regarding the cause of the poor'.[4]

I

It is difficult to identify the first of these towns, much as one would like to mark the place and point at which efforts to cleanse the civic common weal, perhaps with the odd acknowledgement of 'godly' purposes, were swallowed up into the quest for 'thorough reformation', the point at which models drawn from Flanders or even Italy were completely overshadowed by those from Switzerland or the Rhineland. Identification of the earliest examples of the special language of civic godliness requires not only an ear as sensitive as Professor Collinson's but better sources than any of us possess. It would be instructive to know more, for example, about events in Coventry after 1558, to be able to analyse the chemistry of civic reactions when the Edwardian reformers Hales and Thomas Lever returned from exile. Unfortunately, the Coventry leet book fails us at the crucial moment, and we cannot know quite what the gradual building of the Bablake Hospital complex in the 1560s meant for those involved.[5] In other towns too— Colchester and Leicester, for example—the opening years of Elizabeth's reign presented opportunities for Protestant and civic reform which were eagerly seized, though the aspirations and the actors involved are often unclear.[6] The best we can do is to begin with what appears to be the first fullblown example of the godly rhetoric of civic reformation.

It occurs in Kingston-upon-Hull at the end of 1563, two years after the arrival from Boston of the town preacher, Melchior Smith. The council then promulgated a set of orders whose switch from old to new is evident from its preamble: 'Forasmuch as in every well ordered commonwealth most principally is sought out the heinous offenders and insensible persons which be delighted in drunkenness, excess, riot, whoredom, wantonness, lightness, idleness and scolding . . .'. These were, as they had individually often been in the past, 'great infections and enormities', but they were now to be suppressed together by 'godly ordinances . . . for punishing of vice'. Three years later, in 1566, there were no fewer than fifty-three ordinances—later extended to sixty-four—all 'to the glory of God and well ordering of this commonwealth': they added 'cards, dice, tables, bowls' to the offences and misdemeanours already attacked, prescribed that at least one member of each household should attend sermons on Sundays, Wednesdays, and

---

[4] Jenison, *Cities Safetie*, 25, 20.　　　　　　　　　　　　　　　　　　[5] Above, p. 21.

[6] Cf. the ordinances of 1562 in Leicester and Colchester: M. Bateson et al. (eds.), *Records of the Borough of Leicester*, iii. 100–3; M. S. Byford, 'The Price of Protestantism: Assessing the Impact of Religious Change on Elizabethan Essex: The Cases of Heydon and Colchester 1558–94', D.Phil. thesis, Univ. of Oxford, 1988, 149–50. For the complexities of the situation in Colchester, see the excellent analysis ibid. ch. 2.

Fridays, and included 'old ancient orders' regulating marketing and weights and measures, imposing a curfew after 9 p.m., and prohibiting rubbish in the streets and ditches, and fire-risks such as unshielded candles. In 1574 there were further detailed by-laws against 'detestable sins and enormities' and 'for reformation of disorders in alehouses', all to ward off 'the manifold grievous and terrible plagues of God hanging over the . . . town, if speedy reformation be not had'.[7]

By 1574 the quest for speedy reformation was being pursued in other towns, and directing attention particularly to the poor. In 1568 the councillors of King's Lynn formalized arrangements for their employment, and for a corn stock for 'labouring poor householders and artificers', 'God moving their hearts thereto by the preaching of the gospel'. The preacher was William Sanderson, who had arrived in 1564.[8] In 1571 the aldermen of Norwich famously brought reformation of manners and relief of the poor together, in this case three years *before* the arrival of their 'Apostle', John More. Having completed their great census of the poor, they had orders for 'the reformation of . . . evils' and especially idleness printed, read in churches, and set up in 'divers places' around the town with a view to 'the practising of youth . . . in work, in learning and in the fear of God'. They appointed a committee to view the state of the poor, two deacons — 'civil and expert men that will be painful' — to supervise the poor in every petty ward, and 'select women' to teach children 'to work and learn letters'. In all, 950 children, 64 men, and 180 women were said to be profitably employed by these means.[9]

Variations on these themes, employing much the same rhetoric, were common in English towns from 1570 through to the Interregnum. As the above examples suggest, they cluster first down the east coast and especially in East Anglia: we could add Ipswich and Bury St Edmunds to the list.[10] In the early seventeenth century it was the turn of towns in the south-west: Dorchester, Salisbury, and Plymouth, for example, where it is possible to

---

[7] Hull City RO, Bench Book 4, fos. 50, 51ᵛ, 56ʳ, 66ᵛ-70, 117ᵛ–121ʳ. On Melchior Smith, see *VCH East Riding*, i (1969), 95; C. Cross, *Urban Magistrates and Ministers: Religion in Hull and Leeds from the Reformation to the Civil War* (Borthwick Paper 67, York, 1985), 14. One would like to know more about the Boston of the 1560s from which Smith came, but its records are little more informative than those of Coventry at the same time. For what they are worth, they suggest that thorough reformation began there only in the later 1560s: P. and J. Clark (eds.), *The Boston Assembly Minutes 1545–1575* (Lincoln Record Society, 77, 1986), 50, 72. Cf. C. Cross, 'Communal Piety in Sixteenth-Century Boston', *Lincolnshire History and Archaeology*, 25 (1990), 33–8.

[8] King's Lynn Borough Archives, Hall Book 6, fos. 500ʳ–501ʳ, 510ᵛ, 427ʳ.

[9] W. Hudson and J. C. Tingey (eds.), *Records of the City of Norwich*, ii. 344–58; Norfolk RO, Norwich Mayor's 'Booke of the Poore' 1571-9, 4 June 1571. Cf. J. F. Pound, 'An Elizabethan Census of the Poor', *Univ. of Birmingham Historical Journal*, 8 (1962),135–61; J. F. Pound (ed.), *The Norwich Census of the Poor 1570* (Norfolk Record Society, 40, 1971).

[10] P. Collinson, *The Religion of Protestants* (Oxford, 1982), 158, 170–7; D. MacCulloch, *Suffolk and the Tudors: Politics and Religion in an English County 1500–1600* (Oxford 1986), 198; D. MacCulloch and J. Blatchly, 'Pastoral Provision in the Parishes of Tudor Ipswich', *Sixteenth-Century Journal*, 22 (1991), 469.

reconstruct a network of sympathy and connection between leading magistrates and ministers as influential as that evident earlier in East Anglia.[11] In
some places one can detect successive drives for reformation, as in Gloucester in the 1560s, 1580s, 1630s, and 1650s, and in Colchester and Boston at
similarly irregular intervals.[12] Precise details might vary. Hull and Lynn both
used revenue from licences for the export of corn for various new purposes,
including social welfare; Salisbury followed Dorchester in setting up a
municipal brewhouse to provide finance for godly civic projects.[13] But in all
these towns resources were manipulated with an eye to social and moral
reform in recurrent bursts of godly zeal. They articulated a distinctive kind
of civic consciousness.

Quite how distinctive it was has, however, become a matter of historical
debate, with some scholars seeing in it either a programme common to most
Protestants or, more radically, an unremarkable development from earlier
civic and 'humanist' aspirations, without any necessary religious connotation
at all.[14] The issues have been put most clearly by Margaret Spufford in an
important essay which questions the common assumption—taken for granted
in what has been said above—that Puritanism and aspirations towards social
control were intimately connected.[15] She advances two propositions. First,
Puritanism was not 'a necessary condition for a greater enforcement of moral
behaviour on the poor'; that could occur and often had occurred without the
religious impulse. Second, she argues, Puritanism, like other expressions of
Christian faith, was fundamentally concerned about relations with God, not
about relations between men or social groups. Religion and religious belief
are therefore, she concludes, 'a gigantic red herring' for the historian who
wishes to explain spurts of activity for the reformation of manners like those
in Elizabethan Hull.[16]

---

[11] Underdown, *Fire from Heaven*; P. Slack, 'Poverty and Politics in Salisbury 1597–1666',
in P. Clark and P. Slack (eds.), *Crisis and Order in English Towns 1500–1700* (1972), 164–203;
West Devon RO, Plymouth Corporation Records, GP/2. Cf. below, p. 42, n. 56.

[12] Glos. RO, Gloucester Corporation Records, B3/1, 2; Colchester Corporation Records,
Assembly Books, and Byford, 'Price of Protestantism', chs. 2–5; J. F. Bailey (ed.), *Transcrip-
tion of the Minutes of the Corporation of Boston* (2 vols., Boston, 1980).

[13] The idea of a publicly owned brewhouse may have come first from Evesham, where
Lewis Bayly, vicar until 1611, was active in social welfare: S. K. Roberts (ed.), *Evesham
Borough Records of the Seventeenth Century* (Worcestershire Historical Society, new ser., 14,
1994), pp. xiv, xv, 10.

[14] For the latter view, see M. Todd, *Christian Humanism and the Puritan Social Order*
(Cambridge, 1987), ch. 5.

[15] M. Spufford, 'Puritanism and Social Control?', in A. Fletcher and J. Stevenson (eds.),
Order and Disorder in Early Modern England (Cambridge, 1985), 41–57. The contrary view
has been expounded most influentially by Keith Wrightson: see e.g. his *English Society*
(1982), 206–21; 'Two Concepts of Order', in J. Brewer and J. Styles (eds.), *An Ungovernable
People* (1980); and his Ph.D. thesis, 'The Puritan Reformation of Manners, with special
reference to the counties of Lancashire and Essex 1640–1660', Univ. of Cambridge, 1973.

[16] Spufford, 'Puritanism and Social Control?', 47, 57. In what follows, I have presented
Prof. Spufford's case in this stimulating article in particularly stark form for purposes of

It is possible to accept Professor Spufford's two propositions, though with some qualification, without underwriting her conclusion. As we shall see, we can agree that Puritanism was not necessary for all forms of reforming activity in all places while maintaining that it was essential in some places; and we can agree that it is absurd to reduce any variety of religious faith to a mere social message and still hold that religious ideals may shape the kinds of social reform which will be undertaken. But there is a third proposition, implied though not explicit, in Professor Spufford's argument which needs to be cleared out of the way first. The heart of her paper points to the many historical parallels between social attitudes and regulatory policies in the years around 1600 and those which are evident in the years around 1300; and the implication seems to be another kind of reductionism: that these phenomena can be attributed to economic circumstances; that they were reactions to the social disorder and distress which came with overpopulation at these two 'high-pressure' points in English demographic and economic development.

It is not difficult to see the limitations in this kind of economic determinism. The parallels in policy are certainly there. In King's Lynn, as it happens, there were orders against thieves, prostitutes, and forestallers of the market at the very beginning of the fourteenth century which anticipate civic concerns in Lynn three centuries later.[17] But economic circumstances at the two dates were not as similar as they might at first appear. The more we learn about the early fourteenth-century economy, the clearer it becomes that high pressure then was much greater than it was to be in 1600, springing from a larger population and producing a famine in 1315 far worse than the harvest crises of the later 1590s and early 1620s.[18]

There are also particular problems of chronology and economic fit in the later period. Civic reformations beginning as early as the 1560s scarcely coincide with the moment of greatest pressure. It might even be possible to argue that they were associated with declining populations and depressed economies, given their early appearance in some of the east-coast

argument. It is only fair to say that in doing so I have done some violence to the subtleties of her case; and I am aware from helpful discussions with her, as well as from her most recent work, that she is very far from subscribing to the determinist conclusions which it seems to me can be drawn from some of the statements in her article. See esp. *Chippenham to the World: Microcosm to Macrocosm* (Roehampton Institute, London, 1995); and her contributions to M. Spufford (ed.), *The World of Rural Dissenters 1520–1725* (Cambridge, 1995), esp. 42.

[17] D. M. Owen (ed.), *The Making of King's Lynn* (British Academy, Records of Social and Economic History, new ser., 9, 1984), 419, 422.

[18] I. Kershaw, 'The Great Famine and Agrarian Crisis in England 1315–1322', *P&P*, 59 (1973), 3–50. Cf. A. B. Appleby, *Famine in Tudor and Stuart England* (Liverpool, 1978). For further discussion of the relevance of economic circumstances, see below, pp. 151–6, and cf. R. Hutton, *The Rise and Fall of Merry England: The Ritual Year 1400–1700* (Oxford, 1994), ch. 4.

towns from Hull down to Norwich which had suffered particularly badly
from late medieval depression;[19] and it is tempting to add to those cases
similar manifestations in the early seventeenth century in south-western
towns hit by the decline of the broadcloth industry, such as Salisbury. If one
wished to save an economic explanation for the phenomenon, therefore, it
might seem plausible to suggest that it was recession rather than high
pressure which elicited a particularly marked social response. Yet that alternative hypothesis also involves problems when one looks at particular cases.
Colchester was not as depressed as Norwich in the 1570s, for example, and
Dorchester nothing like as depressed as Salisbury in the 1620s. Any single
version of economic determinism fails to carry conviction when confronted
with local conditions on the ground; and if we are reduced to saying that a
variety of economic circumstances, from recession to rapid growth, might
produce identical reactions, that scarcely carries historical understanding
very much further.

All this is not to say that the campaigns of the godly were not informed by
a sense of urgent social and economic problems of one kind or another. On
the contrary, a vivid awareness of critical circumstances was fundamental to
the Puritan mentality, and where it did not exist it had to be created. Jenison's
safety of the godly must rest on constant vigilance, not complacency. John
Northbrook, preacher in Bristol in the 1570s, complained that 'by security
men's minds are brought into a dead sleep, [so] that they be not pierced one
whit with the fear of God's punishment'.[20] The actuality of plague quite
often persuaded magistrates of the need for moral and social hygiene, just as
it commonly gave rise to new orders for the physical cleansing of towns: in
Shrewsbury after 1575, Rye after 1580, Exeter after 1625, Salisbury after
1627. The great fire of Dorchester of 1613 had much the same effect.[21] But it
would be possible to compile a long list of natural disasters which did not
have the same result, beginning with the great mortality crisis of the later
1550s. It was a later influenza epidemic, in 1580 not 1558, which was
nicknamed 'speedy repentance' in Coventry.[22]

We are dealing with a process of active cultural interpretation, and one
which could occur before the event and which had to be maintained after it.
That 'speedy reformation', called for in Hull in 1574 lest God's plagues
descend, came just before an epidemic in 1575 which was quickly followed
by new orders against drunkards and 'excess in apparel', especially 'in

[19] A. Dyer, *Decline and Growth in English Towns 1400-1640* (1991), 21, 42.

[20] John Northbrooke, A *Treatise against Dicing, Dancing, Plays and Interludes with Other Idle Pastimes* (1843 edn.; originally published 1577), 13.

[21] Shrewsbury Guildhall, Assembly Book 1554-83, fos. 221ᵛ, 289ʳ; G. Mayhew, *Tudor Rye* (Filmer, Sussex, 1987), 205, 225; P. Slack, *The Impact of Plague in Tudor and Stuart England* (1985), 261-3; Underdown, *Fire from Heaven*, 3.

[22] Bodl., MS Top Warws. d. 4, fo. 26ʳ.

women'.[23] In order to maintain the pace of reform in Dorchester, the fire of 1613 had to be kept deliberately in mind, by a service of thanksgiving for deliverance every year down to 1634.[24] The association between reformations of manners and critical events was not a reflex reaction but a conscious creation. 'One special *use* of our afflictions is our reformation', said William Whateley, commenting on the great Banbury fire of 1628.[25]

Such events, and the disorder of hard times in general, no doubt made the rhetoric of the godly more persuasive, winning them supporters who might otherwise have been indifferent. It is true also that more secular perceptions of the same circumstances could prompt social regulation in places where the godly had no purchase or before they came on the scene. But earlier clusters of reforming activity, in the 1480s or 1510s, were as dependent as those of the 1570s and 1620s on the ambitions of individuals and the intellectual assumptions which shaped their interpretation of events.[26] One would like to know, for example, who it was in the frankpledge jury of Gloucester in 1504 who took up earlier orders of 1500 against beggars, rogues, and prostitutes, and turned them into a strident indictment of the 'common strumpets and bawds' and their clerical clients, who made 'the common wealth of this town' so 'abominable spoken of in all England and Wales' for 'vicious living'.[27] The councillors of Hull were doing much the same sort of thing in the 1560s when they translated ordinances, some of them going back to 1464, into a complete programme for reformation and in doing so added extra 'sins and enormities' to the earlier list of disorders and nuisances.[28]

This is to say no more than that action cannot be separated from motivation, and motivation may be powerfully influenced by ideology. Once godly ministers had spread the word, zeal for speedy reformation could add a large number of magistrates to that exceptional Gloucester citizen of 1504. Of course, it may be argued that in Gloucester, and even perhaps in Hull, new

[23] Hull City RO, Bench Book 4, fos. 153ᵛ, 157, 164ᵛ.

[24] Underdown, *Fire from Heaven*, 93.

[25] William Whateley, *Sinne no more* (2nd edn., 1628), 22. In Rye, therefore, not only plague but also the silting up of the harbour and 'unseasonable weather' could be interpreted as signs of 'God's great displeasure': A. Gregory, 'Witchcraft, Politics and "Good Neighbourhood" in Early Seventeenth-Century Rye', *P&P*, 133 (1991), 56; Mayhew, *Tudor Rye*, 201.

[26] Above, pp. 15–16. Cf. L. R. Poos, *A Rural Society after the Black Death: Essex 1350–1525* (Cambridge, 1991), 273-5; M. K. McIntosh, 'Local Change and Community Control in England', *Huntington Library Quarterly*, 49 (1986), 219–42; P. J. P. Goldberg, *Women, Work and Life Cycle in a Medieval Economy: Women in York and Yorkshire c.1300-1520* (Oxford, 1992), 116–17, 155.

[27] *VCH Gloucestershire*, iv (1988), 56; Glos. RO, Gloucester Records, B2/1, Red Book, fos. 19–20. Cf. the action against 'adulterers and whoremongers' of John Hooker, late-15th c. mayor of Exeter, described by his descendant: W. J. Harte, *Gleanings from the Commonplace Book of John Hooker* (Exeter, n.d.), 18–19.

[28] William Chambers, *Kingston upon Hull* (facsimile edn., Hull, 1985), iii. 75; Hull City RO, Bench Book 4, fos. 27ᵛ–28.

attitudes only provided a fresh cloak for old purposes, new bottles for old wine; but new slogans can stimulate action before they become in their turn mere rhetorical conventions to which lip-service is paid. In short, returning to the metaphor used in the first chapter, civic godliness had the capacity to produce a new set of determined drivers for the vehicle of social reform, and to accelerate its pace, even if it did not select an entirely new destination. In what follows I want first to look a little more closely at what made these drivers distinctive, and then to turn to their destination in order to ask what, if anything, was peculiar about that.

II

In theory the best way of identifying the distinctiveness of the Puritan drive would be to measure towns where it was present against towns where it was not: to set up a kind of retrospective laboratory experiment, using as controls cities where action for the public welfare was ostensibly secular in motivation. In practice, the exercise turns out to be nothing like as easy as it sounds, but it is instructive to make the attempt.

We might conveniently look for our two experimental samples among the twenty largest English towns in 1600, those with populations over 5,000, from London down to Colchester.[29] As it happens, ten of the twenty towns had at least one episode of what might be called godly rule before 1640: a notable proportion as well as a tidy one. They are Norwich, Plymouth, Salisbury, King's Lynn, Gloucester, Hull, Ipswich, and Colchester, all of which have already been mentioned, plus Coventry and Great Yarmouth.[30] Unfortunately, however, the other ten towns, the potential controls, are far from constituting an uncontaminated sample. Each of them had at some point godly councillors or preachers, exercising a greater or lesser degree of influence, depending on the town.[31] They are a lukewarm rather than a coldly secular group. Nevertheless, several of them started off at the colder end, and therefore repay attention. These were corporations which in the 1550s and 1560s were actively building new welfare facilities on the foundations described in the last chapter—places like Exeter, where there was

---

[29] The towns are those identified in E. A. Wrigley, 'Urban Growth and Agricultural Change in England and the Continent in the Early Modern Period', in R. I. Rotberg and T. K. Rabb (eds.), *Population and Economy* (Cambridge, 1986), 126.

[30] On episodes of Puritan dominance in the two latter, see A. Hughes, 'Coventry and the English Revolution', in R. C. Richardson (ed.), *Town and Countryside in the English Revolution* (Manchester, 1992), 75–6; and R. Cust, 'Anti-Puritanism and Urban Politics: Charles I and Great Yarmouth', *Historical Journal*, 35 (1992), 7–9.

[31] Eight of these towns, with references to a godly input or attempted input, are: London (I. W. Archer, *The Pursuit of Stability: Social Relations in Elizabethan London* (Cambridge 1991), 45–6, 253–4); York (C. Cross, 'A Man of Conscience in Seventeenth-Century Urban Politics: Alderman Hoyle of York', in J. Morrill, P. Slack, and D. Woolf (eds.), *Public Duty and Private Conscience in Seventeenth-Century England: Essays Presented to G. E. Aylmer* (Oxford, 1993), 206–15); Bristol (below, p. 40); Newcastle (Howell, *Newcastle upon Tyne*,

municipal provision of corn in 1562 and a poor rate by 1563, and York, which had rates by 1561, a census in 1566, and a workhouse in St Anthony's Hall in 1567.[32] In Worcester, where the provision of corn had been a 'godly motion' in 1556, no similar epithet was applied to the considerable civic activity of the next five years, which included two censuses in order to 'learn the cause' of poverty, and a committee to 'devise a book and articles' as a remedy.[33] Such cases certainly show that it did not need a Puritan elite to inspire civic interest in the poor.

Yet towns like this did not stand still, or suddenly become isolated from what was happening elsewhere. Even if they were not attending to their preachers, or the example of their hotter neighbours, Exeter and Worcester tended to follow statute, founding or repairing bridewells after the Acts of 1576, 1598, or 1610.[34] When the councillors of York turned again to surveying and employing the poor in 1569 and 1570, they were badgered by the Council in the North urging stricter social control, including compulsory attendance at church.[35] Towns smaller than the top twenty were even more vulnerable to similar pressures. And what makes our controlled experiment fundamentally flawed is the fact that some of the most powerful of these external influences were in one way or another tainted, as it were, by godliness.

This applies most notably to the statutes of the 1570s which shaped the character of relief and regulation of the poor for most of Elizabeth's reign. Something of the radicalism of the 1572 Act emerges from the heated debate which was necessary before the definition of rogues and vagabonds in its first clauses could be extended to minstrels, literally the carriers of an older

---

ch. 3); Exeter (below, p. 46); Chester (below, p. 41); Worcester (below, p. 40); and Canterbury (P. Clark, *English Provincial Society from the Reformation to the Revolution: Religion, Politics and Society in Kent 1500–1640* (Hassocks, Sussex, 1977), 176). The remaining two towns are the special cases of Oxford and Cambridge, where the role of the universities provoked something like the animosities evident in cathedral cities, but was dominant enough to prevent any real civic independence. For the institution of civic preachers in both towns, however, see *VCH Oxfordshire*, iv. 176; J. Twigg, *The University of Cambridge and the English Revolution 1625-1688* (Woodbridge, Suffolk, 1990), 15, 69.

[32] W. T. MacCaffrey, *Exeter 1540-1640* (Cambridge, Mass., 1958), 111–14;. Palliser, *Tudor York*, p. 275; A. Raine (ed.), *York Civic Records*, vi. 110–11.

[33] Above, pp. 11-12; Worcs. RO, Worcester View of Frankpledge 1, fos. 234ᵛ-235 (the returns from one of the censuses are at fos. 50-4); Chamber Order Book 1, fos. 73ᵛ, 83ᵛ. There was a third census of the poor in 1563: View of Frankpledge 1, fos. 117ᵛ-123.

[34] MacCaffrey, *Exeter*, p. 114; Worcs. RO, Worcester Chamber Order Book 1, fo. 201ʳ; S. Bond (ed.), *The Chamber Order Book of Worcester 1602-50* (Worcestershire Historical Society, new ser., 8, 1974), 41.

[35] Raine, *York Civic Records*, vi. 150-3, 159, 179; vii. 10, 19-20. This example makes one wonder whether the 'book' for 'the ordering of the poor' discussed in Shrewsbury in 1559 as well as in Worcester in 1561 was prompted by the Council in the Marches: Shrewsbury Guildhall, Assembly Book 1554-83, fos. 32ᵛ-34ʳ. The Shrewsbury book was compiled by a Mr Eastwyke, who has not been identified.

culture now unmistakably under attack.[36] The debt of the second half of the statute to the practice of continental Reformed cities is equally plain: its insistence that every parish should have both collectors of the new rates for the poor and 'overseers' of their behaviour followed a division in the office of deacon recommended by Calvin and Bucer.[37] The statute of 1576 similarly provided two sets of officers for its new houses of correction, while also punishing the parents of bastards as offenders 'against God's law and man's law'.[38] This was portmanteau legislation put together by committees, and by committees which allowed various interests to have their say. Their members included hard-headed urban magistrates like Recorder Popham of Bristol, for long famous as a hammer of vagrants; but they also included representatives of reforming cities—Norwich, Gloucester, and Ipswich—and municipal recorders from the same stable, such as Robert Bell of King's Lynn, Speaker of the Commons in 1572, and Roger Manwood, who founded a new grammar school in the famously clean streets of 'godly' Sandwich.[39]

Similar figures closer to the centre of power backed the bills in Parliament and then pulled their weight in the localities: William Fleetwood, the new recorder of London; Sir Francis Knollys, promoter of a house of correction in Oxford in 1579; Walsingham, who sponsored one in Hampshire and admired the bridewell in Norfolk as 'good work . . . in the time of the gospel'.[40] The earl of Leicester recommending employment schemes in

[36] 14 Eliz. I, c. 5. For the debates, see T. E. Hartley (ed.), *Proceedings in the Parliaments of Elizabeth I* (3 vols., Leicester, 1981-95), i. 312-13, 367, 384; P. Roberts, 'Elizabethan Players and Minstrels and the Legislation of 1572 Against Retainers and Vagabonds', in A. Fletcher and P. Roberts (eds.), *Religion, Culture and Society in Early Modern Britain: Essays in Honour of Patrick Collinson* (Cambridge, 1994), 29-55.

[37] 14 Eliz. I, c. 5, s. xvi; Martin Bucer, *De Regno Christi* (Basle, 1557), 124-6; *The Lawes and Statutes of Geneva* (1562), fo. 9. The close supervision of the poor aimed at in some German towns was publicized immediately after the 1572 Act in [Andreas Gerardus or Hyperius,] *The Regiment of the Pouertie* (1572), translated by Henry Tripp, who praised the recent statute for 'the weal public of this realm' (sig. A3ᵛ). Hyperius himself, however, probably drew more on the humanist heritage than on new strands in Protestant theology: R. Jütte, 'Andreas Hyperius (1511-1564) und die Reform des frühneuzeitlichen Armenwesens', *Archiv für Reformationsgeschichte*, 75 (1984), 113-38.

[38] 18 Eliz. I, c. 3. An unsuccessful amendment would have made the Act one against bigamy as well as bastardy: Hartley, *Proceedings in the Parliaments of Elizabeth*, i. 496.

[39] For the committees, see *Commons Journal*, i. 85, 105, and for biographies of their members, P. W. Hasler, *The History of Parliament: The House of Commons 1558-1603* (3 vols., 1981). The representatives from Norwich, Gloucester, and Ipswich were John Aldrich, Sir Nicholas Arnold, and Edward Grimston. On Sandwich, see BL, Lansdowne MS 6/71, fo. 172.

[40] W. H. Turner (ed.), *Selections from the Records of the City of Oxford . . . [1509-83]* (Oxford, 1880), 404; A. Rosen, 'Winchester in Transition, 1580-1700', in P. Clark (ed.), *Country Towns in Pre-industrial England* (Leicester, 1981), 158-9; BL, Cotton MS, Titus BV, fos. 424-7; H. Ellis, 'Letter from Secretary Walsingham', *Norfolk Archaeology*, 2 (1849), 92-6. The influence of Norwich perhaps explains the early county bridewell at Acle: John More preached there (A. Hassell Smith, *County and Court. Government and Politics in Norfolk 1558-1603* (Oxford, 1974), 104-5). The Hampshire house of correction, which had 40 beds, 6

Warwick, and the earl of Huntingdon introducing a clothier from Gloucester in order to give a similar push in Leicester, were equally convinced that religious reform and regulation of the poor must advance hand in hand in the decade after the Rising in the North.[41] Even Norwich heard the same message, from Cecil's agent, Dru Drury, sent in after a threatening local conspiracy in 1569. It was scarcely news to the reforming mayor and MP, John Aldrich, who had been an alderman in the camping times of 1549, and who must have had his own reasons for embracing the godly rhetoric of 1571 and the legislation of 1572 and 1576.[42]

Faced with these pressures from inside and outside, town councils had choices available to them, and local circumstances determined a multiplicity of different outcomes. Protestant refugee communities, as in Sandwich and Norwich, might influence both attitudes and welfare practices. Reformations of manners could get an official boost when bishops recognized the particular problems of ports, and effectively delegated jurisdiction over 'sin and wickedness' to the secular authority, as Parkhurst did in Yarmouth, Curtis in Rye, and Hutton in Hull.[43] In towns with a single parish, or what amounted to a single parish—Hull, Lynn, early Stuart Plymouth and Strat-ford—a minister could sometimes dominate, and determine policy, more easily than in towns with several parishes.[44] But some densely structured places like Norwich, Ipswich, or Colchester might already have had religious reformations at the parish level and early experiments in social welfare,

looms, and a dyehouse, and set 80 rogues to work as well as providing spinning work for non-residents, may have been the first county house founded after the 1576 Act. For the part played by Fleetwood, Knollys, and Walsingham in the origins of the 1572 and 1576 legislation, see G. R. Elton, *The Parliament of England 1559–1581* (Cambridge, 1986), 269–71, though Elton mistook Walsingham for Strickland (*Commons Journal*, i. 84). Both central and local interests had a role in framing these statutes, and it is impossible to disentangle them. For another example of how projectors and central and local politicians might interact to stimulate legislation, see G. R. Elton, 'Piscatorial Politics in the Early Parliaments of Elizabeth I', in *Studies in Tudor and Stuart Politics and Government*, iv (Cambridge, 1992), 109–30, and Robert Hitchcock, *A Pollitique Platt for the honour of the Prince . . .* (1580), sigs. Fiv–v.

[41] A. L. Beier, 'The Social Problems of an Elizabethan Country Town: Warwick, 1580–90' in P. Clark (ed.), *Country Towns in Pre-industrial England* (Leicester, 1981), 75; C. Cross *The Puritan Earl* (1966), 126.

[42] Pound, *Norwich Census of the Poor*, 9; Hasler, *House of Commons 1558–1603*, i. 333. Aldrich had been mayor for the first time during the great mortality crisis of 1557-8, when his colleagues fell like flies around him: Slack, *Impact of Plague*, 128.

[43] Collinson, *Religion of Protestants*, 160 (n. 65), 173–4; Hull City RO, Bench Book 4, fos. 326ᵛ–327ʳ. In Rye, authority was delegated to the town preacher but he worked 'hand in glove with the magistrates'.

[44] Hull had two churches, both technically mere chapelries, and King's Lynn (after 1555) one and a half parishes, but there was no doubt about the dominance of Holy Trinity in the first and St Margaret's in the second: Cross, *Urban Magistrates and Ministers*, 2, 8; *VCH East Riding*, i. 95; V. Parker, *The Making of King's Lynn* (1971), 21–2; Norfolk RO, C/GP 13/2. For the troubles caused by Thomas Wilson's attempt to dominate Stratford, see Hughes, *Politics, Society and Civil War in Warwickshire*, 83–4, and A. Hughes, 'Religion and Society in Stratford on Avon 1619-1638', *Midland History*, 19 (1994), 58–84.

which were taken over and reshaped by the clerical and magisterial alliances of the 1570s and after.[45] At the same time, one might have a small town like Warwick with little civic provision for the poor at all, until Leicester and Cartwright came on the scene, or Lincoln in the 1580s, where those pushing for religious and social reform seem essentially to have been engaged in a first religious reformation, not, as in Norwich, embarking on a second.[46]

These were all, for one reason or another, and at some point or other, reforming towns. At the permanently lukewarm end of the spectrum were cities which had well-developed welfare facilities by the 1570s and where godly preachers had only a modest influence. One was Bristol, with its increasingly rich endowment of schools and hospitals, where Northbrook's sermons seem not to have inspired a civic campaign for the reformation of manners, or at least not immediately: in the 1580s there are some signs of a 'new tone', godly in character, in municipal ordinances.[47] A comparable case, rather later, was Worcester, where Robert Abbot's impact was similarly muted.[48]

Shrewsbury may have gone further down the Norwich road. At the beginning of Elizabeth's reign the bailiffs engaged in a civic reformation, appointing a Protestant schoolmaster, confiscating church plate 'for the use of the poor', taking surveys, beginning a poor rate, and appointing six 'provosts' to supervise paupers. In essence it was perhaps less a new departure than the continuation of the kind of civic activity considered in the last chapter. It coincided with the appointment as recorder of John Throckmorton, already recorder of Coventry and Worcester, which suggests interesting connections, and a crucial element in it may have been the long experience of Adam Mytton, alderman in 1559, who had been a contact of Cromwell's and an

[45] Cf. Byford, 'Price of Protestantism', ch. 5; and for Ipswich, MacCulloch and Blatchly, 'Pastoral Provision', 473–4, and Collinson, *Religion of Protestants*, 175–7.

[46] Beier, 'Social Problems of an Elizabethan Country Town', 74–5; J. W. F. Hill, *Tudor and Stuart Lincoln* (Cambridge, 1956), 101–6.

[47] Northbrooke, *A Treatise;* M. C. Skeeters, *Community and Clergy: Bristol and the Reformation c.1530–c.1570* (Oxford, 1993), 134–8; M. Stanford, *The Ordinances of Bristol 1506–1598* (Bristol Record Society, 41, 1990), pp. xxiv, 72–3, 84–5. It is unfortunate that the 16th-c. records of the corporation are so sparse. Popham's influence may be more important than Northbrook's in explaining the house of correction of 1577 (S. Seyer, *Memoirs, historical and topographical, of Bristol . . .* (2 vols., Bristol, 1821-3), ii. 248); but it is at least possible that in the 1580s, with John Carr's endowment of Queen Elizabeth Hospital, modelled on Christ's Hospital, London, there was some effort at a reformed citadel. See the hints in W. K. Jordan, *The Forming of the Charitable Institutions of the West of England* (Transactions of the American Philosophical Society, new ser., 50, pt. 8, Philadelphia, 1960), 29, 37; Hasler, *House of Commons 1558–1603*, i. 628–9; Stanford, *Ordinances*, 103-4. On Bristol generally, see D. H. Sacks, *The Widening Gate: Bristol and the Atlantic Economy 1450–1700* (Berkeley, Calif., 1991).

[48] There are only faint signs of sabbatarianism in the city, and another 'godly' provision of corn for the poor in 1597, echoing that of 1556: A. Dyer, *The City of Worcester in the Sixteenth Century* (Leicester, 1973), 238–9; Worcs. RO, Worcester View of Frankpledge II, 1569–1608, fo. 221ᵛ.

MP back in the 1530s and active in providing corn for the town in 1550.[49] In the later 1570s, however, the bailiffs began a second reformation in a rather different key. They sought advice on 'the best course for the suppressing of inmates, idle persons, drunkards', appointed a 'godly' lecturer, Edward Bulkeley, and surveyed the poor on more than one occasion in the 1580s with an eye to identifying 'all idle persons and inmates or other disordered persons meet to be reformed'.[50] Yet Shrewsbury was never taken over by a godly alliance. The power struggles which occupied the élite were still, as they had been for decades, between rival economic interest groups, between the drapers and the mercers, for example, just as those in Bristol were between merchants and retailers; they were not replaced by, or transmuted into, contests between the upright and the profane.[51]

The kinds of choice available to town councils are perhaps best illustrated by the case of Chester. There, as in Norwich, there was a survey of the poor and a project for their employment just before the 1572 statute; and in 1575 the city had a 'godly, overzealous' mayor, Henry Hardware, attacking the mystery plays and Shrove Tuesday games, and founding a workhouse run by 'governors and collectors' and 'censors and wardens' just as the 1576 statute prescribed.[52] In 1583, however, the offer by an anonymous 'well-wisher' of £100 for the poor, communicated by the town preacher, Christopher Goodman, was turned down, and turned down because of the conditions attached. These were that the number of city brewers be reduced, 'that no citizen resort to any tippling or alehouse', 'that the poor be provided for as not to go abroad', and that all holders of city funds be called to account. The last of these stipulations, with its implication of corruption, may have caused most offence, but together they constituted a programme of civic reform which some cities would have welcomed. The Chester council thought them 'not

[49] Shrewsbury Guildhall, Assembly Book 1554–83, fos. 32ᵛ, 33, 34ʳ, 42ᵛ; *VCH Shropshire*, ii (1973), 154; Hasler, *House of Commons 1558–1603*, iii. 494–6; S. T. Bindoff, *The History of Parliament: The House of Commons 1509–1558* (3 vols., 1982), ii. 653–4; Shropshire RO, Shrewsbury Records, MS 2696. One of the younger men involved as a 'provost' of the poor in 1559, Robert Ireland, was, however, later renowned as 'a stout protestant and a furtherer of the poor' who died 'godly': Hasler, *House of Commons 1558–1603*, ii. 370. The confiscation of church plate for civic purposes has parallels elsewhere in the early 1550s: e.g. HMC, *Salisbury (Cecil)*, i. 119-20 (Stamford).

[50] Shrewsbury Guildhall, Assembly Book 1554–83, fos. 221ᵛ, 232ʳ, 353ʳ, 360ʳ; Shropshire RO, Shrewsbury Records, MSS 728, 2624. For correspondence between the corporation and Bulkeley, see MS 2699. Cf. P. Williams, *The Council in the Marches of Wales under Elizabeth I* (Cardiff, 1958), 183, 191.

[51] Cf. T. C. Mendenhall, *The Shrewsbury Drapers and the Welsh Wool Trade in the XVI and XVII Centuries* (Oxford, 1953), 40–6; Sacks, *Widening Gate*, chs. 6 and 7.

[52] Chester Corporation Records, A/B/1, fo. 126ᵛ; Collinson, *Birthpangs*, 54–5; R. H. Morris, *Chester in the Plantagenet and Tudor Reigns* (Chester, n.d.), 319–22; BL, Harleian MS 2150, fo. 198. Hardware was the son-in-law of Henry Gee, on whom see above, p. 11: A. M. Kennett, E. J. Shepherd, and E. Willshaw, *Tudor Chester* (Chester, 1986), 14. For the impact of another reforming mayor, in 1592, compare the ordinances in Chester Corporation Records, A/F/4/30 with those of 1591 in M/L/1/26.

requisite nor convenient neither yet some of them sufferable by law'. Thereafter they followed the law, summoning a 'general meeting' of overseers and churchwardens in 1598 to study the new poor law brought down by one of their MPs.[53]

Yet the welfare legislation of 1598, which even the lukewarm had to take on board, was as much a product of reforming instincts and fears of popular disorder among MPs as was that of the 1570s. Framed by a committee chaired by a 'promoter of further reformation' and 'practical godliness', Robert Wroth, the 1598 statutes show that the godly continued to contribute to new national prescriptions.[54] They also continued to implement them once they were in place with greater enthusiasm and elaboration than their colleagues. Houses of correction were again in fashion after the 1610 statute encouraging their use,[55] but it was John Cotton's Boston which produced a 'jersey-school' employing poor children in 1614, and John White in Dorchester and his friends in Plymouth who planned ambitious new workhouse-hospitals in 1616.[56] The Book of Orders of 1631, whose origins will be considered in the next chapter, had a similar impact: simply confirming what the councillors of Dorchester and Gloucester were already doing, prompted by high prices in 1630; stimulating the councillors of Lynn to yet another discussion of novel means of employing the poor 'as it shall please God to

---

[53] Chester Corporation Records, A/B/1, fos. 186ᵛ-187, 254. The MP was Alderman Peter Warburton, subsequently an active reforming justice in the county palatine: S. Hindle, 'Aspects of the Relationship of the State and Local Society in Early Modern England with special reference to Cheshire c. 1590–1630', Ph.D. thesis, University of Cambridge, 1992, 412-13.

[54] P. Slack, *Poverty and Policy in Tudor and Stuart England* (1988), 126; Hasler, *House of Commons 1558–1603*, iii. 663; J. Walter, 'A "Rising of the People"? The Oxfordshire Rising of 1596', *P&P*, 107 (1985), 138. On Wroth, see Hasler, *House of Commons 1558-1603*, iii. 663, but also N. Tyacke, 'Wroth, Cecil and the Parliamentary Session of 1604', *Bulletin of the Institute of Historical Research*, 50 (1977), 120-5.

[55] 7 James I, c. 4. This statute seems to have been intended to clear up legal doubt about whether magistrates had the power to commit the 'idle and disorderly' to houses of correction, and to encourage county foundations. Among those specially named to the committee on the bill, in addition to all knights of the shire, were the Puritans Sir Francis Hastings and Sir Nathaniel Bacon: *Commons Journal*, i. 429.

[56] Bailey, *Minutes of the Corporation of Boston*, ii. 162, 196; Underdown, *Fire from Heaven*, 109–10; F. Rose-Troup, *John White: The Patriarch of Dorchester* (1930), 30-1; R. N. Worth, *Calendar of the Plymouth Municipal Records* (Plymouth, 1893), 257-8; R. N. Worth *History of Plymouth* (Plymouth, 1890), 194, 273-4, 286–90; M. Stoyle, *Loyalty and Locality: Popular Allegiance in Devon during the English Civil War* (Exeter, 1994), 196. Cf. the new house of correction in Exeter and ordinances for the poor in Salisbury in 1613: MacCaffrey, *Exeter*, 114; P. Slack (ed.), *Poverty in Early-Stuart Salisbury* (Wilts. Record Society, 31, 1975), 83-6; and for connections between these West Country towns, see: Underdown, *Fire from Heaven*, 131; *William Whiteway of Dorchester: His Diary 1618–1635* (Dorset Record Society, 12, 1991), p. 180 n.; Slack, *Impact of Plague*, 305. In 1612 there were also stringent regulations for Colchester's new workhouse: P. Morant, *The History and Antiquities of the County of Essex* (Chelmsford, 1816), i. Appendix to the History of Colchester, pp. 17–18; Colchester Corporation Records, Assembly Book 1601-20, fos. 119ᵛ–121ᵛ.

give the best success thereunto'; quickly left behind in Hull, where the great Charity Hall of May 1631 was designed to set 100 poor children to work.[57]

This process might have continued. The early Stuarts were perfectly capable of borrowing the clothes of the godly if it looked as if they might be tailored to fit: not perhaps sabbatarianism after the Book of Sports,[58] but certainly campaigns against the 'odious sin' of 'profane swearing and cursing', attacked in a proclamation of 1635, and attempts to regulate brewing and alehouses, not least because both could be the basis of profitable patents.[59] Conversely, the godly continued to hope for the support of the state, like Samuel Ward of Ipswich, Robert Jenison's tutor, who thought the 'epidemical pestilence' of drunkenness only curable 'by sovereign power and the king's hand', or William Mott, a Colchester justice, seeking Privy Council authority in 1632 for his own remedy, a common brewhouse and an official licenser of alehouses.[60] Cooperation between the Crown and the godly might be an unlikely prospect in the 1630s, when the Laudian programme threatened both the powers of Puritan councils in cathedral cities and the survival of those Stranger churches which still provided models of how social welfare should be managed.[61] But if Henry Sherfield of Salisbury had succeeded in getting his bill for the purpose through Parliament in 1626, municipal brewhouses might have been as common as houses of correction, and as worthy of Archbishop Laud's support as the Reading workhouse proved to be;[62] and if the proposal to 'reduce' the poor relief statutes 'into one law', backed by Sherfield and William Noy, had not also failed, the

---

[57] Underdown, *Fire from Heaven*, 116–19; Glos. RO, Gloucester Records, B3/1, fos. 549ᵛ–550ʳ; King's Lynn Borough Archives, Hall Book 9, fo. 340ʳ; Hull City RO, Bench Book 5, 241, 253–4, 255–6.

[58] Charles had, however, supported sabbatarian legislation in 1625 which had its origin in bills sponsored by John White's friend, Sir Walter Earl: K. L. Parker, *The English Sabbath* (Cambridge, 1988), 170, 175; *Commons Journal*, i. 511, 521–2.

[59] J. F. Larkin and P. L. Hughes, *Stuart Royal Proclamations* (2 vols., Oxford, 1973–83), ii, nos 200, 240; PRO, SP 16/332/67; S. K. Roberts, 'Alehouses, Brewing and Government under the Early Stuarts', *Southern History*, 2 (1980), 45–71.

[60] Samuel Ward, *Woe to Drunkards* (1624), 41, 48–9; APC 1630–1, 358–9; HMC, *Verulam* 31–5. On the Mott family, see B. W. Quintrell, *The Maynard Lieutenancy Book 1608–1639* (Chelmsford, 1993), 362, n. 152.

[61] K. Fincham, *Prelate as Pastor: The Episcopate of James I* (Oxford, 1990), 96; A. Foster, 'Church Policies of the 1630s', in R. Cust and A. Hughes (eds.), *Conflict in Early Stuart England* (1989), 208–9. In London Sir Thomas Middleton, sponsor of a scheme for parish employment for the poor, was a member of the Dutch Church: Slack, *Poverty and Policy*, 154; O. P. Grell, *Dutch Calvinists in Early Stuart London: The Dutch Church in Austin Friars 1603–42* (Leiden, 1989), 47, 99.

[62] *Commons Journal*, i. 833, 837; Hants RO, J. L. Jervoise, Herriard Collection, M69/S6/xxi.4 (I am grateful to Mr J. T. L. Jervoise for permission to consult and cite this collection); M. Hinton, A *History of the Town of Reading* (1954), 89–91; J. M. Guilding (ed.), *Reading Records: Diary of the Corporation* (4 vols., 1892–6), iii. 389.

Parliament of 1626 might have been as formative in the development of social welfare as those of 1572 and 1597.[63]

We are dealing therefore with municipal policies and practices which evolved by accretion, so that what were once the peculiar enthusiasms of godly cities might be assimilated into a general consensus, whether through legislation or simple emulation. That is what invalidates our proposed laboratory experiment. But it also highlights the particular contribution of godly zeal in maintaining the momentum: occasionally ratcheting up the regulatory machinery by another notch, more often creating a new spurt of local reform when earlier bursts of energy had flagged.

It was never possible to sustain the momentum for long. Too much depended on individual personalities. In the 1570s they might be experienced hands like Aldrich in Norwich, facing new challenges and adopting new language late in life with perhaps a tongue half in cheek. In the more embattled citadels of the 1620s some of them were originally 'new men' in a town, like John Ivie in Salisbury, who had waited years for the chance to topple a cautious old guard.[64] In either case, much depended also on maintaining a godly party: hence the rarity of bursts of thorough reformation in towns like London and Bristol with alternative political alignments, and their relative frequency in some (though not all) cathedral cities, where there were familiar antagonists in the Close. The rhetoric of reformation needed to encounter resistance if it was to be as hot and all-embracing as it sometimes was. The reforming party in 'all the contentions in Lincoln' in the 1580s, for example, not only claimed to be enforcing sobriety and the sabbath against opponents who wished to set up 'maypoles and maygames' and preferred 'a tale of Robin Hood' to a sermon; they also prided themselves on remodelling the town school, regulating the assizes of bread and beer, and 'bridling' the poor by setting 180 potential beggars and thieves to work.[65] In the simultaneous faction fights in Rye, John Fagge and his allies suppressing whoredom and drunkenness were equally keen to secure bequests for the poor, for highway repairs and for a new water conduit.[66]

The propaganda employed in these struggles could be deceptive, and mask

---

[63] *Commons Journal*, i. 699, 714, 833, 853; W. B. Bidwell and M. Jansson (eds.), *Proceedings in Parliament 1626* (4 vols., New Haven, Conn., 1991–6), iii. 125, 199.

[64] T. A. Kent, 'John Ivie, Goldsmith', *Hatcher Review*, 3 (1987), 130–1. Cf. Underdown, *Fire from Heaven*, 41–3. Ignatius Jorden, the Exeter Puritan, was also a newcomer to the town as a youth: Ferdinando Nicolls, *The Life and Death of Mr. Ignatius Jurdain* (2nd edn., 1655), 3–4.

[65] PRO, SP 12/192/67; Hill, *Tudor and Stuart Lincoln*, 90, 101-6; HMC, *Lincoln*, 65, 68–70. Robert Monson, recorder immediately before the Lincoln disturbances, and much interested in schools, a 'house of industry' and the town conduit, had been an MP and a member of the committee on the poor bill of 1571: Hill, *Tudor and Stuart Lincoln*, 90, 102–3; Hasler, *House of Commons 1558–1603*, iii. 66.

[66] Mayhew, *Tudor Rye*, 128, 132-4. On factions in the town, see also Gregory, 'Witchcraft, Politics and "Good Neighbourhood"'.

more sordid motives: that was part of its purpose. Dr Craig has shown that the 'stirs' in Elizabethan Bury St Edmunds set the godly against the town feoffees in what was essentially a fight for command of charitable resources; and that perceptions of a 'cosmic drama' between good and evil were imposed on similar disputes in Thetford by prejudiced outside observers.[67] The brewers who persistently opposed restrictions on customary forms of sociability in more than one town were defending their livelihoods, and wrestling with rival networks of patronage and power.[68] But perceptions of the religious credentials of ambitious civic reformers were not always inaccurate, even if they could be manipulated, by insiders as well as outsiders. In many civic troubles the godly were defining their own identity through contentions with the ungodly, as in the Yarmouth of the 1630s, where they accused their adversaries of misappropriating funds for the repair of the harbour, or in Norwich at the same time, where a 'silly Puritan mayor' blamed unemployment on Bishop Wren, who had driven honest employers overseas.[69] Henry Sherfield's notes for his speeches in Salisbury show that he adjusted his tone when he was there, talking much more in terms of 'wars' against the reprobate than he did in Parliament or in private correspondence; he was appealing to those striving to achieve their local 'Sion' and rejoicing in the divisions that 'a true and real reformation' caused. Such men laid claim to what Dr Ingram rightly describes as the 'moral high ground', and to the civic high ground as well.[70]

When they succeeded, their occupation was always temporary, rarely lasting more than a decade; but it might nevertheless have lasting consequences. The Norwich of the 1570s was hailed as a model of how social welfare should be organized for at least a century, and town councils from Nottingham to Oxford regularly recruited Norwich men to run their workhouses, much as they looked to certain Cambridge colleges for their preachers.[71] A copy of Salisbury's storehouse for the poor seems to have

---

[67] J. S. Craig, 'The Bury Stirs Revisited: An Analysis of the Townsmen', *Proceedings of the Suffolk Institute of Archaeology and History*, 37 (1991), 208–24; J. S. Craig, 'The "Godly" and the "Froward": Protestant Polemics in the Town of Thetford, 1560-1590', *Norfolk Archaeology*, 41 (1992), 279–93.

[68] Slack, 'Poverty and Politics in Salisbury', 186–7; Gregory, 'Witchcraft, Politics and "Good Neighbourhood"', 44–5; and for a later example, C. Lee, '"Fanatic Magistrates": Religious and Political Conflict in Three Kent Boroughs, 1680–1684', *Historical Journal*, 35 (1991), 45. Cf. Underdown, *Fire from Heaven*, 114. Alderman Hodgson of Lincoln, a brewer and a member of the reforming party in the 1580s, is an exception: Hill, *Tudor and Stuart Lincoln*, 231; HMC, *Lincoln*, 69.

[69] Cust, 'Anti-Puritanism and Urban Politics', 7 and n.; Bodl., Tanner MS 68, fo. 147.

[70] Slack, 'Public Conscience of Henry Sherfield', 164–8; M. Ingram, 'Reformation of Manners in Early Modern England', in P. Griffiths, A. Fox, and S. Hindle (eds.), *The Experience of Authority in Early Modern England* (1996), 69.

[71] J. Thirsk and J. P. Cooper (eds.), *Seventeenth-Century Economic Documents* (Oxford, 1972), 753–4; Thomas Firmin, *Some Proposals For the imploying of the Poor* (1678), 6; below, p. 97; W. H. Stevenson et al. (eds.), *Records of the Borough of Nottingham*, v. 124–5, 173

been planned in Bristol in 1635, and the Dorchester brewhouse was thought by several 'ministers and householders' to be a remedy for Lynn's problems as late as 1658.[72] It was a brewhouse also, as in 'some adjoining corporations', which John Baber, recorder of Wells, wanted in 1631. But if such projects were to get anywhere quickly, they needed godly motivation too, which Baber conspicuously lacked. At about the same time the mayor of Southampton, bogged down in a long legal struggle to secure an endowment for a workhouse, was writing to Sherfield for advice on how to 'procure reformation' when the town's 'great men' were dragging their feet—how in effect to be like Plymouth, Dorchester or Salisbury.[73]

While we must agree with Professor Spufford that godly zeal was not a necessary condition for any kind of social reform, therefore, we must also respect the opinion of those contemporaries who thought that it was essential for the speedy reformation of their own communities. It was what Jenison was trying to inculcate in Newcastle and what 'the Arch-Puritan', Ignatius Jorden, looked for in Exeter but could only impose when other councillors fled from the plague of 1625.[74] Without that 'forwardness in well-doing' which distinguished men such as Jorden, civic reformation would have been even slower and more piecemeal than it actually was.

III

That said, however, it leaves us with the question of whether we are observing only a change of speed or also a change of direction and destination. If the godly essentially brought fresh enthusiasm to things like workhouses which had been tried before and which might be revived for a host of secular reasons, was there in the end anything peculiar in their contribution to public welfare? If we look for specific innovations in practice, the answer must be a scarcely qualified 'no'. There is only one indisputably Puritan novelty in our story, and this chapter would have a very dry conclusion if it had to end in the municipal brewhouse. The claim of the godly to special attention might better rest not on particular items on their menu, but on the

(1627); M. G. Hobson and H. E. Salter (eds.), *Oxford Council Acts 1626–1665* (Oxford Historical Society, 95, 1933), 165 (1649). For other examples, see Bailey, *Minutes of the Corporation of Boston*, ii. 281 (1619); Hull City RO, Bench Book 5, fos. 253–4 (1631) and BRK/3/12/1 (1655); Chester Corporation Records, A/B/2, fos. 182ᵛ, 184ʳ (1675).

[72] Bristol AO, Common Council Proceedings 1627–42, between fos. 59 and 60; King's Lynn Borough Archives, Hall Book 11, fo. 7. Cf. P. Clark, *The English Alehouse* (1983), 193, n. 72, for another possible copy, in Bridport.

[73] PRO, SP 16/194/19; Hants RO, J. L. Jervoise, Herriard Coll., 44M69/xxxv/35, 59, 62; W. J. Connor (ed.), *The Southampton Mayor's Book of 1606–1608* (Southampton Records Series, 21, 1978), 27–8, 30. On Baber, see W. Prest, *The Rise of the Barristers* (Oxford, 1986), 342, and cf. T. G. Barnes, *Somerset 1625–40* (Oxford, 1961), 137 and n.

[74] Nicolls, *Jurdain*, sig. A7ᵛ, p. 65; Slack, *Impact of Plague*, 258, 261–2. For Jorden's career, see M. Stoyle, *From Deliverance to Destruction: Rebellion and Civil War in an English City* (Exeter, 1996), 19–43. Nicolls, Jorden's biographer, had been a colleague of White's in Dorchester, and his elder brother was Rector of Plymouth: Whiteway, *Diary*, p. 180.

voracious appetites which could encompass everything from profane words to water supply in pursuit of speedy reformation: on the comprehensive civic ambition which made a sabbatarian mayor of Coventry demand weekly reports from his constables on the cleanliness of the streets in 1655, and which persuaded the council of Stafford to convert their maypole into ladders for fighting fires in 1612.[75]

We might also make something of the reformation of manners, of course, a force whose long-term contribution to Professor Hutton's 'Fall of Merry England' it is difficult to deny.[76] But that too was compounded out of older ingredients, and in local practice it had a tendency to run into the sand, to lose some of its peculiarities when constables and magistrates found more familiar and urgent targets. In the court records of Norwich, for example, the most numerous practitioners of 'ill rule' were not the sabbath-breakers, drunkards, or harlots identified by magisterial rhetoric, but people simply living 'out of service', idly, unemployed, and in Colchester they were suspicious immigrants and lodgers.[77] Orders for the Bury St Edmunds house of correction in 1589 concentrated on vagrants, petty pilferers, and especially hedge-breakers, a persistent problem in an area beset by timber famine.[78] Only in the remarkable Offenders' Book of early Stuart Dorchester do we find many cases of profane swearing, thanks to the sharp ears of exceptionally committed constables, and a preponderance of offences relating in one way or another to drink.[79] The more usual pattern was that described by Dr Archer in Elizabethan London, where an initial campaign against illicit sexuality, pursued by Puritan governors of Bridewell in the later 1570s, quickly degenerated into an attack on vagrants and the disorderly poor.[80]

[75] Hughes, 'Coventry and the English Revolution', 92; D. Underdown, *Revel, Riot and Rebellion* (Oxford, 1985), 54. On Mayor Beake of Coventry, see also Hughes, *Politics, Society and Civil War in Warwickshire*, 283–4, 291; L. Fox (ed.), 'Diary of Robert Beake, Mayor of Coventry, 1655-6', *Miscellany I* (Dugdale Society, 31, 1977), 114.

[76] Hutton, *Rise and Fall of Merry England*, ch. 4. See also Collinson, *Birthpangs*, ch. 4; P. Collinson, *From Iconoclasm to Iconophobia: The Cultural Impact of the Second English Reformation* (Stenton Lecture, Reading, 1985); Ingram, 'Reformation of Manners'.

[77] Cf. Norfolk RO, Orders to the overseers, before the 1577–8 account in Norwich Mayor's 'Booke of the Poore' 1571–9, with Norwich Mayor's Court Books; and Colchester Corporation Records, Assembly Book 1576–99, 14 and 21 June 1590, 17 June 1591, fos. 149ʳ–150ʳ, with Sessions of the Peace Bk. ii, 1630-63. On Norwich, see also P. Griffiths, 'Masterless Young People in Norwich, 1560–1645', in Griffiths et al., *Experience of Authority*, 146–86.

[78] F. M. Eden, *The State of the Poor* (3 vols., 1797), vol. iii, pp. cxxxvi–cxlvi. For other references to pilfering of wood, see J. A. Sharpe, *Crime in Seventeenth-Century England: A County Study* (Cambridge, 1983), 170; West Suffolk RO, Sudbury Town Book D, 1618-34, fo. 122ʳ; Norfolk RO, 'The Charge given to the Overseers', in Norwich Mayor's 'Booke of the Poore' 1571–9.

[79] Dorset RO, Dorchester Records, B2/8/1; Ingram, 'Reformation of Manners', 80; Underdown, *Fire from Heaven*, 72. Of 320 offenders coming before the court between July 1629 and July 1630, 110 (34%) were presented for tippling or drunkenness, and 30 (9%) for swearing profane oaths.

[80] Archer, *Pursuit of Stability*, 249–50, 253, 256; Slack, *Poverty and Policy*, 93–4.

A much stronger case can be made for singling out for attention the *mechanisms* adopted by the godly to realize their ideals, mechanisms which were more persistent because they could be applied specifically to the poor. According to the printed orders in London in 1582, vestrymen were to visit the poor 'daily if it may be . . . to see how they apply their work'. In Norwich the overseers were to do the same every Saturday night or Sunday morning, and to search houses 'several times in every week' for suspect persons and stolen goods. In early Stuart Salisbury there were weekly surveys in order to 'counsel and direct' the poor 'how to order themselves'. Mott's project of 1632 for Colchester envisaged 'certain new beadles, qualified with . . . good courage', and trusted women in each parish who would 'espy and discover the tricks and frauds' of the poor.[81] The distinction between parish collectors and overseers of the poor in the 1572 statute was intended to provide the manpower for exactly this kind of monitoring of behaviour. It is often forgotten—because it remained precept rather than practice—that the 1598 poor relief statute prescribed *four* overseers in every parish, and that the Act of 1601 assumed that the number would range from two to four depending on its size. Sherfield's brewhouse bill of 1626 would have restored four overseers everywhere in order to correct the 'unskilfulness, idleness and falsehood of the poor'.[82]

Once again, however, this tightening of the screws of social discipline was easier to inscribe on paper than in parochial practice. It was impossible in the countryside where, one of Baxter's correspondents complained, people were not 'at home upon any of the weekdays' to be supervised or catechised. It was difficult even in towns, despite John White's view that 'bodies nearly compacted' were 'more easily and better governed'.[83] Hence the importance attributed to institutions, like the Sudbury house of correction, where the inmates in 1624 prayed daily for 'a reformation of our former lives', or the Plymouth workhouse-hospital with its 'religious orders and exercises', where 'continual watch' could be kept 'for avoiding all profaneness and vice whatsoever'.[84] Yet workhouses, conventionally admired as examples of

---

[81] *Orders appointed to be executed in the Cittie of London, for setting rogues and idle persons to worke, and for releefe of the poore* [n.d.; 1582 according to *STC*], sig. Aiv[v] (the orders were first drawn up in 1579: Archer, *Pursuit of Stability*, 98); Norfolk RO, 'Charge given to the Overseers', in Norwich Mayor's 'Booke of the Poore'; Slack, *Poverty in Early Stuart Salisbury*, 91; HMC, *Verulam*, 34.

[82] 39 Eliz. I, c. 3, s. 1; 43 Eliz. I, c. 2, s. 1; Hants RO, J. L. Jervoise, Herriard Coll., M69/S6/xxi.4. Cf. L. Botelho, 'Aged and Impotent: Parish Relief of the Aged Poor in Early Modern Suffolk', in M. Daunton (ed.), *Charity, Self-Interest and Welfare in the English Past* (1996), 97, 107.

[83] N. H. Keeble and G. F. Nuttall, *Calendar of the Correspondence of Richard Baxter* (2 vols., Oxford, 1991), i. 313; Underdown, *Fire from Heaven*, 91.

[84] West Suffolk RO, Sudbury Town Book D, 1618–34, fo. 122[r]; West Devon RO, Plymouth Corporation Records, GP/2. Ordinances drawn up by Sir Richard Martin for Bridewell in 1596 proposed catechizing, prayers, and psalm-singing for the inmates: Huntington

'justice and mercy meeting together',[85] usually failed to deliver the goods. It was not only Bridewell which became a nursery of rogues, despite the ringing declaration in 1582 that its purpose was 'reformation and not . . . perpetual servitude'. Within a decade of the erection of Hull's Charity Hall, its children were removed and boarded with 'some good orderly women' because they were 'so unwholesomely fed and ill-ordered, not brought up in any religious course of life'.[86]

The ideal was practicable only in very special circumstances. In 1635, having already founded sermons 'for the poor' alongside the usual town lecture, the council of Gloucester set about another complete reformation; but it was now to be realized within the confines of the civic hospitals, reorganized under common management, and decked out with a range of officers. The newcomer among them was an 'overseer of the manners of the poor'. He may well have had little to do in the old people's home of St Bartholomew's, whose carefully selected paupers—no 'common scolds' or 'common slanderers'—in 'fit and sweet' lodgings were paid the remarkably generous pension of 2s. 6d. a week and went to prayers twice a day.[87] That shows what civic reformation was supposed to be about, and why even godly cities fell far short of the ideal.

It shows too that the ultimate purpose of Puritan social reform, of the fashioning of welfare according to the dictates of justice and mercy, was public edification. Leaving speed on one side, that was the peculiar destination of the godly; and it was one they were bound never to reach. Margaret Spufford is right, therefore, to stress the centrality of religion, although it was as much a matter of reforming lives as of saving souls. The trouble was that it brought with it all the familiar tensions of Puritanism: that quest for universal reform whose unpopularity and impracticality separated the elect from the reprobate quite as effectively as its Calvinist doctrine. In the real world of the small cities of the godly, one logical if severely limited conclusion was a narrowing of vision to the tidy hospitals we encountered at the end of the last chapter: to the reformed Wigston's of 1576, for example, where a remnant might be 'trained in learning of godliness'.[88] It was in the end, though certainly unwittingly, a cloistered rather than a wholly public virtue.

Library, Calif., Ellesmere MS 2522, fo. 11ᵛ, no. 8. (I owe this reference to the kindness of Ian Archer.)

[85] Nicolls, *Jurdain*, sig. A8.

[86] *Orders appointed to be executed in the Cittie of London* [1582], sig. Biiᵛ; Hull City RO, Bench Book 5, p. 460.

[87] Glos. RO, Gloucester Records, Council Minutes 1565-1632, fos. 560ʳ, 561ʳ; K1/2; P. Clark, 'The "Ramoth-Gilead of the Good": Urban Change and Political Radicalism at Gloucester 1540–1640', in P. Clark, A. G. R. Smith, and N. Tyacke (eds.), *The English Commonwealth 1547–1640* (Leicester, 1979), 189.

[88] A. H. Thompson, A *Calendar of Charters and other Documents belonging to the Hospital of William Wyggeston at Leicester* (Leicester, 1933), 77.

IV

One might have expected some broadening of vision after 1640, some effort to recreate what Robert Burton called whole cities, not mere houses, of correction, once the 'declining days' for the godly of the 1630s were over.[89] But Professor Hirst has amply demonstrated the sporadic and fragile quality of godly rule in the Interregnum.[90] Whatever the impact of millenarianism on national politics, it seems seldom to have rekindled the hottest sort of civic activism. Gloucester was a partial exception. There the necessary tension and godly solidarity were maintained by its escape from the royalist siege of 1643, by its sense of being 'a city assaulted by man and saved by God'—the message inscribed over the south gate and hammered home by the town clerk in his speeches at every subsequent mayor-making. The mayor of this 'Virgin City' must aim at its 'common welfare', see the sabbath observed and 'provisions . . . made for the poor, provisions of work for the idle and of relief for the needy'.[91] The united hospitals, which had been threatened by Laud, were put in place again.

There were somewhat similar 'pious works' elsewhere: in Bristol, Exeter, and Winchester in the 1650s, and in London, with the new workhouses of its Corporation of the Poor, after 1649.[92] Except in the case of London, however, where there were new inputs which will be considered in Chapter 4, the old confidence had gone. Godly schemes continued to be opposed by threatened vested interests; and the godly side itself was now fragmented, literally so in Holy Trinity, Hull, where Baptist soldiers worshipped in the chancel while the town's lecturer kept his congregation isolated from their infection in the nave. In Salisbury the Cromwellian charter of 1656 put in a new recorder ready to 'punish sin, suppress alehouses and administer justice with greater courage' even than his Presbyterian predecessor; but the new regime seems to have had little enthusiasm for the old brewhouse and workhouse, which probably looked like relics of a campaign which had failed.[93] The new generation showed more interest in another inheritance from John White, the wider 'propagating of the gospel', into the counties, into Wales,

[89] Robert Burton, *Anatomy of Melancholy*, ed. H. Jackson (Everyman edn., 1932), i. 92–3. 'Declining days' is Nicolls's phrase: *Jurdain*, sig. A5ᵛ. In 1645 Samuel Fairclough of King's Lynn, for one, looked for rapid progress in 'church purging, and state reforming policy': *The Troublers Troubled* (1641), 53.

[90] D. Hirst, 'The Failure of Godly Rule in the English Republic', *P&P*, 132 (1991), 33–66.

[91] J. Dorney, *Certain Speeches Made upon the day of the Yearly Election of Officers in the City of Gloucester* (1653), 10, 57, 72.

[92] Bristol AO, Common Council Proceedings 1649–59, 59–60; Devon RO, Exeter Records, B1/10, 67; Rosen, 'Winchester in Transition', 168–9; below, pp. 84–7. According to Dr Rosen, the Interregnum rulers of Winchester displayed 'great energy but very little originality' in record-keeping, cleaning the streets, and managing the poor.

[93] John Shawe, *Memoirs of the Life of John Shawe* (Hull, 1824), 54–5; *VCH Wiltshire*, vi (1962), 119; Slack, 'Poverty and Politics in Salisbury', 193.

to the American Indians; and that may have dispersed energies which might otherwise have gone into internal civic reform.[94]

There was in any case a lack of municipal resources for it. Corporations had much more difficulty finding the money to purchase and convert confiscated ecclesiastical property in the 1640s than in the 1540s.[95] The costs of civil war, direct and indirect, were too great, not only in towns 'ravished by violence' like Gloucester's 'sister cities', Bristol and Worcester, but in Gloucester itself, its municipality virtually bankrupt and its trade depressed. According to the town clerk in 1652, people attributed the decay of trade to the garrison which kept gentry visitors away. They attributed it also in proto-Weberian fashion to the flight of religion: 'When this city had more zeal in religion, then here was more quickness in trade.'[96] But the converse turned out not to be true. Zeal had little place in Restoration towns when garrisons disappeared, the gentry returned, and marketing and service sectors revived.

The end of godly cities with a whimper rather than a bang does not mean that they had had no effect. They had pushed mechanisms for the regulation and relief of the poor further than they would otherwise have gone, and the influence of that will be evident in later chapters. Whether they had succeeded in transforming popular manners more generally is doubtful, though the question merits further research. Professor Underdown shows that the illegitimacy rate in the Puritan hothouse of Dorchester fell even more rapidly than the national trend, but it would be risky to argue with confidence from a single case.[97] We do not know whether the national trend itself owed anything to regulation, alongside the many other factors depressing fertility generally. It seems on the face of it unlikely, and if it did we should probably look for an explanation to Dr Ingram's church courts rather than to the efforts of a few civic magistrates.[98] There is obviously every reason to be sceptical about the contemporary claim that in Ignatius Jorden's time Exeter citizens living near the market 'did not hear an oath sworn for many years together'. If the disciplines of the godly were effectively imposed

[94] [John White,] *The Planter's Plea* (1630), 83. The wider aspirations are evident in e.g. Baxter's correspondence: Keeble and Nuttall, *Calendar of Correspondence of Baxter*, i. 193–4, 207, 256; ii. 7, 9, 19, 40.

[95] See e.g. *VCH Wiltshire*, vi. 119. Chichester took over a small hospital formerly belonging to the dean and chapter, but such cases are few: M. James, *Social Problems and Policy during the Puritan Revolution 1640–1660* (1930), 254. In 1656 the Gloucester corporation acquired the cathedral, along with other property, but had to raise a subscription to cover the cost: *VCH Gloucestershire*, iv. 283.

[96] Dorney, *Certain Speeches*, 71, 77; *VCH Gloucestershire*, iv. 98–9.

[97] Underdown, *Fire from Heaven*, 106–7. I have been unable to detect anything comparable in the admittedly less helpful parish registers of Salisbury.

[98] M. Ingram, *Church Courts, Sex and Marriage in England, 1570–1640* (Cambridge, 1987), 238, 276–81. Some reasons for the decline of bastardy rates are suggested in K. Wrightson, 'The Nadir of English Illegitimacy in the Seventeenth Century', in P. Laslett, K. Oosterveen, and R. Smith (eds.), *Bastardy and Its Comparative History* (1980), 176–91.

or internalized, we must surely follow Dr Wrightson and find the victims or beneficiaries among local élites, legitimizing their status by distancing themselves from the 'great unjust rude rabble'.[99]

The wider inculcation of godly discipline remained an impossible goal; and the greater the acceleration of civic reform, the more divisive, unpopular, and unattainable that ultimate destination became. Norwich in its Elizabethan heyday had been described as 'another Utopia: the people . . . so orderly, the streets kept so cleanly, the tradesmen, young and old, so industrious, the better sort so provident and withal so charitable, that it is . . . rare to meet a beggar there'; but Samuel Ward confessed that the similar vision which he presented to the Bury assizes in 1618 might be 'an Utopia, I fear some will say, too good to be true'.[100] The constant supervision and repression which is a theme of all early modern Utopias — 'servitude, loss of liberty, punishment', in Robert Burton's words — could not be achieved.[101] John Eliot of Massachusetts wrote to Baxter soon after the Restoration hoping still that 'all the world would become a divine college' — a hospital or city of correction writ large. Baxter commented in reply that so few were 'reformed', and so few of them had 'the power of godliness', that 'we shall have what we would, but not in this world'. We may conclude where we began, with Robert Jenison. Warning against 'the too immoderate love of these earthly habitations, though we enjoy peace in them', he turned his eyes to 'that better city, the heavenly Jerusalem', because 'here', experience showed, 'we have no abiding city'.[102]

---

[99] Nicolls, *Jurdain*, 46; K. Wrightson, *English Society 1580-1680* (1982), 170, 212–15; K. Wrightson and D. Levine, *Poverty and Piety in an English Village: Terling 1525-1700* (1979), 178-81; Slack, *Poverty in Early-Stuart Salisbury*, 122. Cf. R. von Friedeberg, 'Reformation of Manners and the Social Composition of Offenders in an East Anglian Cloth Village: Earls Colne, Essex 1531–1642', *Journal of British Studies*, 29 (1990), 368.

[100] J. Pound, *Tudor and Stuart Norwich* (Chichester, 1988), 67; Samuel Ward, *Iethro's Ivstice of Peace* (1618), 62. For contemporary praise of the civic amenities of Hull and Leicester, akin to the commonplace admiration for Norwich, see B. Capp, *The World of John Taylor the Water-Poet 1578–1653* (Oxford, 1994), 108.

[101] J. C. Davis, *Utopia and the Ideal Society: A Study of English Utopian Writing 1516–1700* (Cambridge, 1981), 104. Cf. Northbrooke, *A Treatise*, 13: 'It is better to be a subject to a magistrate under whom nothing is lawful, than under him to whom all things is lawful.'

[102] Keeble and Nuttall, *Calendar of Correspondence of Baxter*, ii. 39–41; Jenison, *Cities Safetie*, 188.

3

ABSOLUTE POWER

In December 1586 a group of justices of the peace met in 'conference' at Maidstone to discuss recent letters from the Privy Council. The harvest had failed and the Council had written ordering searches of barns, provisioning of markets, and the setting of 'reasonable' prices for grain. One of the magistrates, William Lambarde, said afterwards that he had spelt out what was in all their minds: these were 'commandments proceeding from absolute authority'. He did not say they were improper. The word for that would have been 'arbitrary'. But Lambarde was in no doubt that naked exercises of executive authority—which is what he meant by 'absolute'—were unpopular: there was 'nothing more hardly digested by the common man', and nothing less likely to be 'earnestly attempted' or 'willingly obeyed'. 'To say the truth,' he wrote to the local power-broker and Privy Councillor, Lord Cobham, 'I wish that absolute power should not be extended where ordinary laws may effect our desires.'[1]

Over the next fifty years, however, absolute power was more and more extended, and put to a variety of uses for the public welfare. By 1609 the Council could write to sheriffs and justices pointing out 'how great a portion of power and government' was left to their care, not only in enforcing ordinary laws but in executing 'extraordinary directions derived from the prerogative power of his Majesty by proclamations, letters and commissions', all 'much importing the common weal of this kingdom'. According to a proclamation of the same year, James I had learnt from observing other Christian princes 'how far the absoluteness of sovereign power extendeth itself'.[2] Here was another reforming drive, and one with considerable potential. If its policies had had the coherence and conviction of those of godly magistrates, the Crown might have put forward a distinct strategy for social reform; and if it had had real power, it might have implemented it.

Simply to present these conditions is, of course, to suggest that neither

---

[1] Staffs. RO, Sutherland MSS, D593/S/4/18/7. Lambarde made much the same point about 'absolute authority' in a letter written the same day to his colleague, Sir John Leveson: D593/S4/14/16. (I am grateful to the Countess of Sutherland for permission to cite these papers.)
[2] HMC, *Buccleugh*, iii. 140; J. F. Larkin and P. L. Hughes, *Stuart Royal Proclamations* (2 vols., Oxford, 1973–83), i. 217, no. 98.

result occurred. Scepticism about the authority and consistency of purpose of the Elizabethan and early Stuart monarchy no doubt explains why there has been surprisingly little recent discussion of the state and state-building in this period, as compared with the eighteenth or nineteenth centuries. The subject cannot be avoided in any account of the history of social policy, however. It is important to ask how far England travelled down the road of purposeful, centrally directed social engineering, a road on which the monarchy seemed to be embarking from the 1580s, and one which was followed by other countries then and later, whether one calls their goal an absolute, a police, or a cameralist state.[3] In order to try to shed some light on this question, I shall look in turn at the development of the social policies promoted by absolute power, at their local implementation, and at the consequences which followed from the limitations of both.

I

The 'very Cato of the commonwealth',[4] William Cecil, again provides a hinge with the past. Just as he welcomed good towns, without foreseeing the trouble they might cause, so he saw the need for the Council also to attack the problems caused by plague, famine, and the sword, without expecting that there might be any doubt about it among lesser governors. Lambarde's conference of December 1586 came at the very moment when Burghley was designing the printed book of dearth orders, published in January 1587, in response to an emergency. He had heard of 'extreme famine' and crowds of 'starving' beggars in Wales and the Marches, with 'lean cheeks and pale faces', uttering 'pitiful cries' and 'woeful moans'. At the same time the government victualler was finding it impossible to provision the navy for the first major war for a quarter of a century, and Recorder Fleetwood was worried about the food supplies of London, and predicting riots by apprentices 'as like unto ill May Day as could be devised'.[5] The parallels with Wolsey are obvious. In 1586 Burghley consulted documents about the cardinal's dealings with the London bakers and about the corn commissions of 1556 which were modelled on those of 1527. In 1578 he had already in-

---

[3] Cf. H. Ballon, *The Paris of Henri IV: Architecture and Urbanism* (Cambridge, Mass., 1991), introd.; S. Cavallo, *Charity and Power in Early Modern Italy: Benefactors and their Motives in Turin, 1541–1789* (Cambridge, 1995), 86–94; M. Raeff, *The Well-Ordered Police State: Social and Institutional Change in the Germanies and Russia, 1600–1800* (New Haven, Conn., 1983), 169–79. For comments on the turning of English politics generally in a more absolutist and less consensual direction from the 1580s, see P. Collinson, 'The Elizabethan Exclusion Crisis and the Elizabethan Polity', *Proceedings of the British Academy*, 84 (1994), 82; J. Guy (ed.), *The Reign of Elizabeth I: Court and Culture in the Last Decade* (Cambridge, 1995), 12–13; and for fears of absolutism in the Sidney circle, B. Worden, *The Sound of Virtue: Philip Sidney's* Arcadia *and Elizabethan Politics* (1996), 241–2, 279.

[4] I. W. Archer, *The Pursuit of Stability: Social Relations in Elizabethan London* (Cambridge, 1991), 38.

[5] BL, Lansdowne MS 49/3–5, 10, 77.

corporated current defences against plague, begun by Wolsey in 1518, into a first printed book of orders. Not for nothing had he been musing at the beginning of the reign on the past 'miseries of the realm . . . the many rebellions . . . the dearth, the famine, the plagues'.[6]

As with Wolsey, moreover, what began as a response to critical circumstances was quickly extended to items of continuing government concern, especially in London. As the rapid growth of the capital became evident from the 1570s, there was an increasingly one-sided dialogue between Council and City in which the Council's voice became ever more peremptory. Besides printed orders for the poor in 1582, and about plague in 1583, it produced in July 1580 the first proclamation banning new building and the subdivision of houses in London and within three miles around. The intention was clear in Burghley's mind: to attack together 'the excess prices of victuals and fuel', 'the danger of plague and infection', and London's 'over-peopling for governance, especially of the worst and basest sort'.[7] In 1586 there followed the first of a complementary series of orders sending justices of the peace back from London to keep hospitality in their counties.[8] It looked as if the social and economic tides which upset the balance of the common weal and aggravated the miseries of the realm were to be firmly held at bay by direction from the top, by printed books of orders and proclamations.

None of this necessarily ruled out political consensus and cooperation, least of all with rulers of good towns, such as Fleetwood and his successors.[9] Neither did it exclude what Lambarde called 'ordinary law'. Another ongoing Cecil concern, the military problem of maimed soldiers, was attacked by

[6] P. Slack, 'Dearth and Social Policy in Early Modern England', *Social History of Medicine*, 5 (1992), 3–5; BL, Lansdowne MS 48, fos. 122, 142; P. Slack, 'Books of Orders: The Making of English Social Policy, 1577–1631', *Trans. Roy. Hist. Soc.*, 5th ser., 30 (1980), 3–4; HMC, *Salisbury*, i. 153.

[7] Archer, *Pursuit of Stability*, 98, 229, 244; Slack, 'Books of Orders', 4; BL, Lansdowne MS 30/18, fo. 44; P. L. Hughes and J. F. Larkin, *Tudor Royal Proclamations* (3 vols., New Haven, Conn., 1964–9), ii. no. 649. The 1580 proclamation may first have been prompted by suggestions from the City, in connection with the orders for the poor drawn up in 1579 and printed in 1582 (BL Add. MS 48019, fo. 152[r]), but the idea was clearly grasped with enthusiasm by Burghley. On the enforcement of the proclamation and its successors, see T. G. Barnes, 'The Prerogative and Environmental Control of London Building in the Early Seventeenth Century: The Lost Opportunity', *California Law Review*, 58 (1970), 1332–63.

[8] *APC 1586–7*, 120. Cf. F. Heal, 'The Crown, the Gentry and London: The Enforcement of Proclamation, 1596–1640', in C. Cross, D. Loades, and J. J. Scarisbrick (eds.), *Law and Government under the Tudors: Essays Presented to Sir Geoffrey Elton* (Cambridge, 1988), 211–26.

[9] The addition of articles against alehouses when the dearth orders were reprinted in 1594 may reflect interchange of this kind: Slack, 'Books of Orders', 3, n. 8; BL, Lansdowne MS 76/4, fos. 87–8. See also the continuing discussion of social problems and policies between government and City in the same decade: Lansdowne MS 74/27–8, fos. 55, 57; 26/73, fos. 205[v]–206[r]; Archer, *Pursuit of Stability*, 56; Huntington Library, Ellesmere MS 2522, fos. 10–13. (I am grateful to Dr Archer for showing me a copy of this last document.)

statute in 1593, when a machinery of assessments, county treasurers, and pensions was erected which persisted in its essentials for a century. Burghley also contemplated commissions of inquiry into hospitals and almshouses, in order to secure housing for disabled veterans, but it was typical of his caution that his inquiries did not proceed as far as allocating vacant places for them.[10] It was typical of him too that he called the dearth orders a 'godly service'; and that he responded rapidly to a suggestion from Lambarde that any threat to fix the price of grain could only be based on an obscure statute of 1534: a proclamation of January 1587 referred to that 'special law of parliament' as well as to the Queen's 'prerogative royal'.[11]

Yet it was plain in all these cases where initiative and authority really lay. Lambarde had learnt the lesson by 1594 when he told jurors searching for corn in Kent to obey 'her Majesty's most princely commandment'. Fleetwood similarly thought the queen might 'by her prerogative' appoint officers to enforce quarantine regulations in London.[12] Strictly speaking, successive editions of dearth and plague orders no doubt rested on the Crown's emergency powers in what Chief Justice Richardson later called any 'emergent cause of state that many times cannot await [a] parliament'. In the case of the dearth orders, however, no new statute was ever thought necessary; and in the case of the plague orders it had to wait until 1604, although rates for the infected had been levied since 1578.[13]

There was also a sufficiently grey area around the prerogative to permit its extension to something as non-emergent as the growth of London, though the Crown was careful to appeal to ordinary law where it could. A search for medieval precedents under the common law of nuisance having proved unfruitful, the 1580 proclamation warned that 'more new jurisdictions and officers' might be needed to prevent new building, and a supporting statute was passed in 1593. But when the Act was not renewed on its expiry in 1601, regulation continued, by proclamations and royal commissions. As Profes-

[10] 35 Eliz. I, c. 4; D. Dean, *Law-Making and Society in Late Elizabethan England: The Parliament of England, 1584–1601* (Cambridge, 1996), 174; BL, Lansdowne MS 103/75, fo. 216. There was in the event a commission of inquiry in 1594: C. Read (ed.), *William Lambarde and Local Government* (Ithaca, NY, 1962), 179. G. Hudson, 'Ex-Servicemen, War Widows and the English County Pension Scheme, 1593–1679', D.Phil. thesis, Univ. of Oxford, 1995, ch. 1, provides the most thorough account of policy with respect to maimed soldiers.

[11] E. M. Leonard, *Early History of English Poor Relief* (Cambridge, 1900), 326; Staffs. RO, Sutherland MSS, D593/S/4/18/7; Hughes and Larkin, *Tudor Royal Proclamations*, ii, no. 686, p. 534; 25 Henry VIII, c. 2. On this statute, see G. R. Elton, *Reform and Renewal: Thomas Cromwell and the Common Weal* (Cambridge, 1973), 111. It was also cited in support of the Crown's dearth policy in 1550 (R. W. Heinze, *Proclamations of the Tudor Kings* (Cambridge, 1976), 229) but not in 1556 (N. S. B. Gras, *The Evolution of the English Corn Market* (Cambridge, Mass., 1915), 448–9).

[12] Read, *Lambarde and Local Government*, 167 (and cf. Lambarde's more hesitant remarks in 1587, ibid. 163); BL, Lansdowne MS 38, fo. 23.

[13] Barnes, 'Prerogative and Environmental Control', 1350; P. Slack *The Impact of Plague in Tudor and Stuart England* (1985), 211–12.

sor Barnes has shown, it was justified, according to inclination and occasion, either by reference to the common law or on the elevated view of the royal prerogative which, according to Ellesmere, might 'restrain things against the commonweal': 'And what is against the commonweal, the king and his council are to judge and determine.'[14]

Parliament, of course, also thought itself a judge of the interests of the common weal, and if we are to understand the increasing prominence of absolute power we need to explain why the Commons found itself willy-nilly taking a back seat. While the executive was relearning the advantages of certain kinds of command, the legislature was backing away from some types of regulation, partly voluntarily, partly because it was pushed. One difficulty was that increasing use of the prerogative power could only exacerbate parliamentary unease about regulatory statutes which necessarily depended on the executive for their enforcement. Joan Kent showed some years ago the difficulties which the Commons had when debating the regulation of 'personal conduct' between the 1570s and 1620s. Members worried about the mechanisms, about creating new summary jurisdictions, conciliar powers, and opportunities for common informers. That may explain the collapse in 1601 of the statute against London building, which Coke said was held to be 'dangerous'. It explains also the demise of those long-lived bastions of common-weal policy, the sumptuary laws, which were always cited as the prime example of unenforceable legislation, and which the Commons chose to repeal altogether in 1604, rather than replace them with something more effective and intrusive.[15]

Equally disabling for parliamentary action were new uncertainties about the direction which economic and social regulation should take. The 1624 Usury Act shows a Parliament finally coming to terms with covetousness, but unwilling of course to go the whole hog and embrace thorough-going *laissez-faire*.[16] Ralegh was in a minority when arguing for the repeal of enclosure laws in 1601 in order to 'leave every man free, which is the desire of a true Englishman'. Yet the seesaw fate of enclosure legislation—repealed in 1593, restored in 1597, relaxed by royal commission in 1618, partially repealed in 1624—reveals total uncertainty about how to respond to agrarian

---

[14] BL, Lansdowne MS 30/21, fos. 52–4; Barnes 'Prerogative and Environmental Control', 1358, 1360–1, and *passim*. Fleetwood refers to the legal doubt about prerogative action in this area in BL, Lansdowne MS 30/22, fo. 55.

[15] J. R. Kent, 'Attitudes of Members of the House of Commons to the Regulation of "Personal Conduct" in Late Elizabethan and Early Stuart England', *Bulletin of the Institute of Historical Research*, 46 (1973), 53, 56–8; Barnes, 'Prerogative and Environmental Control', 1360. On the dubious efficacy of sumptuary laws, see e.g. R. H. Tawney and E. Power, *Tudor Economic Documents* (3 vols., 1924), iii. 334–5; BL, Lansdowne MS 55/12, fo. 34ʳ; S. Burtt, *Virtue Transformed: Political Argument in England, 1688–1740* (Cambridge, 1992), 113.

[16] On public ambivalence about usury, see N. Jones, *God and the Moneylenders: Usury and Law in Early Modern England* (Oxford, 1989); Dean, *Law-Making and Society*, 151–2.

change.[17] So also does the fact that the 1621 Parliament considered both a proposal for a bill supporting the Council's project for public granaries in every county and a bill repealing the Edwardian legislation against regrating, forestalling, and engrossing, a measure which would have been unthinkable in the 1580s.[18] The complex economic crisis of the 1620s, as formative for economic thinking as that of the 1540s, could produce a Misselden visualizing the economy as a self-regulating mechanism, but it did not leave policymakers convinced that no regulation was needed. It undermined some old certainties about the kinds of offender who should be attacked in the name of the common weal—about middlemen, for example—but it offered no obvious replacement. It left confusion—in the Council, it should be said, as much as in Parliament—as debate moved this way and that between various vested and 'concessionary' interests; and it left to historians a policy tangle which only the pen of that great scholar J. P. Cooper could properly unravel.[19]

Parliament was sometimes able to surmount confusion and achieve consensus, when it had the time. The most conspicuous example, despite its lack of practical bite, was wage legislation, which was successfully adapted between 1563 and 1604 so as to fit industry as well as agriculture, and to accommodate the reality of inflation while retaining customary notions of justice and hierarchy.[20] One might also point to Elizabethan legislation on poverty and vagrancy which, while being the immediate result of crisis circumstances and dealing with symptoms rather than causes, showed that where there was room for lengthy debate, contentious issues could be resolved with productive effect. That had happened in 1572 and again, though there was less contention, with the great clutch of poor laws of 1597–8, based on a dozen unofficial bills 'all . . . tending to a like end and purpose', 'a thing scarce to be patterned', D'Ewes thought. It was not patterned again, however, for a century, not even in the 1620s, when circumstances were similar and Sherfield and Noy, among others, would have welcomed a repeat. For

[17] A. McRae, *God Speed the Plough: The Representation of Agrarian England, 1500–1660* (Cambridge, 1996), 12; J. Thirsk (ed.), *The Agrarian History of England and Wales*, iv: *1500–1640* (Cambridge, 1967), 228–37; v: *1640–1750* (2 vols., Cambridge, 1985), ii. 317–21. McRae, *God Speed the Plough*, ch. 2, provides a good account of changing public attitudes on agrarian issues.

[18] W. Notestein, F. H. Relf, and H. Simpson (eds.), *Commons Debates 1621* (7 vols., New Haven, Conn., 1935), ii. 97; Gras, *English Corn Market*, 246–8; Jones, *God and the Moneylenders*, 192–3. A 1552 statute against middlemen in the wool trade was repealed in 1624: B. E. Supple, *Commercial Crisis and Change in England 1600–1642* (Cambridge, 1964), 247.

[19] On the intricacies of economic policy and its formation in the 1620s, see ibid. ch. 10; J. O. Appleby, *Economic Thought and Ideology in Seventeenth-Century England* (Princeton, NJ, 1978), ch. 2; J. P. Cooper, 'Economic Regulation and the Cloth Industry in Seventeenth-Century England', *Trans. Roy. Hist. Soc.*, 5th ser., 20 (1970), 73–85.

[20] The authoritative account is M. F. Roberts, 'Wages and Wage-Earners in England, 1563–1725: The Evidence of the Wage Assessments', D.Phil. thesis, Univ. of Oxford, 1981, 26–40, 334–40.

by then uncertainty about policy was compounded by a further, and decisive, political obstacle: by the reluctance of the early Stuarts, as Professor Russell has shown, either to initiate legislation or to allow parliamentary time for it.[21]

Against this background, the would-be philosopher-statesman of the Jacobean common weal, Francis Bacon, looks like a figure marooned: caught between old and (in his case) family pieties and new political and economic realities, the last defender of an unsustainable common-weal position. As a young man in the 1593 Parliament, he had sat on committees on the bills for London and for maimed soldiers, and he had introduced enclosure bills for 'the benefit of the common wealth' at the opening of the 1597 Parliament.[22] Twenty years later, in government, he tried to pursue the same tack. He had 'some commonwealth bills' ready for the Parliament of 1621, modelled in part on a list of proposals already prepared in 1614. They covered such matters as usury and 'the beautifying and better government of the city of London, and the suburbs of the same', and they included a measure against brewers and tipplers being magistrates in corporate towns which would have appealed to their godly opponents in places like Salisbury. These were not 'wooing bills', Bacon assured Buckingham, but 'good matter to set the parliament on work, that an empty stomach do not feed upon humour'.[23] King and Council nevertheless thought empty parliamentary stomachs safer than debate on a legislative programme, and Bacon had to toe the line. His speech to the 1621 Parliament echoed that of keepers to Parliaments since the 1590s: there were more than enough laws already; what was needed was their enforcement.[24]

In the new climate, Bacon's proposals for royal commissions for a multitude of purposes had more of a future, but there was none for his title for them: 'commonwealth commissions'. As he recognized, 'the care of the commonwealth' was now suspect on all sides, 'the world' thinking it 'but a pretext in matters of state'.[25] Neither was there any prospect of agreement

[21] S. D'Ewes, *Journals of all the Parliaments of Elizabeth* (1682), 561; Dean, *Law-Making and Society*, 170; above, pp. 42–4; C. Russell, *Parliament and English Politics 1621–1629* (Oxford, 1979), 45.

[22] D'Ewes, *Journals*, 519, 551; P. W. Hasler, *The History of Parliament: The House of Commons 1558–1603* (3 vols., 1981), i. 376–7; A. J. Pollard and M. Blatcher, 'Hayward Townshend's Journals', *Bulletin of the Institute of Historical Research*, 12 (1934), 10. Cf. J. Martin, *Francis Bacon, the State and the Reform of Natural Philosophy* (Cambridge, 1992), 6, 71, on Bacon's place in a 'commonwealth' tradition.

[23] J. Spedding (ed.), *The Letters and the Life of Francis Bacon* (7 vols., 1861–74), vii. 116; T. L. Moir, *The Addled Parliament of 1614* (Oxford, 1958), 69, 202–4; Notestein et al., *Commons Debates 1621*, vii, esp. 18–20, 209–10, 273–7. Cf. J. Marwil, *The Trials of Counsel: Francis Bacon in 1621* (Detroit, 1976), 16–17, 136–9. For some similar bills proposed for 1604, see W. Notestein, *The House of Commons 1604–1610* (New Haven, Conn., 1971), 47, 50–3.

[24] Spedding, *Letters and Life of Bacon*, vii. 178; Russell, *Parliaments*, 45.

[25] Spedding, *Letters and Life of Bacon*, vii. 70–3.

on new initiatives in areas where policy was lagging behind economic conditions. Bacon's bills and commissions identified the problem topics, notably agrarian change and urban growth; and the most prominent Jacobean projects and policies to tackle them will be considered later in this chapter. But there was no generally agreed vision of a newly modelled common weal, acceptable alike to Council and Parliament, much as Bacon would have liked it, because there was neither the political space to achieve the necessary consensus nor the political will to overcome the obstacles which economic and social change was putting in its way.

For want of anything better, therefore, Jacobean social policy for the most part ploughed on in grooves well worn by Elizabethan practice. Absolute power continued to extend itself. Sometimes it modestly innovated, as with the new books of orders for the regulation of alehouses, issued in 1608 and 1609 after Parliament failed to legislate on the subject.[26] But more often it sought to improve the mechanisms which might deliver familiar and limited ends. That was the burden of James I's great Star Chamber speech, made at Bacon's suggestion to the judges about to go on circuit in 1616. He asked for reports on the state of the country, urged a clampdown on alehouses and rogues, a revival of country hospitality, and the control of London building, and commended the usual charitable purposes: highways and bridges, relief of the poor, schools and hospitals. The king thought he 'could not more fitly begin a reformation than here to make an open declaration of my meaning'.[27]

In fact, the Jacobean reformation of local government, by numbered articles and instructions, by peremptory commands and cautious reports back, had begun earlier. There are signs of it in the lord keeper's regular charges to assize judges, which had been revived in 1595, and in the activities on circuit of men such as Chief Justice Popham, once recorder of Bristol, MP in the 1570s, veteran of discussions about the first dearth orders, and author in 1598 of one of the first of those sets of articles to high constables which ensured the wider implementation of the poor laws.[28] The campaign gained momentum after 1603 — there were fierce circular letters in 1605 — and especially after the Midland Rising of 1607. Although much of the historical record disappeared in the Whitehall fire of 1619, Dr Quintrell has

[26] Slack, 'Books of Orders', 3, n. 8; Kent, 'Attitudes of Members of the House of Commons', 58.

[27] C. H. McIlwain (ed.), *The Political Works of James I* (Cambridge, Mass., 1918), 326–45. On Bacon's role, see Spedding, *Letters and Life*, vii. 70–1.

[28] Heal, 'Crown, Gentry and London', 215. On Popham, see Hasler, *House of Commons 1558–1603*, iii. 234–6; Dean, *Law-Making and Society*, 171; above, p. 38; BL, Lansdowne MS 48/52, fos. 122–4; Archer, *Pursuit of Stability*, 229; A. Fletcher, *Reform in the Provinces: The Government of Stuart England* (1986), 137–8. Cf. Lord Treasurer Dorset's interest in surveying local corn supplies and grain prices in 1604: *Sir Henry Whithed's Letter Book, i: 1601–1614* (Hampshire Record Ser., 1, 1976), 33 (and cf. p. 6); Hull City RO, BRL 148; and his earlier involvement (as Buckhurst) in discussions of dearth policy in 1586: Staffs. RO, Sutherland MSS, D593/S/4/10/3.

documented its vitality in Lancashire in the second decade of the seventeenth century. It can be traced in Cheshire in 1610 and 1611, where the impetus came from Serjeant Warburton, once an active councillor of Chester.[29] It left its mark in other counties where that tireless bureaucrat, Henry Montagu, formerly recorder of London, was active as lord chief justice. In 1620, reflecting on his experience, Montagu drafted a commission to supervise local government as one of Bacon's proposed 'commonwealth commissions'; and in 1630, now earl of Manchester, he returned to it when the whole Jacobean programme was polished up at the outset of Charles I's Personal Rule. He made his 1620 commission the basis of a new and final Book of Orders.[30]

There was therefore nothing very surprising about the Caroline Book of Orders of January 1631, any more than there was about the other items in the cluster of royal pronouncements on social policy which accompanied it, including reprints of Burghley's plague and dearth orders. Manchester had checked the Book's detailed subject-matter, its *Directions*, with his brother Edward, the very epitome of the godly magistrate in Northamptonshire, and they can have given little offence: vagrants, alehouses, houses of correction, highways added as an afterthought. As Dr Quintrell rightly remarks, they have 'a scratch look about them'. What did cause offence were the two changes introduced into the supervisory commission first drafted in 1620: it was now to comprise the whole of the Council, and to be able to appoint deputies—'spies', Manchester confessed—to act for it in the localities. But that too was the logical conclusion to much that had gone before. It might have been foreseen by Bacon, Popham, and even Lambarde. The Book of Orders, like much else in the social policy of the Personal Rule, was a predictable sheep in wolf's clothing. The question we must ask now is whether the howl of the wolf before and after 1630 succeeded in giving life to what were by then somewhat venerable Elizabethan sheep: whether exercises of absolute power 'quickened' local government, to use Manchester's favourite image, in the ways that were intended.[31]

II

There is no doubt that there was some quickening. The difficulty is to know its speed and extent. The hundreds of reports in the State Papers elicited by

---

[29] *Whithed's Letter Book*, 35–7; Slack, 'Books of Orders', 19; B. W. Quintrell, 'Government in Perspective: Lancashire and the Privy Council, 1570–1640', *Trans. Historical Soc. Lancs. and Cheshire*, 131 (1982), 50; B. W. Quintrell (ed.), *Proceedings of the Lancashire Justices of the Peace at the Sheriff's Table during Assizes Week, 1578–1694* (Lancs. and Cheshire Record Society, 121, 1981), 41, 171–8; above, p. 42, n. 53.

[30] B. W. Quintrell, 'The Making of Charles I's Book of Orders', *Eng. Hist. Rev.*, 95 (1980), 560. For an example of Montagu's activity as LCJ, see Longleat House, Wiltshire, Whitelocke MSS, i. 199–200. (I owe this reference to the kindness of Prof. Derek Hirst.)

[31] Slack, 'Books of Orders', 13–15; Quintrell, 'Making of Charles I's Book of Orders', 568.

the various books of orders in the 1620s and 1630s show bushels of corn being surveyed, households quarantined, vagrants punished, alehouses suppressed, children put out as apprentices, all in their scores. They do not show that these practices were either continuous or universal. Almost 1,000 certificates returned in the 1630s in response to the 1631 Book of Orders still survive; there should be ten times that number. It is impossible to know how many have been lost and how many were never written; and we cannot tell whether the non-reporters were non-actors, or whether they were simply reluctant to give hostages to fortune, to say anything at all lest, as one of the Northamptonshire justices put it, it 'produce an unexpected prejudice' in high places.[32] It is similarly difficult to gauge how exceptional those magistrates were whose papers happen to survive and show them busily riding round enforcing the dearth orders: Lambarde in the 1580s and 1590s, for instance, or Sherfield's friend, Sir Thomas Jervoise, in the 1620s.[33] Where the evidence is partial—as it is also in the case of quarter sessions and, still more, petty sessions—any conclusion is bound to be inference rather than certainty.

Conclusions are easiest with respect to the plague orders. Plague was a largely urban phenomenon and the records of towns are plentiful. It is possible to show corporations adopting new habits after 1578, raising plague rates, listing the infected, in some cases adopting or developing bills of mortality. In the early seventeenth century one can trace the spread of the same habits into rural areas, as quarter sessions also raised special rates for infected villages and sought to isolate them. Contemporaries were dealing with real emergencies, and those emergencies are measurable by the historian, thanks partly to the records they generated. It can be demonstrated that magistrates were most active, as one might expect, at the beginning of an outbreak, or in milder epidemics, when victims were few, readily identifiable, and easily regulated in socially differentiated neighbourhoods; but also that direction from the top had encouraged new administrative habits and a new public consciousness about the management of public health.[34]

The situation is quite otherwise with respect to the dearth orders. In their case the vital administrative activities took place in locations ill served by the

---

[32] Quintrell, 'Making of Charles I's Book of Orders', 569; Slack, 'Books of Orders', 21. The most thorough account of the certificates is now H. A. Langelüddecke, 'Secular Policy Enforcement during the Personal Rule of Charles I: The Administrative Work of Parish Officers in the 1630s', D.Phil. thesis, Univ. of Oxford, 1995, ch. 2. Dr Langelüddecke puts the number of surviving reports at 1412 (p. 336), but his total includes some which were in response to the reissue of the dearth orders in 1630. I am most grateful to him for a copy of his thesis, and for permission to cite his conclusions.

[33] P. Clark, *English Provincial Society from the Reformation to the Revolution: Religion, Politics and Society in Kent 1500–1640* (Hassocks, Sussex, 1977), 232–3; Staffs. RO, Sutherland MSS, D593/S/4/10/2, 4/17, 4/36/1, 4/60/9; C. Russell, *The Fall of the British Monarchies* (Oxford, 1991), 6; Hants RO, J. L. Jervoise, Herriard Coll., 44M69/012, 013.

[34] Slack, *Impact of Plague*, chs. 8, 10.

historical record, in markets, and they involved negotiation between more equal parties, between farmers and magistrates or special jurors who were often farmers themselves. Worse than that, the very phenomenon of dearth is elusive. Studies of parish registers have undermined Professor Bowden's dark picture of 'suffering and extreme hunger' almost throughout the 1620s and 1630s. After 1625 there might be small increases in mortality when grain prices rose, but there were not subsistence crises as severe as those of the early 1620s or later 1590s, problematic as even their identification is.[35] The confident use of price fluctuations by W. G. Hoskins to show the degree of deficiency in a harvest is no longer persuasive either. Contemporaries thought prices might be artificially inflated by panic, sometimes brought on by the proclamation of the dearth orders themselves.[36] Less speculatively, recent work on the large stocks of grain necessarily carried over from one harvest to the next for seed and animal feed suggests that it only needed 'a relatively small decline in the supply of grain' to produce 'a sharp rise in prices'. Professor Robert Fogel concludes, and Amartya Sen's work on entitlements would support him, that famines were not natural calamities caused by bad weather; they were 'man-made—the consequence of failures in the system of food distribution'.[37] Dearth in early modern England is like the Cheshire cat: appearing, and then vanishing, just as one thinks one has the measure of it.

We must continue to pursue it, however, because if dearth was man-made, it follows that it was humanly preventable. Is it conceivable that the crises of 1622–3 would have been worse and that there might have been famine in 1630, if the Council and its dearth orders had not intervened? Would the whole body of the Cheshire cat have appeared if the Queen of Hearts and the executioner had not turned up? There are, of course, facets to that

---

[35] P. Bowden, 'Agricultural Prices, Farm Profits and Rents', in Thirsk, *Agrarian History*, iv. 632–3; A. B. Appleby, *Famine in Tudor and Stuart England* (Liverpool, 1978), 155 and *passim*; R. B. Outhwaite, *Dearth, Public Policy and Social Disturbance in England, 1550–1800* (1991), 31–2, 57–8; R. B. Outhwaite, 'Dearth and Government Intervention in English Grain Markets, 1590–1700', *Econ. Hist. Rev.*, 2nd ser., 33 (1981), 401–2.

[36] W. G. Hoskins, 'Harvest Fluctuations and English Economic History, 1480–1619', *Agricultural History Review*, 12 (1964), 28–46, and 'Harvest Fluctuations and English Economic History, 1620–1759', ibid. 16 (1968), 15–31, which should be compared with C. J. Harrison, 'Grain Price Analysis and Harvest Qualities, 1465–1634', ibid. 19 (1971), 135–55; Slack, 'Dearth and Social Policy', 12; T. Gray (ed.), *Harvest Failure in Cornwall and Devon: The Book of Orders and the Corn Surveys of 1623 and 1630–1* (Sources of Cornish History 1, 1992), 86; BL, Lansdowne MS 51/41, fo. 87. For some evidence the other way, that proclamation of the book reduced prices in the later 16th c., see Lansdowne MS 71/38, fo. 71[r].

[37] R. W. Fogel, 'Second Thoughts on the European Escape from Hunger', in S. R. Osmani (ed.), *Nutrition and Poverty* (Oxford, 1992), 260, 280; A. Sen, *Poverty and Famines: An Essay on Entitlement and Deprivation* (Oxford, 1981), ch. 5. For differing views on the extent of the carry-over of grain from one year to the next, see E. A. Wrigley, *People, Cities and Wealth: The Transformation of Traditional Society* (Oxford, 1987), 92–130, and K. G. Persson, 'The Seven Lean Years, Elasticity Traps, and Intervention in Grain Markets in Pre-industrial Europe', *Econ. Hist. Rev.*, 49 (1996), 692–714.

question which cannot be pursued here. Rising agricultural productivity is obviously one. Another is the fact that the dearth orders, with their emphasis on local self-sufficiency, could do little for pastoral areas like the north-west, were indeed in some respects counterproductive, which is why historians have often followed Adam Smith in thinking that free trade would have been better. But if the dearth orders had contributed even a little to averting famine, it would suggest that here, as with plague, new administrative habits had caught on. If they contributed massively, it would suggest much more: that it was not only the famed 'moral economy' of the crowd which could hold out against the interests of private property, but that what might be called 'the political economy of absolutism' was powerful enough to do the same. It would suggest that the Crown could command the distribution of resources, even if only temporarily, if only in crises.[38]

Unlikely as it seems, that is exactly what Professor Fogel infers from his econometric analysis of grain prices. He shows that the degree to which wheat prices deviated from trend was much smaller between 1600 and 1640 than it had been between 1541 and 1599, and smaller even than it was to be between 1641 and 1699; and the differences are too great to be the product of chance, that is, of fluctuations in the weather. They lead Professor Fogel to conclude that 'the food distribution policies of James I and Charles I' — though not those of Elizabeth — 'apparently succeeded in reducing the variability of wheat prices by over 70 per cent'.[39] Since even the early Stuarts' most devoted admirers have scarcely thought them capable of that, the empirical historian must here raise a sceptical eyebrow.

The trouble is that the evidence, such as it is, does not suggest that the dearth orders were more rigorously enforced in the early seventeenth century than in the later sixteenth. When prices rose in 1637–8, as Dr Outhwaite has pointed out, the orders were not proclaimed at all.[40] In 1630–1 there was a good deal of noise about the local (and in some cases conciliar) punishment of a few offenders against them.[41] But detailed surveys of corn holdings, on which the policy strictly depended, seem no more common in the 1620s and early 1630s than in Elizabeth's reign or even before.[42] On the contrary, there was an increase in complaints about the broad-brush quality of the orders in the 1620s and especially in 1630–1, and there are many more suggestions

[38] Slack, 'Dearth and Social Policy', 10–14, 17.

[39] Fogel, 'Second Thoughts', 265, 280.

[40] Outhwaite, 'Dearth and Government Intervention', 398, 405.

[41] See e.g. *Cal. SP Dom. 1629–31*, 445, 491, 499; *APC 1630–1*, 148, 168–9, 175, 222, 243, 371–2.

[42] Such a conclusion is bound to be impressionistic, but see the particularly full listings from the 16th c. discussed in P. Slack, *Poverty and Policy in Tudor and Stuart England* (1988), 64–6, and the comparative numbers of returns of grain stocks listed for the 1520s, 1580s, and 1620s in W. Ashley, *Bread of our Forefathers* (Oxford, 1928), app. IV. Further examples are cited in Slack, 'Dearth and Social Policy', 3, n. 3.

that the strict letter of the book was being evaded: rather than regulate the whole marketing system, justices were choosing to target the poor, either by putting money in their pockets through poor rates or by ordering that they be supplied with grain free or at reduced prices at their own doors. That had always happened in the champion parts of Norfolk, one of the certificates of 1631 significantly remarked, because there was no statute to justify the forced provisioning of markets.[43]

Such activities were essentially extensions to smaller places of the policies of provision and relief which had characterized sixteenth-century cities.[44] They would have had a real impact by directly adjusting the entitlements of the poor. Along with restrictions on malting and brewing in dearth years, which may have grown more rigorous after 1600,[45] some of them would have served to release part of Professor Fogel's grain stocks, and hence have reduced prices in some parts of England. But there are also other possible reasons for the greater stability of wheat prices between 1601 and 1640, notably a reduction in two kinds of bulk purchase of grain which had distinguished the late Elizabethan period: first for the armed forces in war-time and second for the provision of London by the livery companies. The problem deserves further study, but it is possible that it was a withdrawal rather than a tightening of some kinds of public interference in the market which reduced the turbulence of prices after 1600.[46]

The government certainly never had the power totally to command market relations, and it knew it. Price-fixing, which Lambarde was so suspicious of, was often threatened by the Council between 1550 and 1630 but never embarked upon. Even Jacobean attempts to introduce county granaries following 'the example of foreign nations' got nowhere, much to the later regret of Charles Davenant, who thought these protections against famine essential 'for the public welfare'.[47] Instead, what we seem to have in England in the 1620s and early 1630s is a policy still giving rise to some dispute between competing claims on grain resources, but gradually being locally

---

[43] J. Thirsk and J. P. Cooper (eds.), *Seventeenth-Century Economic Documents* (Oxford, 1972), 346. Cf. Slack, 'Books of Orders', 14; B. W. Quintrell, *The Maynard Lieutenancy Book 1608–1639* (Chelmsford, 1993), 281–2.

[44] Slack, 'Dearth and Social Policy', 4; Slack, *Poverty and Policy*, 146; Archer, *Pursuit of Stability*, 202–3.

[45] Cf. Slack, 'Dearth and Social Policy', 9–10; P. Clark, *The English Alehouse* (1983), 172–6; K. Sharpe, *The Personal Rule of Charles I* (New Haven, Conn., 1992), 466.

[46] On the London Companies, see Gras, *English Corn Market*, 85–7. As for the increased turbulence of prices again after 1640, that may have been a reflection of the exercise of consumer preferences, given the greater availability of other grains by then. I am grateful to Prof. Fogel for his generosity in suggesting these alternative hypotheses, which arise from his recent work, in correspondence. The brief discussion above ignores municipal purchases of corn from abroad, which were, of course, net additions to food stocks; but there is no evidence that these were greater in the early 17th than in the later 16th c.

[47] Slack, 'Dearth and Social Policy', 9; Larkin and Hughes, *Stuart Royal Proclamations*, i, no. 248, pp. 585–6; Thirsk and Cooper, *Seventeenth-Century Economic Documents*, 813–15.

adjusted in the light of experience: coming to terms with middlemen so far as the provisioning of towns was concerned, but being fine-tuned to pay particular attention to the needs of the poorest consumers in small towns and villages. An uneasy balance between respect for individual property rights and the dictates of charity and prudence operated in the 1640s and later when prices rose, and it seems wholly consistent with the evidence to argue that it was already taking shape when the dearth orders were enforced for the last time between 1630 and 1632.[48] Targeting the poor, with all that followed from it, was the price grain-holders willingly paid for a relatively free market.

Targeting the poor was also a central theme of the Caroline Book of Orders of January 1631, which had many of the same effects. It was another stimulus to one of the real achievements of conciliar direction, the spread of what had once been almost entirely urban practices beyond the boundaries of corporate towns. Elizabethan councillors had already sponsored the migration of houses of correction from town to country, and they had been taken up by county justices, some of them godly, some of them supporters of the 1610 statute which encouraged their multiplication.[49] Judges' exhortations to justices and justices' articles to constables had induced several rural parishes to appoint overseers of the poor. To judge by the certificates which came in, the Book of Orders now added pauper apprenticeships to the repertoire of some of them, although suspiciously rounded figures prevent any accurate assessment of the number of children who benefited. It was no mean feat, however small in scale initially, given the reluctance of many masters to take them on; it required full judicial backing; and it may have made some modest contribution to dealing with the unemployed bulge in a relatively youthful population.[50]

The Book also did something to encourage rating for the poor, though its impact should not be overstated. Some places which already had assessments increased them, as the Book required,[51] but many country parishes remained hostile to regular taxation and thought annual poor rates an unnecessary imposition. Justices of the peace in Essex reported in 1629 that there was a

---

[48] Slack, 'Dearth and Social Policy', 15, 17. I am therefore wholly in agreement with Persson's conclusion that 'the historical record suggests an evolution away from intervention in markets and towards selective entitlement protection', and would want to argue for an early rather than later start to that process: Persson, 'Seven Lean Years', 712.

[49] Above, pp. 38, 42. For examples of later houses of correction or workhouses prompted by, respectively, assize judges, local justices, and an ambitious lawyer (John Maynard), see *Whithed's Letter Book*, 105 (Hants, 1613); Bodl., Bankes MS 52/13 (Halifax, 1635); PRO, PC2/48, 321–2 (Devon, 1637). On the latter, see also S. K. Roberts, *Recovery and Restoration in an English County: Devon Local Administration 1646–1670* (Exeter, 1985), 191, 193–4.

[50] Fletcher, *Reform in the Provinces*, 137–8, 215–16; Slack, 'Books of Orders', 20.

[51] W. L. Sachse, *Minutes of the Norwich Court of Mayoralty 1630–31* (Norfolk Record Society, 15, 1942), 106, is a clear case, and certificates to the Council claimed similar compliance: *Cal. SP Dom. 1629–31*, 386; PRO, SP16/176/55, 185/70.

'general averseness in the country' to paying rates in aid for the unemployed in clothing towns, it being assumed (even by some of the magistrates) that the statutes authorized assessments only for the 'lame, impotent, old, blind and such others as being poor are not able to work', and for putting out apprentices. In 1634 the Herefordshire justices received legal advice on how to 'prevent the charge of poor upon every parish', which implied that rates would be unnecessary if fines on drunkards, swearers, and absentees from church were properly imposed and redirected, and if masters took on poor apprentices in place of 'charmen and charwomen' hired by the day, another sign of current structural problems in the economy.[52] There is no evidence at all of rates in rural Northumberland before 1640, and even further south the practice of regular annual rating does not seem to have caught on quickly in the generality of parishes, to judge by an admittedly fallible indicator: the survival of overseers' account books. There are few of them in some Midland counties until the 1650s and 1660s, and only a handful in Essex before the 1680s.[53] By that time, it is relevant to note, the structural problem was one of an increasingly elderly population, for whom annual pensions were an appropriate provision.[54]

Nevertheless, the ground had been firmly laid by 1640. Alongside the minority of parishes with annual rates and overseers' accounts by 1650 were others where occasional assessments and disbursements, especially in difficult years, were entered in churchwardens' accounts or 'parish books'.[55] New habits were gradually catching on, and can only have been encouraged by all those exercises in targeting which the books of orders had demanded: the lists of infected houses and rates for them, of vagrants and apprentices, and in particular of the poor and mouths to be fed which, once an urban innovation, were produced under the dearth orders in several country parishes from the 1580s through to the 1620s.[56] As early as 1601, a guide for

---

[52] Quintrell, *Maynard Lieutenancy Book*, 260; Herefords. RO, W52/2.

[53] Fletcher, *Reform in the Provinces*, 184–7. I am indebted to Joanna Innes for information on surviving accounts in 10 Midland counties. For Essex, I have relied on F. G. Emmison, *Catalogue of Essex Parish Records 1240–1894* (Chelmsford, 1966). Overseers' accounts surviving in the Carlisle RO for the ancient county of Cumberland are numerous only from 1700 onwards.

[54] Cf. R. Smith, 'Charity, Self-Interest and Welfare: Reflections from Demographic and Family History', in M. Daunton (ed.), *Charity, Self-Interest and Welfare in the English Past* (1996), 37–9.

[55] See e.g., *Essex Parish Records*, 70, 121, 135, 185, 220, 238, 242. Cf. W. Hunt, *The Puritan Moment: The Coming of Revolution in an English County* (Cambridge, Mass., 1983), 248–9. Dr Langelüddecke ('Secular Policy Enforcement', 90, 102–3) argues for a quicker and more widespread adoption of rates than is suggested above, but I am not persuaded that annual rating was practised in the majority of country parishes before 1650. The view adopted by *An Ease for Overseers of the poore* (Cambridge, 1601), 29, that overseers had 'discretion' to impose or not impose rates 'as the time serveth', seems to me accurately to represent rural practice into the Interregnum.

[56] Slack, *Poverty and Policy*, 65–7; Slack, 'Dearth and Social Policy', 16.

overseers provided a printed model of how censuses of the poor should be drawn up, and there were little Montagus in the parishes testing them out: parish notables like George Sawer of Cawston, Norfolk, compulsive compiler of household listings and, we happen to know, a 'precisian' in his religion.[57]

In their results, books of orders thus pointed in much the same direction as the regulatory drive of the godly. They created a wider sense of public responsibility for the poor, and the mechanisms by which the latter might be identified. But they did not create the command economy which absolute power might have promised or threatened. Any prospect of that had been dispelled well before the political collapse of the Stuart monarchy, by the accommodation of policy to circumstance.

III

There was, however, another side to royal reformation and particularly Jacobean reformation, no less ambitious or impractical in its rhetoric but rather different in its focus. In some respects the Crown welcomed new circumstances, not reluctantly coming to terms with social and economic change but enthusiastically embracing it, with an inconsistency which, while no doubt common to most governments, generally does nothing for the credibility or practicability of their policies. On the one hand are endeavours to restore, for example, country hospitality, manly sports, and the keeping of Lent, betraying what Dr Heal calls a 'romantic nostalgia . . . for a good old world' long gone. On the other, we have the government Dr Thirsk's Ford Lectures showed us, sponsoring with a different kind of illusion a host of projects and inventions for the common weal.[58]

They covered a vast range, from new crops and industrial processes to drainage schemes in the countryside and waterworks—a new enthusiasm of the period—in towns. They included most of the elements which fed Utopian visions, like that of Robert Burton quoted in the introduction to this book; and they had behind them the reality of a whole new world of private enterprise which required public sanction and regulation: either because it provided public amenities and services, or because it threatened in one way or another the public welfare, or because it did both. It made new demands on prerogative government and common law, stretching existing regulatory devices like patents of monopoly and the law of nuisance.[59] It also offered

---

[57] *Ease for Overseers*, 4; S. D. Amussen, *An Ordered Society: Gender and Class in Early Modern England* (Oxford, 1988), 23, 26–8. On the Cawston listings, see also T. Wales, 'Poverty, Poor Relief and the Life-Cycle: Some Evidence from Seventeenth-Century Norfolk', in R. M. Smith (ed.), *Land, Kinship and Life-Cycle* (Cambridge, 1984), 369–81. It is possible that Sawer was a surveyor: Amussen, *Ordered Society*, 28, n. 45.

[58] Heal, 'Crown, Gentry and London', 223; J. Thirsk, *Economic Policy and Projects* (Oxford, 1978).

[59] R. Cizdyn, 'Monopolies in England 1603–1630', M.Litt. thesis, Univ. of Oxford, 1982,

opportunities for profit as well as power to public authorities willing to seize them.

Royal determination to harness innovation was keenest in the two locations where the Crown's private and public interests met: the Crown lands and the capital city. But it had a publicly acceptable face, best expressed by Bacon in a New Year letter to James I in 1618, flattering his achievements. One was that local reformation of government which we have already dealt with, and it was phrased with notable care: 'Your gentlemen and justices of peace willing to apply your royal mandates to the nature of their several countries, but ready to obey.' Two others were: 'the fields growing every day by the improvement and recovery of grounds, from the desert to the garden'; and 'the city grown from wood to brick'.[60] Absolute power was making a bid to shape even the landscape.

An announcement of the proposed drainage of Sedgemoor, also in 1618, roundly affirmed that 'improvement and enclosure . . . ought greatly to tend to the good of our commonwealth, the relief and right of the . . . lawful commoners . . . and the just increase of the revenue of the Crown'.[61] Though the three causes were not universally agreed to be compatible, least of all by threatened commoners, they were persistently yoked together by interested parties, from Armagil Waad in 1558, advocating disafforestation and the cultivation of wastes 'barbarous and barren for want of culture', to the projects for a 'general permanent improvement' of land which survive in the Bankes papers of the later 1630s. Fens could be drained, marshes made fertile, commons and wastes enclosed to employ the 'industrious poor' and prevent another Midland Rising. All this could be achieved, John Shotbolt thought, and the king's revenue increased, by 'his princely command or as a man may say his fatherly enforcement'.[62]

Yet the revenue motive was increasingly prominent, as Dr Hoyle and others have shown, especially after Burghley's cautious hand was removed; and it made the Crown a player rather than an arbiter in a game where the stakes were high, and for which it had neither the necessary capital nor the necessary skill. Local opposition sank the Sedgemoor scheme and much else

provides a useful list of Jacobean patents, and calculates (p. 30) that while 45 patents of monopoly were current in 1610, 112 were current by 1620 and 134 by 1630. Cf. E. W. Hulme, 'The History of the Patent System under the Prerogative and at Common Law', *Law Quarterly Review*, 12 (1896), 141–54; 16 (1900), 44–55. On the law of nuisance, see J. H. Baker, *An Introduction to English Legal History* (1971), 240–1; Barnes, 'Prerogative and Environmental Control', 1359.

[60] Spedding, *Letters and Life of Bacon*, vi. 452–3.

[61] R. W. Hoyle (ed.), *The Estates of the English Crown 1558–1640* (Cambridge, 1992), 378. Chs. 11 (by Dr Thirsk) and 12 (by Dr Hoyle) of this book are indispensable guides to royal policy, its origins and its implementation.

[62] PRO, SP12/1, fos. 152–3; Bodl., Bankes MS 48/22 (and cf. 48/13); BL, Royal MS, 18.A.xxv, fos. 1–2, 19ᵛ. On Shotbolt, see Hoyle, *Estates of the Crown*, 371–2, 377–81, and for Adam Moore, another projector involved, see ibid. and below, p. 79.

besides. Winnings in Hatfield Chase were mortgaged, and they never materialized from the greatest adventure of all, Charles I's undertaking in the Bedford Level.[63] What the Crown did succeed in doing was discrediting some of the mechanisms for public regulation which had been twisted to its private ends: the Henrician Commissions of Sewers, for example, forest law, and with respect to commons and wastes, the Edwardian 'statute of improvement'. [64] It is ironic but appropriate that in the sixteenth century to 'improve' or 'approve' meant, as in that statute, 'to turn to profit'.[65]

The Crown's interest in urban improvement—though that term had not yet been invented—was less for profit than for prestige, and it looked superficially more promising. The planned towns of Virginia and Ulster, Jamestown and Charlemont among them, were never joined by that other Charlemont projected for the English Fens in the 1630s, 'an eminent town', Dugdale tells us, 'the design whereof' Charles I 'drew himself'.[66] But London might, with a touch of prerogative regulation and a lot of promotion, be made fit to be an 'Imperial city', a 'royal city, the Imperial Seat . . . of this our kingdom'.[67] 'Look abroad,' a proclamation on London building of 1608 directed, to the example of 'other well policed cities of Europe'; and James I and Bacon had done so: to the Paris which Henry IV was then seeking to clean up and adorn.[68]

Another proclamation, drafted by Bacon in 1615, gave a roll-call of the 'ornaments' of London which might already compete with those of Paris:[69]

[63] Hoyle, *Estates of the Crown*, 378–9, 381–3; M. Williams, *The Draining of the Somerset Levels* (Cambridge, 1970), 96–102; H. C. Darby, *The Draining of the Fens* (Cambridge, 1956), 58–63.

[64] J. Thirsk, 'The Crown as Projector on Its Own Estates, from Elizabeth I to Charles I', in Hoyle, *Estates of the Crown*, 350–2; C. Holmes, *Seventeenth-Century Lincolnshire* (Lincoln, 1980), 126–30. Cf. Hoyle, *Estates of the Crown*, 388; K. Fairclough, 'A successful Elizabethan project: The River Lea improvement scheme', *Journal of Transport History*, 3rd ser., 11 (1990), 54–6. On the improvement statute, see 3 & 4 Edw. VI, c. 3; Thirsk in Hoyle, *Estates of the Crown*, 301, 316 n.

[65] In 1510, for example, the Coventry leet met to consider what 'enprowement . . . opprowment or profit might rise unto the common weal of this city' by enclosing the commons: *Coventry Leet Book*, iii. 630. Cf. McRae, *God Speed the Plough*, 136, and for later uses of 'improvement', below, pp. 80–1.

[66] S. M. Bemiss (ed.), *The Three Charters of the Virginia Company* (Williamsburg, Va., 1957), 61; R. J. Hunter, 'Towns in the Ulster Plantation', *Studia Hibernica*, 11 (1971), 40–78; R. J. Hunter, 'Ulster Plantation Towns 1609–41', in D. Harkness and M. O'Dowd (eds.), *The Town in Ireland* (Historical Studies, 13, Belfast, 1981), 58; Darby, *Draining of the Fens*, 60. It is worth noting that the ubiquitous Henry Montagu had a hand in both Ulster and Virginia projects: T. W. Moody, *The Londonderry Plantation 1609–41* (Belfast, 1939), 81–2; *Charters of Virginia Company*, 23.

[67] Larkin and Hughes, *Stuart Royal Proclamations*, i, no. 255, p. 597; T. Rymer, *Foedera* (20 vols., 1704–32), xix. 273. Cf. *APC 1630–1*, 311.

[68] Larkin and Hughes, *Stuart Royal Proclamations*, i, no. 87, p. 193; Ballon, *Paris of Henri IV*. For Crown attempts to influence the urban environment in the provinces, see the 1638 charter for Reading: Bodl., Bankes MS 12/39; *Cal. SP Dom. 1638–9*, 163.

[69] Larkin and Hughes, *Stuart Royal Proclamations*, i, no. 152, pp. 345–7. The roll-call may

Moorfields, newly cleared of encroachments under royal pressure;[70] the New River, model for the piped water supplies then being introduced in most of the largest English towns;[71] the Pesthouse, though that scarcely compared with the Parisian Hôpital St Louis;[72] Sutton's Hospital, the munificent endowment of Charterhouse;[73] 'Britain's Bourse'—Robert Cecil's New Exchange—the perfect example of private enterprise put to public ends.[74] Now, said Bacon, using the grandiose analogy that had first occurred to him in the 1590s, the king intended to turn a London 'of sticks' into one 'of brick', just as Augustus had turned Rome from brick to marble.[75]

Although completely new buildings were still banned, from 1605 any erected on old foundations were to be of brick and stone to avoid fire risks, and 'of uniform order and form' so as to 'adorn and beautify' the city. In 1618, again by proclamation, Inigo Jones, surveyor of the king's works, added specifications for the thickness of walls and floor-heights for the same purpose: the first building regulations, which may have been copied, like adventures in the Fens, from the Dutch.[76] But the total vision came from further south—from Paris, and from the Italian towns which Jones had seen, perhaps including Leghorn, which Evelyn said gave him 'the first hint' for Covent Garden.[77] One vital ingredient of Florentine civic consciousness had

have been influenced by a French publication c.1614 listing royal achievements in Paris: Ballon, *Paris of Henri IV*, 251.

[70] The clearing of Moorfields set a model of *rus in urbe* which influenced Inigo Jones's plans for Lincoln's Inn Fields and possibly Covent Garden: J. Lubbock, *The Tyranny of Taste: The Politics of Architecture and Design in Britain 1550–1960* (1995), 30–6, 166; K. Sharpe and P. Lake (eds.), *Culture and Politics in Early Stuart England* (1994), 8; J. Newman, 'Inigo Jones and the Politics of Architecture', ibid. 245. Fleetwood raised the question of Moorfields with Burghley in 1583: BL, Lansdowne MS 38/8, fo. 23.

[71] B. Rudden, *The New River: A Legal History* (Oxford, 1985), ch. 2. At least 14 provincial towns invested in new conduits and water supplies between 1578 and 1635: P. Slack, 'Great and Good Towns', in P. Clark (ed.), *The Cambridge Urban History of Britain*, ii: *1540–1840* (Cambridge, forthcoming), appendix.

[72] Slack, *Impact of Plague*, 214.

[73] W. K. Jordan, *The Charities of London, 1480–1660* (1960), 151–3; Jones, *God and the Moneylenders*, 179–81. Bacon was in fact dubious about the value of 'one hospital of exorbitant greatness': Spedding, *Letters and Life*, iv. 250.

[74] L. Stone, *Family and Fortune* (Oxford, 1973), 96–8, 103.

[75] Spedding, *Letters and Life of Bacon*, i. 336.

[76] Larkin and Hughes, *Stuart Royal Proclamations*, i, no. 51, p. 112 (and cf. no. 78, p. 174); no. 175; H. Rosenau, *The Ideal City: Its Architectural Evolution* (1974), 77. Larkin and Hughes, *Stuart Royal Proclamations*, ii, no. 9, reinforced the earlier proclamations.

[77] J. Summerson, *Inigo Jones* (Harmondsworth, Middx, 1966), 17–18; F. H. W. Sheppard (ed.), *Survey of London*, xxxvi: *The Parish of St Paul Covent Garden* (1970), 26, 64–5; Newman, 'Jones and the Politics of Architecture', 246; R. M. Smuts, 'The Court and Its Neighbourhood: Royal Policy and Urban Growth in the Early Stuart West End', *Journal of British Studies*, 30 (1991), 117–49. Ballon, however, points to the differences between the Place Royale and Covent Garden: *Paris of Henri IV*, 83, 254. Whatever its origins, and they were no doubt multiple, Jones clearly had an individual vision of a rebuilt London, expressed e.g. in his designs for William Davenant's *Britannia Triumphans* of 1637, discussed in D. Howarth, 'The Politics of Inigo Jones', in idem (ed.), *Art and Patronage in the Caroline*

reached London, and it had entered before the marriage of Charles to the daughter of Henry IV and Marie de Medici.

As in the Tuscany of the later Medici or Bourbon France, or for that matter imperial Rome, however, new urban aesthetics also had political implications.[78] 'The beautifying and better government of the city' went hand in hand, as they had in one of Bacon's proposed bills, and it was easier to disseminate new images for the first than to impose new arrangements for the second, however plain the necessity for them. The early Stuarts could do little more than toy with continental ideas of a 'medical police' in their capital. There was little prospect of implementing Mayerne's proposal of 1631, for example: for a board of health, on foreign models, with 'absolute power' over the whole metropolis, managing every aspect of social welfare, from vagrancy to food supplies.[79] Yet that was the natural culmination of efforts to improve the metropolitan environment; and it was the only obvious solution for social problems which the bills of mortality demonstrated fell increasingly outside the area controlled by the Corporation of the City.

No other solution could be found. Discussions between Privy Council and aldermen from at least 1610 on such projects as the administrative 'quartering' of the suburbs got nowhere.[80] The City was unwilling to extend its jurisdiction to take over the suburbs entirely, an option which was at least half-offered in 1633. The Council's alternative, the separate incorporation of the suburbs of 1636, was a sign of political breakdown, not a practical road to 'better government'.[81] If it had survived, its officers and justices of the peace would have been no more acceptable to the Middlesex bench than to the City whose liberties it invaded; and its immediate effect was scarcely more tolerable: an incorporation of tradesmen, which left winners and losers squabbling over the spoils.

Courts: Essays in Honour of Sir Oliver Millar (Cambridge, 1993), 68–89; L. Manley, *Literature and Culture in Early Modern London* (Cambridge, 1995), 496. See also H. M. Colvin, 'Inigo Jones and the Church of St Michael le Querne', *London Journal*, 12 (1986), 35–9.

[78] For similar ambitions in Turin, see M. D. Pollak, *Turin 1564–1680: Urban Design, Military Culture and the Creation of the Absolutist Capital* (Chicago, 1991), 45–7, 68–9; and for contact between Turin and England *c.* 1612, Sharpe and Lake, *Culture and Politics*, 215.

[79] Slack, *Impact of Plague*, 218–19. For the intimate connection between the exigencies of public health and absolutism, see C. Jones, 'Plague and Its Metaphors in Early Modern France', *Representations*, 53 (1996), 114–17. H. J. Cook, 'Policing the Health of London: The College of Physicians and the Early Stuart Monarchy', *Social History of Medicine*, 2 (1989), 1–33, illustrates the extent of Stuart ambitions, but overstates royal success in manipulating the College as a tool.

[80] R. Ashton, *The City and the Court 1603–1643* (Cambridge, 1979), 164–5; N. G. Brett-James, *The Growth of Stuart London* (1935), 224–5; *Cal. SP Dom. 1623–5*, 157; W. H. Overall and H. C. Overall (eds.), *Analytical Index to the Remembrancia* (1878), 359–60; *Commons Debates 1621*, vii. 332–8; London Corporation RO, Journal 31, fo. 290[v]; Repertory 35, fo. 155[v].

[81] London Corporation RO, Repertory 47, fo. 422; V. Pearl, *London and the Outbreak of the Puritan Revolution: City Government and National Politics 1625–1643* (Oxford, 1961), 34–6; Ashton, *City and Court*, 166–7.

Had it not had similar consequences, the underlying ambivalence of royal policy towards building in London could probably have been lived with. The public pronouncements of the early Stuarts managed to visualize London both as a head too big for the body and as 'the greatest, or next the greatest, city of the Christian world', to try to push the élite back to country hospitality while building a comfortable environment for them in the West End. They never went quite so far as those contemporaries who concluded from the examples of classical Rome, and contemporary Paris and Madrid, that 'the more buildings, the more populous and honourable' London would be.[82] Few property-owners or speculators would have expected so public a U-turn, any more than they would have expected the wholesale abandonment of criticism of enclosure. There was nothing new, after all, in the Crown's left hand apparently not knowing what its right hand was doing, as in the use of the prerogative to license infractions of the penal statutes. But there was something particularly indiscriminate about policies in the 1620s and 1630s, which saw enclosers first licensed to escape enclosure legislation and then, when the legislation had been repealed, fined on the pretext that enclosure was against the common law; and Bedford, licensed to build Covent Garden in 1630, but then proceeded against in 1633 because lack of proper sewers made some of his houses in the neighbourhood a 'public nuisance'.[83]

Such inconsistencies could not survive scrutiny once the fiscal needs of the Crown blatantly dictated policy, as Dr Thirsk and Professor Barnes show they did in the case of fines for enclosure in 1635 and 1636, and fines for new London building from 1634.[84] That was why the social and economic policies of the Personal Rule, which Professor Sharpe has shown to have had a reforming drive reminiscent of that of Cardinal Wolsey, failed in the end to carry conviction. There had simply been too many protestations that 'it was not his Majesty's profit that was sought', that his intention was 'not to enrich himself', that some inducement was necessary if good laws were to be enforced. Sir Robert Heath confessed as much in a comment on an alehouse scheme in 1634: 'It is much better that . . . there be little noise made of any further intention than reformation; but if together with that so

---

[82] Larkin and Hughes, *Stuart Royal Proclamations*, i, no. 152, p. 345; BL, Cotton MS, Titus B.V, fo. 213; *A Briefe Declaration For What Maner of speciall Nusance concerning private dwelling houses, a man may have his remedy by Assise* (1636), 23.

[83] Thirsk, *Agrarian History*, iv. 236–7; T. G. Barnes (ed.), *Somerset Assize Orders 1629–40* (Somerset Record Society, 65, 1959), 57–8; C. Russell, *The Causes of the English Civil War* (Oxford, 1990), 153; Sheppard, *Survey of London*, xxxvi. 33; R. M. Smuts, *Court Culture and the Origins of the Royalist Tradition in Early Stuart England* (Philadelphia, 1987), 128.

[84] J. Thirsk, 'Changing Attitudes to Enclosure in the Seventeenth Century', in *The Festschrift for Professor Ju-Hwan Oh* (Taegu, Korea, 1991), 527–30; Barnes, 'Prerogative and Environmental Control', 1351, 1354–5.

considerable a yearly sum may be added to the King's revenue, I see no inconvenience in it.'[85]

Whatever credibility there might have been in the rhetoric of royal reformation under James I—and I would want to argue that there was more than some historians have allowed—it had largely disappeared by 1640. Without the political breakdown which followed, pursuit of an enlightened absolutism would no doubt have continued, as it did in other countries, compromising with and compromised by private and vested interests, not least the Crown's own. In other countries too, the political, economic, and metropolitan aspirations of absolute power proved flawed ideals which could be realized only in part. But in the England of the 1630s they looked unusually bankrupt, bankrupt intellectually because they were bankrupt financially. Mayerne had written their epitaph in 1631: 'In these declining times of the world,' he told the king, 'the . . . age of gold . . . being long since past, the fairest projects and discourses are but wind' without 'the means to put them in practice . . . to wit a stock or treasure of moneys.'[86]

IV

If we are left with what, it must be confessed, is a familiar picture of a monarchy too weak to be absolute, too ambitious to settle for anything else, it had not all been empty sound and fury. Subsidiary governors had been accustomed to new policies and procedures. If rural England had not become a royally improved garden by 1640, at least a large part of the West End was brick: 60 per cent of houses in Piccadilly in 1650, to be precise, and 72 per cent in Long Acre.[87] Moreover, sound and fury had themselves had an effect, in emphasizing some welfare policies and beginning to jettison others, in accommodating agricultural improvement and trying to mould urban development, not simply resist them. That process undermined many of the assumptions inherent in the common weal. It meant less looking back to a golden age, to 'England's true flourishing common weal far discrepant from that that now is' as it was described in 1574,[88] and a diminishing optimism that anything like it might be recreated in totality. It meant instead emphasis on the provision of a variety of discrete 'public services', a term Lambarde used in the context of the dearth orders of 1587.[89]

[85] Sharpe, *Personal Rule*, 242–62, 403–87; Larkin and Hughes, *Stuart Royal Proclamations*, i, no. 87, pp. 192–3; *Somerset Assize Orders*, 58–9; Bodl., Bankes MSS 64/9, 66/12, p. 17.

[86] PRO, SP16/533/17, fo. 35ᵛ.

[87] M. J. Power, 'The East and West in Early-Modern London', in E. W. Ives, R. J. Knecht, and J. J. Scarisbrick (eds.), *Wealth and Power in Tudor England: Essays Presented to S. T. Bindoff* (1978), 170. Cf. L. Stone, 'The Residential Development of the West End of London in the Seventeenth Century', in B. C. Malament (ed.), *After the Reformation: Essays in Honour of J. H. Hexter* (Manchester, 1980), 180–1.

[88] BL, Lansdowne MS 19/41, fo. 89.

[89] Read, *Lambarde and Local Government*, 164. In 1576 Lambarde had referred to gentry employed in 'the public service': *A Perambulation of Kent* (Chatham, 1826), 7.

Not surprisingly, the 'common weal' itself began to fall out of favour as the ultimate purpose of public service. By the end of Elizabeth's reign it had too many unwelcome political associations, and after 1603 one suspects that it was in any case too rooted in a narrowly English tradition for the early Stuarts to be entirely comfortable with it. An alternative was needed which gave fewer hostages to fortune, was less old-fashioned, sounded more agreeable to educated and Scottish ears. 'The general good and welfare of our people'—the declared purpose of the incorporation of the suburbs—was one attempt.[90] But 'public' became the more usual adjective: partly by analogy with 'public health', imported from abroad into discussion of plague policy,[91] partly because the private/public distinction was at issue in many of the Crown's policies, and more obviously as a straight translation of *pro bono publico*. There was a gradual return to the fifteenth-century 'bien publique', now translated as 'the public good'.

The Parliament of 1597, meeting, the Speaker said, 'for the public good of the whole land', may have started the process;[92] but the term acquired wider currency after 1603. It was appealed to in the proclamation against new buildings in London in 1608 and in the draft bill on the subject of 1621, in the proposal for granaries in 1623, and in relation to every part of the package of 1630 and 1631: dearth, plague, the regulation of London, and the relief of the poor.[93] In 1607 Coke described our old friend Chief Justice Popham as a man active for the 'public good of the realm', and Ben Jonson made Justice Overdoo claim the same distinction soon afterwards.[94] By 1620 Henry Montagu was harnessing the new slogan to Lambarde's notion of public service: his draft local-government commission referred to 'services for the public good'.[95] That phrase nicely summarizes one consequence of the developments described in this chapter.

There were still frequent references to the common weal in the proclama-

---

[90] Larkin and Hughes, *Stuart Royal Proclamations*, ii, no. 234, p. 551.

[91] Slack, *Impact of Plague*, 218. Cf. Fynes Moryson, *Itinerary* (1617), cited in *OED sub.* 'health' 2b.

[92] Hartley, *Proceedings in the Parliaments of Elizabeth*, iii. 230. For other uses, in this parliament and then in 1601, see ibid. 312, 397 (both speeches by Robert Cecil); Hughes and Larkin, *Tudor Royal Proclamations*, iii. 236, 242; *Whithed's Letter Book*, 6 (Buckhurst on corn policy); HMC, *House of Lords*, new ser., xi: *Addenda 1514–1714*, 63.

[93] Larkin and Hughes, *Stuart Royal Proclamations*, i, no. 87, p. 194; *Commons Debates 1621*, vii. 273; *Stuart Royal Proclamations*, i, no. 248, p. 587; ii, no. 136, p. 281, no. 141, p. 298; *APC 1630–1*, 274; PRO, SP16/533/17, fo. 47ᵛ; *Orders and Directions* (1630), 13.

[94] Hasler, *House of Commons 1558–1603*, iii. 236; 'Bartholomew Fair' in B. Jonson, *Works*, ed. C. H. Herford, and P. and E. Simpson (Oxford, 1938), vi. 39, 67. For other Jacobean uses of the term, see McRae, *God Speed the Plough*, 246 (1610); T. Mun, *England's Treasure by Forraign Trade* (Oxford, 1928), 1 (1621?); *The Sermons of John Donne*, ed. G. R. Potter and E. M. Simpson (10 vols., Berkeley, Calif., 1957), iii. 363 (1621); Quintrell, *Maynard Lieutenancy Book*, 314 (1622). Cf. Robert Burton, above, p. 3.

[95] Quintrell, 'Making of Charles I's Book of Orders', 568.

tions of the 1630s,[96] a reflection of the ambivalence which has been another theme of this discussion. In the 1631 Book of Orders the 'services for the public good' of 1620 reverted to 'public services for God, the King and the Commonwealth', in a search for broad consensus.[97] But the advantages of the alternative were fully appreciated by projectors advocating agrarian improvement and looking to their own and the Crown's, not the common, profit. One of them founded his arguments on 'the royal prerogative in the exercise of her paternal and divine power in all things touching the public good' of the realm. Sovereign power was not to be encumbered by the cultural and political baggage of the common weal but free to pursue what was at once a modern, abstract, and infinitely malleable ideal: what another project called 'the public good and welfare of the kingdom'.[98] The fruitful development of that theme, however, belongs to the period after 1640, to projectors addressing a different sovereign power, and to the next chapter.

[96] e.g. Larkin and Hughes, *Stuart Royal Proclamations*, ii, pp. 461, 520, 636.
[97] *Orders and Directions*, 19.
[98] Bodl., Bankes MSS 48/13, 48/22.

4

THE PUBLIC GOOD

In *The Poor Man's Friend*, a tract published in 1649, Rice Bush celebrated a new beginning in 'reformation of and provision for the necessitous poor'. He dismissed the reformations of the past more quickly than previous chapters have done. 'Experience' showed that the 'many excellent orders and directions' in 'that book set forth by King Charles'—the Book of Orders—had failed to 'put life' into the poor laws. As for godly cities, some towns—'as Norwich, Ipswich, Dorchester'—had managed to suppress idleness and beggary, but they were few in number. Much more promising now was the special Corporation of the Poor, established in 1647 to organize workhouses and employment in London; and Bush wished for further 'progress . . . in that godly work', in London and beyond. The poor should be surveyed: 'first number your poor'. They should have access to loan funds, to stocks of materials on which to work at home, to free 'physic and surgery' and free education for their children. What had been wanting so far, Bush said, was 'an improvement': 'an improvement' in 'laws, officers, time, materials, poor &c'. Now all was possible, if men would only 'improve their interest for the public good'.[1]

I

The Poor Man's Friend was one of a dozen tracts published between 1645 and 1653, all concerned with the problem of poverty, and all employing the same language to the same kinds of end. Their authors or publishers were without exception connected with the Hartlib circle, some at its centre, some on its fringes, and hence all influenced by that Baconian 'Great Instauration' whose all-embracing ambition Charles Webster has monumentally described.[2] Their particular interest for us lies in the way that they

[1] Rice Bush, *The Poor Man's Friend* (1649), title-page, sig. A2ᵛ, pp. 2, 3, 10, 12, 17, 18–20, 21. Samuel Hartlib also had a copy of the Book of Orders; and he knew of the Dorchester brewhouse, perhaps directly from John White: Sheffield University Library, Hartlib Papers [hereafter HP], 15/2/14; 28/1/21A, Ephemerides, 1649. (The Hartlib Papers are quoted from transcripts prepared by the Hartlib Papers Project, Sheffield, by permission of the Project Directors and the University Librarian.)

[2] C. Webster, *The Great Instauration: Science, Medicine and Reform 1626–1660* (1975). For tracts on the poor, see pp. 360–3, 368.

yoked together aspects of public welfare, from poor relief to reform of the
environment, which have been considered in previous chapters often as
discrete items, and imbued them with a common sense of purpose.

Connections with the past were sometimes explicit. Leonard Lee, author
of the first of my dozen pamphlets, claimed that the Caroline Privy Council
had approved, as it well might have done, his project for a committee
supervising social welfare over the whole metropolis, including Westminster,
Middlesex, and Southwark, where 'most of the poor do live'. Peter Chamberlen said that his proposal for a public fund to subsidize employment had
similarly been recommended by Charles I to Archbishop Laud; but Chamberlen had taken that 'as a providence to desist from it'.[3] Now providence
had changed everything, delivering Church and then Crown lands into
public hands, and presenting opportunities for exploitation as great as in the
dissolutions of a century before. These pamphleteers rushed to put forward
new projects while the sun shone: for the erection of 'Collegiate habitations
. . . for . . . workhouses, schools, hospitals &c' from Chamberlen; for
public pawnshops—'lombards' or 'mounts of piety'—from several hands;
for teaching hospitals and free medical services from John Cooke, Henry
Robinson, and William Petty; for work on hemp, nets, and ropes for the
advancement of navigation, from Thomas Jenner; and for an 'Office of
Public Address', a combined trade centre and employment exchange, from
Balthasar Gerbier, and Samuel Hartlib himself, whose pet scheme this was.[4]

The agenda was a long one. Never a man to miss a reforming bandwagon,
Hugh Peter ran through the whole of it: from hospitals and relief for poor
debtors to a Baconian 'improvement of nature' in agriculture and inland
navigation. He ended with proposals for 'London in particular': broader
streets, cleaned and paved like those in Holland, houses of brick and stone,
not wood, a fire brigade, and a large Thames-side quay like that in Rotter-
dam. His jumbled postscript added three other things to 'be minded': Bedlam; 'the army diseased', i.e. maimed soldiers; and hospitals.[5]

Though long in particulars—and many others could be added from Hartlib's voluminous papers—the projects in these tracts were all part of a single

[3] Leonard Lee, *A Remonstrance Humbly presented to the High and Honourable Court of
Parliament* (1644; 13 Mar. 1644/5 according to Thomason), sig. A2, pp. 11, 12; [Peter
Chamberlen,] *The Poore Mans Advocate* (1649), sig. A4ʳ, p. 5.

[4] Ibid. 5; John Cooke, *Unum Necessarium: or, The Poore Mans Case* (1648), 41, 49; Henry
Robinson, *Certain Proposals in order to the Peoples Freedom* (1652), 22, 26; [William Petty,]
The Advice of W.P. to Mr Samuel Hartlib (1648) in *Harleian Miscellany* [hereafter *Harl.
Misc.*] (10 vols., 1808–13), vi. 147, 149; Thomas Jenner, *London's Blame If not its Shame*
(1651), title-page, p. 10; Balthazar Gerbier, *A New-Years Result, In favour of the Poore*
(1652), 10; [Samuel Hartlib,] *A Further Discovery of the Office of Publick Address for
Accommodations* (1648) in *Harl. Misc.*, vi. 164–5. On earlier proposals for lombards, see
above p. 24;. D. Dean, *Law-Making and Society in Late Elizabethan England: The Parliament of England, 1584–1601* (Cambridge, 1996), p. 152.

[5] H[ugh] P[eter], *Good Work for a Good Magistrate* (1651), 18, 75–7, 101–8, postscript.

vision. Hartlib intended to build upon 'leading examples of the present promoting . . . of public works' and so to make 'the whole kingdom . . . a city of God'. His reformed workhouses were to be schools for 'civilising' the children that 'lie all day in the streets in playing, cursing and swearing . . . which is an excellent step to reformation'. His Office of Address was to take the bourses and exchanges for merchants and extend the exchange of information to 'the whole society of all men'.[6] Total reformation, Gerbier explained, would no longer be 'confined within the walls of hospitals or almshouses, nor under the gowns of a small number of old men or women' in them. The employment and training of the poor, the protection of public health and reformed hospitals, a clean environment, and reformed cities should all contribute to one end. The aim, said Bush, was to 'unite the several streams that run this way, bringing them into one channel'.[7]

That channel might well be called the *public good*. The term echoes throughout the writings of the Hartlib circle, almost as a party slogan. It was added, for example, to two of the poor relief pamphlets of 1645–53 which had been written thirty years before—*Stanley's Remedy* and Adam Moore's *Bread for the Poor*—in order to mark the stable they now came from.[8] The Hartlib group did not coin this alternative to the ideal of the common weal. As we have seen, the Privy Council was using it in 1630, when it occurs in a letter from Hartlib to John Dury. Gabriel Plattes, who brandishes it in *Macaria*, his Utopian tract of 1641, might have heard it being applied long before to the New River enterprise on which he had worked as engineer.[9] But it was an indispensable image for a group of writers keen to publicize and realize solutions to the nation's ills, all of them, Hartlib assured Sir Thomas Roe in 1640, for 'the public good of these countries'.[10]

---

[6] HP, 28/2/50B, 53/28; S[amuel] H[artlib], *Londons Charitie Stilling the Poore Orphans Cry* (1649), 5; S[amuel] [H[artlib], *Londons Charity inlarged* (1650), 10, 15; S[amuel] H[art-lib], *The Parliaments Reformation* (1646), in C. Webster (ed.), *Samuel Hartlib and the Advancement of Learning* (Cambridge, 1970), 113. For earlier projects for registers of foreigners and shipowners' contracts, which in some respects anticipate parts of the Office of Address, see BL, Lansdowne MS 66/55, 73, fos. 156–9, 198ʳ; Bodl., Bankes MS 60/7; D. Woolf, 'Conscience, Constancy and Ambition in the Career and Writings of James Howell', in J. Morrill, P. Slack, and D. Woolf (eds.), *Public Duty and Private Conscience in Seventeenth-Century England: Essays Presented to G. E. Aylmer* (Oxford, 1993), 246, n. 12.

[7] Gerbier, *New-Years Result*, 5; Bush, *Poor Man's Friend*, sig. A3ᵛ.

[8] *Stanley's Remedy* (1646), title-page; Adam Moore, *Bread for the Poor* (1653), sig. A4ᵛ. For Stanley, see A. L. Beier, *Masterless Men: The Vagrancy Problem in England 1560–1640* (1985), 151, 167: the original tract was published *c.* 1621 (*STC* 23228.5). For Moore, see HP, Ephem. 1652; above, p. 69, n. 62.

[9] Above, p. 75; Webster, *Hartlib and the Advancement*, 78, 81, 88 (and see also 99, 121); C. Webster, *Utopian Planning and the Puritan Revolution: Gabriel Plattes, Samuel Hartlib and Macaria* (Wellcome Unit for the History of Medicine, Oxford, 1979), 15–16; B. Rudden, *The New River: A Legal History* (Oxford, 1985), 15. Hartlib would also have found the term in a 1611 pamphlet on the proposal of Arthur Gorges and Walter Cope for a 'Public Register for General Commerce': HP, 48/2/10B. Dury defined 'a public good' as 'nothing else but the universal private good of every one in the life of God': Webster, *Hartlib and the Advancement*, 99.

[10] Ibid. 12.

As in the 1630s, the subsequent appeal of the term lay partly in its elasticity. It could readily be used to justify determined government action, while at the same time implying that there were limits to what might otherwise be unrestrained prerogative rule.[11] That would have been wholly congenial to Hartlib, given his background in the Calvinist second Reformation in Germany, where godly princes engaged in energetic state-building.[12] In the particular context of England in the 1640s, where the Commonwealth was coming to have real political meaning, it also gave its advocates an alternative ideal which would not tar them with a republican or egalitarian brush, and which might enable them to harness the support of Crown, Parliament, or army as circumstances dictated. Whether eirenicist philosophers or more insular projectors, none of them was in any doubt that they needed what Dury called 'the authority of the state itself' to advance their programme.[13] They picked up the public good and ran with it, and in doing so put it once and for all into the currency of public discourse.

Gabriel Plattes was also in at the birth of another new and related concept, that of *improvement*. In the early seventeenth century the word was just beginning to move by analogy beyond its initial association with the land. Francis Bacon took the lead. In *The Advancement of Learning*, published in 1605, and in related letters, learning might be improved: 'improved and converted by the industry of man' in order to 'correct ill husbandry'. The *Oxford English Dictionary* tells us that time could be improved in 1617, that is, turned to greater profit; so could the nation's commodities in an unpublished tract written a few years later.[14] Successive editions of *The Advancement* (in 1629 and 1633) stood almost alone, however, until 1639, when Plattes trumpeted the virtues of 'new inventions and improvements' for 'the general good' loud and long. In *A Discovery of Infinite Treasure, Hidden Since The Worlds Beginning*, he enumerated a host of improvements, most of them agrarian, like enclosure, planting of orchards, and conservation of timber; and he gave the concept general application in his conclusion. Just as 'it was an excellent improvement to teach horses and oxen to do the works of men', so his readers should 'consider well in what case their posterity will

<hr>

[11] Cf. P. N. Miller, *Defining the Common Good: Empire, Religion and Philosophy in Eighteenth-Century Britain* (Cambridge, 1994), 36–7, 50–1, 128; and on discussion of the relationship between public and private interests, J. A. W. Gunn, *Politics and the Public Interest in the Seventeenth Century* (1969), esp. ix, 219, 281.

[12] M. Greengrass, M. Leslie, and T. Raylor (eds.), *Samuel Hartlib and Universal Reformation* (Cambridge, 1994), 15–16.

[13] M. J. Braddick and M. Greengrass (eds.), 'The Letters of Sir Cheney Culpeper (1641–1657)', in *Camden Miscellany* xxxiii (Camden Society, 5th ser., 7, 1996), 236.

[14] B. Vickers (ed.), *Francis Bacon* (Oxford, 1996), 174, 114, 577; *OED sub* 'improve'; John Keymer, *Original Papers regarding Trade*, ed. M. F. Lloyd Prichard (New York, 1967), 36. According to George Hakewill in the 1630s, 'country boars' thought 'nothing can be improved by industry': quoted in V. Harris, *All Coherence Gone: A Study of the Seventeenth Century Controversy over Disorder and Decay in the Universe* (Chicago, 1949), 52.

be in two or three ages hence, if no new inventions and improvements shall be from henceforth put in practice'.[15]

Other writers in the Hartlib circle seized on the theme, hoping like Sir Cheney Culpeper that Plattes's ingenuities might themselves 'be improved to the public good'.[16] As has often been pointed out, their interest in both agriculture and education encouraged the transfer of ideas of enclosing, nurturing, and improving from one to the other;[17] and once 'what is good in children' and their 'intellectual abilities' could be improved, so, by 1650, could the poor and the machinery for their relief, as with Bush, the whole of nature, as with Peter, and the whole nation. 'England's Improvement' was part of the running head of Walter Blith's agricultural tract of 1649, *The English Improver*, itself to be *Improved* in 1652.[18] Dictionary definitions began slowly to catch up with usage. In 1613 'to improve' had simply meant 'to raise rents'. In 1658 a definition of improvement included 'a thriving, a benefiting in any kind of profession'. It might just as well already have added, as a dictionary of 1721 did, 'bettering, progress'.[19]

Given all this, it seems to me legitimate to apply to the Hartlib group the comment which Hartlib himself made in 1634 about Puritan divines, including John White of Dorchester, whose works he had been reading: 'They have made a new language as it were, using new terms and a new phraseology.'[20]

---

[15] G[abriel] P[lattes], *A Discovery of Infinite Treasure Hidden Since The Worlds Beginning* (1639), 20, 81, 86–7, 88, 92.

[16] Braddick and Greengrass, 'Letters of Culpeper', 208.

[17] Webster, *Hartlib and the Advancement*, 10; Webster, *Great Instauration*, 466–8; M. Leslie and T. Raylor (eds.), *Culture and Cultivation in Early Modern England: Writing and the Land* (Leicester, 1992), 5, 9, and *passim*.

[18] Petty, *Advice of W.P.*, 145; Webster, *Hartlib and the Advancement*, 149; Walter Blith, *The English Improver* (1649), running headline; Walter Blith, *The English Improver Improved or the Survey of Husbandry Surveyed* [1652]. For other examples, see Hartlib, *Further Discovery*, 172; Webster, *Hartlib and the Advancement*, 87; Bush, *Poor Man's Friend*, 3; G. H. Turnbull, *Hartlib, Dury and Comenius* (Liverpool, 1947), 26 (1645); Webster, *Great Instauration*, 74 (1655). OED sub 'improvement' 5 has Clarendon in 1647 on the 'improvement of his education'.

[19] Robert Cawdrey, *A Table Alphabeticall* (3rd edn., 1613) *sub* 'improve'; Edward Phillips, *The New World of English Words or a General Dictionary* (1658); Nathan Bailey, *An Universal Etymological English Dictionary* (1721), *sub* 'improvement'. In 1688 Guy Miège's *Great French Dictionary* gave the French for 'improvement' as 'culture, bonne Education; progrès, avancement'. (I am grateful to Prof. Janet Bately for this reference.) The new meanings given to improvement exemplify a process lucidly explained by Quentin Skinner: new additions to vocabulary often arise from 'turning a neutral description into a favourable evaluative-descriptive term (usually by means of a metaphorical extension of its uses) and then applying it in virtue of this extended meaning to describe some course of action which one wishes to see commended': 'Some Problems in the Analysis of Political Thought and Action', in J. Tully (ed.), *Meaning and Context: Quentin Skinner and His Critics* (Cambridge, 1988), 114.

[20] HP 29/2/25A, Ephem. 1634. Hartlib was commenting on the need to translate these works, for which a new 'lexicon' would be needed; unfortunately, he does not specify which 'new terms' he had in mind. On Hartlib's admiration for White, see Webster, *Great Instauration*, 34.

Hartlib and his friends developed their own new language, not without some deliberation;[21] and in doing so they contributed to that complicated shift in modes of expression and sensibility which occurred in mid-seventeenth-century England, and which literary scholars as well as historians of science and political thought are beginning to unravel.[22] Students of language and the processes of translation may indeed have more to tell us if I am right to think that foreigners—Hartlib, Dury, and perhaps Plattes—played a role in the story. For there seem to me to be obvious parallels between Hartlib and those later self-conscious stylists, the latitudinarians studied by Isobel Rivers: Hartlib, necessarily distancing himself from the style of some Puritan divines in a search for an exact and practical language; and the latitudinarians, determined to replace the obscure vocabulary of godly fanatics with a 'plainer' English more suited to 'practical godliness'.[23]

There is certainly material in the poor relief tracts which are my chief concern which anticipates later sensibilities. There is a sensitivity to the sufferings of the poor, and particularly of children, for example, which it is difficult to find earlier. Bush asks us to attend to 'the secret mournings of poor families, to the heart-breaking of the truly pitiful and compassionate Christians'. Hartlib's *Londons Charitie* had a woodcut illustration of poor starving children—'pictures of pity to every pious heart'—very different in impact from the threatening rogues depicted in earlier tracts.[24] The same pity lay behind Hartlib's concern for 'the poor that are shamefaced', perhaps the first English use of that common European category, and it inspired the names he suggested for his reformed workhouse: not 'house of correction' but 'Nursery' or 'Magazin of Charity'.[25]

It is difficult now to identify the resonances which such language conveyed in the 1640s and 1650s. What seems to modern ears a cooler, even a more secular tone, when compared with the hot rhetoric of the godly,

---

[21] For the linguistic interests of the reformers, see Webster, *Hartlib and the Advancement*, 17–18, 68, 156–7; Greengrass, *Hartlib and Universal Reformation*, ch. 7.

[22] See e.g. K. Sharpe and S. N. Zwicker (eds.), *Politics of Discourse: The Literature and History of Seventeenth-Century England* (Berkeley, Calif., 1987), 1–8; B. Shapiro, *Probability and Certainty in Seventeenth-Century England* (Princeton, NJ, 1983), ch. 7; N. Smith, *Perfection Proclaimed: Language and Literature in English Radical Religion 1640–1660* (Oxford, 1989); Q. Skinner, *Reason and Rhetoric in the Philosophy of Hobbes* (Cambridge, 1996), 308, 361, 436; M. Hunter, *Science and Society in Restoration England* (Cambridge, 1981), 118–19.

[23] I. Rivers, *Reason, Grace and Sentiment: A Study of the Language of Religion and Ethics in England 1660–1780*, i: *Whichcote to Wesley* (Cambridge, 1991), chs. 1 and 2, esp. pp. 54–6. The parallels should not, of course, be exaggerated. Latitudinarians would have been profoundly out of sympathy with some expressions of mystical enthusiasm in the Hartlib circle, and Hartlib found more to admire in the writings of the godly than they did. Nevertheless, their concerns for language seem to me to point in the same direction.

[24] Bush, *Poor Man's Friend*, 13; Hartlib, *Londons Charitie*, 4.

[25] Hartlib, *Further Discovery*, 165; HP, 15/2/9. For the shamefaced poor, see also [Edward Chamberlayne,] *Englands Wants* (1667), 28.

probably seemed to contemporaries something that was simply more direct and more intelligible, and no more hostile to religion than it was to warmth of feeling. Hartlib, after all, had his own pan-sophic mystical enthusiasm, though it may be significant that its expression was muted in his publications.[26] Equally restrained were references to the millenarian religious excitements of the 1640s, which it is conventional to assume had some connection with optimism about progress: they are only hinted at in these tracts, in the odd remark about 'England's glorious days . . . approaching' and hopes of a 'year of Jubilee'.[27] Rather more prominent are reflections of the associated radical notion of the perfectibility of the world, partly because that could be allied with Baconian advancement and with the pursuit of 'felicity', 'happiness', which was also to become a latitudinarian aspiration.[28] Hearing Petty discuss Chamberlen's poor relief projects, Hartlib noted privately: 'from hence the whole world may be enhappined, and all at last come to live in plenty and peace &c and all wars cease.' For Plattes the ultimate aim was 'the World's Happiness'; and since *felicitas* might also be translated as 'welfare', that could easily shift to Blith's goal, 'the public welfare'.[29] Whatever the origins, public welfare was acquiring new conceptual clothes. It was coming to be seen in terms of felicity and improvement, instead of—or rather as well as—in its older guises of correction, restoration and edification.

The more robust economic historian, suspicious of these linguistic turns, would look for an explanation of confidence in improvement to the example of the Dutch; and there were, of course, foreign models, practical as well as intellectual, on which these tracts drew. Dutch achievements were never far from the pens of their authors, to be copied and even exceeded. 'Though Holland seem to get the start of us,' says Hugh Peter, 'yet we may so follow as to stand at length upon their shoulders, and so see further.' And if Dutch towns seemed admirable—'their streets and buildings so fairly and orderly set forth'—so did the 'brave cities, towns and villages' of 'France, Italy . . .

---

[26] Cf. Hartlib's note of 1649, à propos of Chamberlen's expectations of parliamentary support: 'The City of Peace tending so much to community, he dares not yet divulge, lest people should be too much frightened': HP, 28/1/19B, Ephem., 1649.

[27] Cooke, *Unum Necessarium*, p. 29; Chamberlen, *Poor Mans Advocate*, sig. A4ᵛ; Hartlib, *Londons Charity inlarged*, 1. On millenarian influences on the Hartlib group, see Webster, *Great Instauration*, ch. 1; and on the Jubilee, H. R. Trevor-Roper, *Religion, the Reformation and Social Change* (1967), 264–5; M. Chase, 'From Millennium to Anniversary: The Concept of Jubilee in late Eighteenth- and Nineteenth-Century England', *P&P*, 129 (1990), 135.

[28] *Advice of W.P.*, 142; Rivers, *Reason, Grace and Sentiment*, 79–85. Cf. Webster, *Great Instauration*, 19–27, 33; Peter, *Good Work*, 73; Hartlib, *Further Discovery*, 159. Some Leveller tracts share the same aspirations to the nation's 'happiness' (D. M. Wolfe (ed.), *Leveller Manifestoes of the Puritan Revolution* (1944), 113, 388) but not the same concern for social improvement, though Overton showed an interest in hospitals and schools (ibid. 155, 194).

[29] HP, 28/1/17A, Ephem. 1649; Webster, *Hartlib and the Advancement*, 79; Plattes, *Infinite Treasure*, 89; Blith, *English Improver*, sig. a2ᵛ. For another (1645) reference to 'the public welfare', see B. Worden, 'Providence and Politics in Cromwellian England', *P&P*, 109 (1985), 67.

and other places', where the poor were properly employed.[30] Hartlib looked
as much to Paris as the early Stuarts had done, especially when he wanted
models of purposeful state enterprise for the public good, admiring Richelieu
for sponsoring Theophraste Renaudot's version of his 'Office of Address',
noting that the French trained their physicians in hospitals, as Petty
proposed for England, and later on seeking for information about the
Parisian Hôpital Général.[31] No one was more aware than Hartlib that there
was a European context to the turning of social and welfare policies in the
direction of public improvement.

The most striking example of this intellectual shift which the Hartlib
papers provide is perhaps a project to 'improve the design . . . for the poor'.
It was probably by Benjamin Worsley, since its purpose was to associate
workhouses with his much-publicized scheme for making saltpetre. Drawing on chemical and Paracelsian theory, and noting the fertilizing properties
of the 'corruptible parts of our aliments which nature daily separates from
us as excrementitions', the author proposed to use them to 'generate . . .
something for human use'. He calculates that a workhouse with 150 people
might furnish sufficient human waste to produce ten tons of saltpetre a year,
if properly managed. We need not dwell on the details. But there could be no
better example of how what had once been regarded as inevitable sources of
corruption and decay—like the poor, or towns, or indeed private interests—
could be turned to public use. Rather than condemn it, writes the author, 'I
know not why we may not translate corruption into policy and', he adds
optimistically, 'into action'.[32]

II

Though not as malleable as Worsley and Hartlib would have liked, public
policy proved easier to influence than public action. Some of the projects of
the Hartlib group were like the contemporary Utopias Hartlib himself
dismissed as 'impossible to be put into practice'.[33] Several were embarked
upon, but not concluded, because their authors lacked the necessary political
influence. Many remained on the agenda, persistent issues for public debate,
as much because circumstances so dictated as because of the eloquence of
their sponsors. All three points are best illustrated by the London Cor-

[30] Peter, *Good Work*, sig. A4; Jenner, *Londons Blame*, 6; Lee, *Remonstrance*, 6. Cf.
Braddick and Greengrass, 'Letters of Culpeper', 250.

[31] Hartlib, *Further Discovery*, 172; HP, Ephem. 1648; HP, 27/21.

[32] HP, 15/2/5, n.d. but probably c.1646. For Worsley's saltpetre project, see Webster, *Great
Instauration*, 377–80; C. Webster, 'Benjamin Worsley: Engineering for Universal Reform
from the Invisible College to the Navigation Act', in Greengrass, *Hartlib and Universal
Reformation*, 215–16; and for Hartlib's interest, Braddick and Greengrass, 'Letters of Culpeper', 226–7.

[33] HP, Ephem., 1640. For Hartlib's correspondents on More (*Utopia* was reprinted in
1639), Bacon, and Burton, see Ephem., 1649, HP, 21/1/19B; HP, 28/2/56B; and for doubts
about Utopian 'fictions', Cooke, *Unum Necessarium*, 36; *Advice of W.P.*, 148.

poration of the Poor: a major innovation in public welfare, in many ways the greatest concrete achievement of these projectors, but a flawed and incomplete achievement nonetheless.

Most of the poor relief pamphlets of 1645–53 were intended to contribute to the Corporation's erection or its perfection; but they did not invent it. In 1641 and 1642 the Common Council of London was already considering a draft bill for the poor to be submitted to the Long Parliament, which probably included all the essentials;[34] and the rationale for a new Corporation sanctioned by statute emerged naturally from past events. It could restore central management of municipal poor relief, which the united hospitals of the 1550s had half-enjoyed, and which the 1598 Poor Law had destroyed through its insistence on parochial autonomy. A Corporation could facilitate new civic workhouses, which the City had been considering since the 1620s, and remove the legal doubt about whether rates might be levied in support, a question recently debated before the Privy Council.[35] Incorporation would also allow the new organization to receive and manage charitable bequests in perpetuity: one of the reasons why hospitals had been incorporated by statute or letters patent in the past. The advantages would have been clear to any lawyer, and certainly to Matthew Hale and John Maynard, who were employed to redraft the 1641 bill when the City picked it up again in 1645.[36]

Nevertheless, though not in at the beginning, it was Hartlib who was responsible for the Common Council's return to the subject in 1645, along with influential allies who joined him in petitioning for a Corporation. Some of them were merchants 'to the Western parts', including Thomas Andrewes, prominent among Professor Brenner's 'new merchants', and Nicholas Corselis, from the Dutch Church at Austin Friars, another pressure group for welfare reform with which Hartlib had contact.[37] Some of them contributed

---

[34] London Corporation RO, Journal 40, fos. 6^r, 31^v. In the following description of the founding of the Corporation I have added information from the Hartlib Papers to the account given in V. Pearl, 'Puritans and Poor Relief: The London Workhouse, 1649–1660', in K. Thomas and D. Pennington (eds.), *Puritans and Revolutionaries: Essays in Seventeenth-Century History Presented to Christopher Hill* (Oxford, 1978), 206–32.

[35] P. Slack, *Poverty and Policy in Tudor and Stuart England* (1988), 129; Pearl, 'Puritans and Poor Relief', 214–15 (Hartlib knew of one of these schemes: HP, 15/2/14); *APC 1630–1*, 329. The description 'Corporation of the poor' had antecedents: it was used in a 1589 statute with reference to an incorporation of almsmen in a Berkshire almshouse: House of Lords RO, 31 Eliz. I, OA 20.

[36] Bush, *Poor Man's Friend*, 4. As Recorder of Plymouth, Maynard would have known of the corporation of the Poor's Portion there (above, pp. 42, 48), and Hale had been a pupil of William Noy, on whom see above, p. 43.

[37] LCRO, Journal 40, fo. 145^v; HP, 15/2/35, 47; R. Brenner, *Merchants and Revolution: Commercial Change, Political Conflict and London's Overseas Traders, 1550–1653* (Princeton, NJ, 1993). The involvement of Andrewes is clear from Bush, *Poor Man's Friend*, sig. A2^r. On Corselis, see O. P. Grell, 'From Persecution to Integration: The Decline of the Anglo-Dutch Communities in England 1648–1702', in O. P. Grell, J. I. Israel, and N. Tyacke (eds.),

to the extraordinary twice-weekly public meetings advertised by the lord mayor as open to anyone 'well-affected to so pious and charitable a work'. Rice Bush himself managed the passage through Parliament of the 1647 ordinance setting up the Corporation, together with an apothecary, Edward Odling, later to be its solicitor.[38]

Yet Odling's account makes it clear that they had to make concessions to opposition in the Commons, and Hartlib's papers show how far their initial ambitions had been cut down to size, largely no doubt before the bill ever left the Guildhall for Westminster. They had hoped for Bush's whole programme for what was virtually a welfare state: free medical assistance and education;[39] encouragement to cultivate wastes and grow flax to employ the nation's poor; a London Corporation to cover the whole metropolis, either within the bills or within the new military 'lines of communication'. What they got in 1647 was a Corporation confined to the old City and to the provision of workhouses and houses of correction within it, with an additional clause permitting similar Corporations in boroughs or counties which wanted them.[40]

Their chances improved after Pride's Purge. A new Act for the Corporation in 1649 increased its corporate authority and enhanced its autonomy. Among the new governing assistants were Bush and Odling, Thomas Jenner, Corselis, and Thomas Andrewes.[41] But they could not look beyond the City, and the reins of power were still held by old political Presbyterians who remained as deputy president and treasurer. If we are to believe the Corporation's propaganda—its official records do not survive—Bush and his friends may have achieved some of their purposes. There was a register of the poor; children (up to eighty at a time) were sent to the workhouse to be taught as well as employed; up to 1,000 adults were set to work, most of

From Persecution to Toleration: The Glorious Revolution and Religion in England (Oxford, 1991), 111, 113; O. P. Grell, 'Godly Charity or Political Aid? Irish Protestants and International Calvinism, 1641–1645', *Historical Journal*, 39 (1996), 747; Brenner, *Merchants and Revolution*, 617.

[38] HP, 57/4/5A; *To the Right Honourable the President and Governors of the Corporation . . . The humble Remonstrance of Edward Odling* (1652; BL, 190.g.12(185)). For the input of the City's recorder, William Steele, see House of Lords RO, Main Papers 1641, fos. 194–9 (undated but, as Pearl points out ('Puritans and Poor Relief', 215), of 1646 or later).

[39] Neither the Hartlib group's petition nor its 'propositions' to the Common Council (HP, 15/2/35 and 47) refer to medical assistance, but the Common Council's committee report (15/2/51) raises the issue as if they expected it to be on the agenda.

[40] C. H. Firth and R. S. Rait (eds.), *Acts and Ordinances of the Interregnum 1642–60* (3 vols., 1911), i. 1042–5, 17 Dec. 1647.

[41] Ibid. ii. 104–10, 7 May 1649. The Act introduced direct elections from the wards to the Corporation in place of nomination of its Assistants by the Common Council: a suggestion put forward earlier by the Hartlib group (HP, 15/2/51) and one which raised issues of wider constitutional importance and much controversy in City politics at this time: see e.g. the debate which set Maynard and Hale against Wildman in *London's Liberties* (1651).

them in their own homes.[42] But there were no similar Corporations elsewhere, and hence no national reformation.

The Corporation of the Poor was the pinnacle of the Hartlib group's practical achievements. Matthew Hale's Law Commission produced some relief for poor debtors, but successive parliamentary committees on the poor laws reached no conclusion.[43] Dr Mark Jenner has described John Lanyon's activity as surveyor-general of London streets, but cleaning and paving were never taken over by the Corporation of the Poor, as had been hoped.[44] Outside London, George Tunstall's scheme for a free medical service in County Durham was rejected by the sessions.[45] Thomas Laurence, keeper of a Marlborough workhouse and pamphleteer for 'the public good', was turned out of office in 1657 when he became a Quaker.[46] In the same year, Hartlib was told that the lord mayor wanted 'a charity school' in every London ward, so that 'Christ's kingdom in little ones may more and more be advanced', but we hear no more of it.[47] By 1659 John Beale, for one, was disillusioned. As sceptical about perfectionism now as Baxter, he retreated to the advocacy of 'Christian societies in small models', such as monasteries had been, or—one might add—such as hospitals and charity schools might be. Only disappointed expectations had resulted from talking 'big of reforming laws and making whole nations churches, and of erecting the kingdom of Christ all over the world'.[48]

Yet contrary to the expectations of the defeated, the Restoration marked a new beginning, not a final blow, for the public good, once it was separated

---

[42] Pearl, 'Puritans and Poor Relief', 223–6.

[43] Firth and Rait, *Acts and Ordinances*, ii. 753–64; M. Cottrell, 'Interregnum Law Reform: The Hale Commission of 1652', *Eng. Hist. Rev.*, 83 (1968), 687; J. Thirsk, 'Agrarian Problems and the English Revolution', in R. C. Richardson (ed.), *Town and Countryside in the English Revolution* (Manchester, 1992), 174–5, 184.

[44] M. Jenner, ' "Another *Epocha*"? Hartlib, John Lanyon and the Improvement of London in the 1650s', in Greengrass, *Hartlib and Universal Reformation*, 343–56. It took the regime until 1657 to produce an ordinance regulating new building in London: Firth and Rait, *Acts and Ordinances*, ii. 1223–34; C. A. Edie, 'New Buildings, New Taxes, and Old Interests: An Urban Problem of the 1670s', *Journal of British Studies*, 6 (1967), 39. Fines were imposed on owners of houses built since 1620 on fewer than 4 acres, and new houses were to be of brick or stone, but the height of storeys and depth of walls were not specified as they had been, by proclamation, before 1640.

[45] HP, 53/12. Cf. D. Harley, 'Pious Physic for the Poor: The Lost Durham County Medical Scheme of 1655', *Medical History*, 37 (1993), 148–66.

[46] Thomas Laurence, *Some Pitty on the Poor* [n.d.], 3 and *passim*; Joseph Besse, *A Collection of the Sufferings of the People called Quakers* (2 vols., 1753), ii. 37. Wing dates Laurence's pamphlet ?1675 (L687A), but it is certainly of earlier date. M. Canney and D. Knott, *Catalogue of the Goldsmiths' Library of Economic Literature* (Cambridge, 1970), no. 1175, suggests 1650. Since part of it is addressed to the Parliament of the three kingdoms, it seems rather to belong to 1654–9, and probably to 1658 or 1659, after Laurence had been dismissed.

[47] HP, 29/6/20B. Might this be the first use of the term 'charity school'?

[48] Quoted in J. C. Davis, *Utopia and the Ideal Society: A Study of English Utopian Writing 1516–1700* (Cambridge, 1981), 316. Cf. above, p. 52.

from any obvious taint of millenarianism. The Royal Society's success in carving out social space for certain parts of the Baconian programme is well known.[49] There were new tracts advocating a 'Poor Man's Office' and 'Mount-pietyes' in 1660 and 1661,[50] and a new boost to improvement in 1663, with the publication of *The Improvement improved* by the parliamentary engineer Andrew Yarranton, and of *England's Interest and Improvement* by the courtier Samuel Fortrey, who wrote to advance the 'public good' and 'the welfare and happiness' of the kingdom.[51] Unlikely as it might have seemed later, Charles II could persuasively present himself as a reforming monarch in 1660, sponsoring the usual clean-up campaign at the start of a reign with a proclamation against profanity and debauchery, and writing to the City to support subscriptions to employ the poor on hemp, and benefit fisheries and the navy.[52] John Evelyn's *Fumifugium* of 1661 catches the same expectant mood. The 'health and felicity' of London could be improved by plantations, by Hugh Peter's wider streets, brick houses, and new quay, given a lead from 'his Majesty's great genius, which studies only the public good'.[53]

It would have taken a greater genius than that of Charles II to deal adequately with the circumstances of the 1660s, of course: the threat of famine in 1662 and the reality of plague, fire, and war soon after. The restoration of the monarchy had not restored confidence in the prerogative powers which had grappled with similar problems in the 1620s, but neither had the restoration of king and lords made legislative solutions to them any easier to achieve. The book of dearth orders was reprinted in 1662, but purely for advice, without conciliar backing. Revision of the plague orders, which all considered necessary in the new intellectual climate of 1665, was delayed, partly by disputes between the two Houses of Parliament on whether peers could be quarantined. Neither king nor Parliament claimed

[49] S. Shapin and S. Schaffer, *Leviathan and the Air-Pump* (Princeton, NJ, 1985), 342 and *passim*; Hunter, *Science and Society*, 91, 92, 118, and see J. A. Mendelsohn, 'Alchemy and Politics in England 1649–1665', *P&P*, 135 (1992), 74.

[50] T.L., *An Appeal to the Parliament concerning the Poor* (1660), 2; *Observations Manifesting the Conveniency and Commodity of Mount-Pietyes* (1661). Cf. Chamberlayne, *Englands Wants* (1667), 7. *An Appeal* has often been attributed to Thomas Lawson; comparison with *Some Pitty* (above, p. 87, n. 46) shows it to be by Thomas Laurence, the Marlborough Quaker. Another reflection on local poor-relief practice, *A Declaration* by John Ivie of Salisbury, was published in 1661.

[51] Andrew Yarranton, *The Improvement improved* (1663), apparently a revision of a lost earlier tract on clover; Samuel Fortrey, *Englands Interest and Improvement* (Cambridge, 1663), sig. A3ᵛ, p. 3. These were the first of a series of economic tracts with 'improvement' titles: see below, n. 89.

[52] R. Steele, *A Bibliography of Royal Proclamations . . . 1485–1714* (Bibliotheca Lindesiana, 5, 1910), i, no. 3211; W. H. and H. C. Overall (eds.), *Analytical Index to the Remembrancia* (1878), 143–4. The latter is referred to by Hartlib: HP, 27/21, fo. 1ʳ.

[53] John Evelyn, *Fumifugium* (1661), sigs. a1, a2. For the context of this work, including the Hartlib circle, see M. Jenner, 'The Politics of London Air: John Evelyn's *Fumifugium* and the Restoration', *Historical Journal*, 38 (1995), 535–51.

the authority to impose the new London street-plan which any of the grand designs of 1666 would have required.[54] Nevertheless, these crises kept questions of public welfare at the centre of public attention for more than a decade;[55] and there remained the continuing problems of poverty and a growing, haphazardly governed metropolis which could only be addressed in the terms established before 1660.

The collapse of the London Corporation of the Poor with the return to the king of the properties it occupied raised both these issues in critical form;[56] and in 1661 two parliamentary bills presented familiar solutions for discussion. One would have set up a single London Corporation for the whole area within the bills of mortality, with no fewer than 200 assistants, Odling and Corselis among them. The other would have constituted Corporations of the Poor 'in the several cities and counties within the kingdom'. Both bills were dropped in the House of Lords, and all that remained were the clauses in the 1662 Act of Settlement authorizing separate Corporations of the Poor in London and Westminster and in urban Middlesex and Surrey.[57]

Yet we know from Matthew Hale's papers that an interest in incorporated workhouses for towns and combinations of rural parishes survived;[58] and from the activities of John Maynard, his partner advising the City back in 1645, that statutory authority continued to be sought for new ventures.[59] Many municipal corporations went ahead without it in the 1660s and 1670s, Exeter getting its first purpose-built workhouse in 1672, Bristol a linen manufactory employing 500 poor spinners, and the once godly cities of Norwich, Dorchester, and Hull new enterprises for indoor and outdoor

---

[54] P. Slack, 'Books of Orders: The Making of English Social Policy, 1577–1631', *Trans. Roy. Hist. Soc.*, 5th ser., 30 (1980), 21; P. Slack, *The Impact of Plague in Tudor and Stuart England* (1985), 222–4; T. F. Reddaway, *The Rebuilding of London after the Great Fire* (1940), ch. 2; S. Porter, *The Great Fire of London* (Stroud, Glos., 1996), 97–105.

[55] In 1663, for example, the Royal Society set up a committee to consider a letter from a Somerset gentleman on 'a way of preventing famine, by dispersing potatoes throughout all parts of England': M. Hunter, *Establishing the New Science: The Experience of the Early Royal Society* (Woodbridge, Suffolk, 1989), 77, 102–4.

[56] Pearl, 'Puritans and Poor Relief', 229. For expectations in 1660 that the London Corporation would continue, see N. H. Keeble and G. F. Nuttall, *Calendar of the Correspondence of Richard Baxter* (2 vols., Oxford, 1991), ii. 9; Overall, *Index to the Remembrancia*, 364.

[57] House of Lords RO, Main Papers, 3 July 1661, 10 Apr. 1662; *Commons Journal*, viii. 345, 366; *Lords Journal*, xi. 390, 439; 14 Car. II, c. 12, s. iv.

[58] Lambeth Palace Library, Fairhurst Papers, MS 3475, fo. 283, the first of an undated list of 'Acts propounded', whose content suggests a date after 1660. The same volume (fos. 129–49) contains a draft bill for the transportation of vagabonds, elaborating on s. xxiii of the Act of Settlement, and apparently considered by the Commons in 1663: *Commons Journal*, viii. 437. Hale advocated incorporated workhouses in *A Discourse Touching Provision for the Poor* (1683; written c.1659), 10.

[59] For the Devon county workhouse, in which Maynard had a long-standing interest, see: 18 and 19 Car. II, c. 9, s. iv; *Commons Journal*, viii. 674, 689; above, p. 66, n. 49.

employment.[60] The London Quakers, with a flax-spinning project for
their poor from about 1677, looked back to earlier projects, and so did
the Socinian Thomas Firmin, employing and training poor children in St
Botolph's Aldersgate at the same time.[61] The London Corporation of the
Poor was not revived, but the 1662 Act produced a new Corporation for
Middlesex, whose Clerkenwell workhouse was applauded by Pepys in terms
Hartlib would have endorsed: 'the many pretty works and the little children
employed, everyone to do something'.[62]

There was continuity in other areas of metropolitan policy too. Another
statute of 1662 set up a commission 'for the streets and ways' within the bills
of mortality, in practice largely for the West End, with Petty and Evelyn
among its members. The rebuilding Acts after the Great Fire authorized a
similar City commission for paving and cleaning with power to levy rates,
widened streets, and took the building regulations of early Stuart proclamations to their logical conclusion, with prescriptions for first-, second- and
third-rate houses, like so many ships in the new dockyards.[63] The City's new
fire regulations, dividing it into quarters, have a familiar ring to them; and
there was even for a time an effort at the long-projected Thames-side quay.[64]
Projects and perspectives from before 1660, and even before 1640, continued
to have practical effect.

In some respects, moreover, the challenge of the Great Fire gave them new

[60] Devon RO, Exeter Chamber Act Book xi, pp. 191, 225, 236–7, 251, 278; Bristol AO,
Common Council Proceedings 1670–87, fos. 128ᵛ–130ʳ; Norfolk RO, Norwich Mayor's
Court Book 24, 1666–77, fo. 46ᵛ; Dorset RO, DOB 16/5, Corporation Minutes 1656–77,
249; Hull City RO, Bench Book 7, 1664–82, 424–5. The Norwich committee inquired into
the rules for workhouses in Holland and Flanders. For other signs of continuing interest in
Dutch workhouses and hospitals, see BL, Harleian MS 7517, fos. 103–8; Lansdowne MS 841,
fos. 27–8; C. D. Van Strien, *British Travellers in Holland during the Stuart Period: Edward
Browne and John Locke as Tourists in the United Provinces* (Leiden, 1993), 196–8.

[61] S. Macfarlane, 'Social Policy and the Poor in the Later Seventeenth Century', in A. L.
Beier and R. Finlay (eds.), *London 1500–1700: The Making of the Metropolis* (1986), 259.

[62] R. Latham and W. Matthews (eds.), *The Diary of Samuel Pepys* (11 vols., 1970–83), v.
289. Cf. ibid. 250, vi. 65–6. The Middlesex workhouse was intended to employ 600 poor and
maintain 100 old and blind paupers: J. C. Jeaffreson (ed.), *Middlesex County Records* (4 vols.,
1886–92), iii. 337. It was soon discredited by allegations of corruption, however: *Commons
Journal*, ix. 211–12; Anchitell Grey, *Debates of the House of Commons From the Year 1667 to
the Year 1694* (10 vols., 1769), i. 403–6; *Lords Journal*, xii. 499. 22 and 23 Car. II, c. 18, tried
to settle the Middlesex controversy. The only other workhouse set up under the 1662 Act was
in St Margaret's Westminster in 1666: Pearl, 'Puritans and Poor Relief', 230. Neither
workhouse can have been run by a separate 'Corporation' after 1685, when the relevant
clause in the 1662 statute was repealed: 1 James II, c. 17, s. ii.

[63] 14 Car. II, c. 2; 18 & 19 Car. II, c. 8 (which describes London in proper Stuart style as
'the Imperial Seat'); 22 Car. II, c. 11. The commission was made perpetual by 22 & 23 Car. II,
c. 17. The implementation of the rebuilding statutes is fully described in Reddaway, *Rebuilding*, which *inter alia* notes Matthew Hale's important role in the Fire Court.

[64] C. F. T. Young, *Fires, Fire Engines and Fire Brigades* (1866), 29; Reddaway, *Rebuilding*,
200, 233–4. On the 'quartering' of London, see above, p. 72; HP, 15/2/47. The Great Fire
made necessary another echo of the Hartlib group: an office for new addresses in Bloomsbury
Square: Porter, *Great Fire*, 84.

impetus and focus. The Fire was an opportunity to be 'improved', Samuel Rolls wrote, for 'the welfare of all England'. Rebuilding was not a matter of 'pomp' and 'pride', but of providing churches, schools, and hospitals in order to show how the moral as well as the physical environment might be reconstructed with 'beauty and decency'.[65] The governors of London's hospitals, as pompous and proud as those of its churches, quickly took the point. The royal hospitals had no special place in Wren's projected vistas or Evelyn's planned piazzas in the new city. They were not listed as beneficiaries from the coal duties, though Bridewell, as a partial prison, got a contribution. But their governors seized the chance to display their wealth, charity, and utility none the less. Christ's Hospital led the way, rebuilding being finally completed thanks to the generosity of Robert Clayton, Firmin's patron and future Whig grandee.[66] Sir William Turner, president of Bethlem Hospital, which had not been destroyed in the Fire, responded with something much more remarkable: the erection of Robert Hooke's new Bedlam of 1676 on the edge of Moorfields, a building whose site, plan, and elevation gave it light, air, and a grandeur which influenced all later hospitals. 'So brave, so neat, so sweet, it does appear,' says a contemporary celebration, 'Makes one half-mad to be a lodger there.'[67]

The new Bethlem was in origin more the product of a competitive building boom than an expression of new sensibilities. But its effect was to put a newly expansive charity on public display, and it was publicized: in engravings in which Bethlem's 500-foot façade, the largest in London, dominated the city, just as Henry IV's Hôpital St Louis or, more recently and influentially, the Invalides dominated printed views of Paris. The Invalides, begun in 1670 and much admired in England, shows, moreover, that the competition was international.[68] In 1665 the Commissioners for Sick and Wounded, trying to find lodging for English veterans of the Dutch War, had resurrected

---

[65] Samuel Rolls, *Londons Resurrection or the Rebuilding of London Encouraged, Directed and Improved* (1668), sigs. A8ᵛ, a2ᵛ, pp. 48–9, 56–8.

[66] Reddaway, *Rebuilding*, 193 n, 258.

[67] *Bethlehem's Beauty* (1676), in R. A. Aubin (ed.), *London in Flames: London in Glory* (New Brunswick, NJ, 1943), 246;. C. Stevenson, 'Robert Hooke's Bethlem', *Journal of the Society of Architectural Historians*, 55 (1996), 252–73; J. D. Thompson and G. Goldie, *The Hospital: A Social and Architectural History* (New Haven, Conn., 1975), 68; M. 'Espinasse, *Robert Hooke* (1956), 91–2. Although the 'ruinous state' of Bethlem was certainly one motive for rebuilding, it scarcely explains the grandeur of the new building or its site: London Corporation RO, Rep. 79, fos. 205ᵛ–206ʳ. Moorfields was, it may be noted, the site of the dialogue in Gabriel Plattes's *Macaria*.

[68] M. I. Batten, 'The Architecture of Dr Robert Hooke FRS', *Walpole Society*, 25 (1937), 92; E. G. O'Donoghue, *The Story of Bethlehem Hospital* (1914), frontispiece; H. Ballon, *The Paris of Henri IV: Architecture and Urbanism* (Cambridge, Mass., 1991), 196; C. I. A. Ritchie, '*The Hostel of the Invalides* by Thomas Povey (1682)', *Medical History*, 10 (1966), 1–22, 177–97. Cf. the rebuilding of public institutions in Turin in the late 17th c.: S. Cavallo, *Charity and Power in Early Modern Italy: Benefactors and Their Motives in Turin, 1541–1789* (Cambridge, 1995), 99.

Burghley's idea of using existing hospitals and almshouses and had failed: a
national survey of facilities demonstrated that it would have cost more effort
than it was worth.[69] Once Ormonde had shown the way with Kilmainham
Hospital, Dublin, in 1680, however, and Stephen Fox found the public funds,
Chelsea Hospital could be begun in 1682 and the model set for Greenwich.
Chelsea was Charles II's version of Henry VII's great work of charity, the
Savoy Hospital; and it was the Crown's contribution to the revival, after
more than a century, of monumental embodiments of public ideals.[70]

Hugh Peter had put Bedlam, maimed soldiers, and hospitals as items to be
minded at the end of his 1651 tract. He would scarcely have approved of the
agents who in the end picked them up, any more than he might have
welcomed the partially baroque city for which the Great Fire had provided
the opportunity. William Petty, however, made the transition with apparent
ease, seeking patrons wherever they might be found in the intricate politics
of the 1660s and 1670s, and then, in the new circumstances of the 1680s,
joining those who looked again to a powerful Stuart monarchy as the only
effective means of translating policy into action, and who were suspected of
Catholic or absolutist tendencies as a result. Petty even acknowledged the
need for a standing army, though Charles II dared not build a barracks (as
opposed to a hospital) for it and used the much-mangled Savoy instead.
Improvement and the public good had proved to be no respecters of political
or sectarian boundaries: they were not vulnerable to 'passion or interest,
faction or party', Petty declared.[71] That was why they had continued to
shape the agenda, even if it was only patchily translated into action. They
had become commonplaces.

[69] C. G. T. Dean, *The Royal Hospital Chelsea* (1950), 19; Lambeth Palace, Sheldon Papers
1664–67, fos. 4^r, 21^r. The returns for 89 institutions, in Lambeth Palace, MSS 639 and 951,
record on average only 7 inmates each. There are related letters in John Norden, *Speculi
Britanniae Pars: A Topographical and Historical Description of Cornwall* (1728), 'Original
Letters Relating to Hospitals . . .' at end.

[70] M. Craig, *Dublin 1660–1860* (Harmondsworth, Middx., 1992), 58–60; Dean, *Chelsea*,
23–41; C. Clay, *Public Finance and Private Wealth: The Career of Sir Stephen Fox, 1627–
1716* (Oxford, 1978), 133–8. A subscription had been begun for a hospital for the poor
'serviceable to the common good' in Dublin in 1669, and even the small 'Scottish box' charity
was funding the building of a Scottish hospital in London in 1676: *A Narrative and an
Accompt Concerning the Hospital on Oxmonton-Green, Dublin* (Dublin, 1673); D. Maclean,
'London in 1689–90', *Transactions of the London and Middlesex Archaeological Society*, n.s.,
6 (1929–32), 488 and n. Charles II's complaint to Fox (Clay, *Public Finance*, 134) that 'he saw
nobody in this age for building hospitals' was scarcely justified.

[71] Hunter, *Science and Society*, 123–9; E. A. O. Whiteman, 'The Census That Never Was',
in E. A. O. Whiteman (ed.), *Statesmen, Scholars and Merchants: Essays in Eighteenth-
Century History Presented to Dame Lucy Sutherland* (Oxford, 1973), 13; Marquis of Lansdowne (ed.), *The Petty Papers* (2 vols., 1927), i. 268; R. Somerville, *The Savoy. Manor:
Hospital: Chapel* (1960), 74. Cf. M. Goldie, 'Sir Peter Pett, Sceptical Toryism and the Science
of Toleration in the 1680s', in W. J. Sheils (ed.), *Persecution and Toleration* (Studies in Church
History, 21, Oxford, 1984), 261–2, 269–71; T. C. Barnard, 'Sir William Petty, Irish Landowner', in H. Lloyd-Jones, V. Pearl, and B. Worden (eds.), *History and Imagination: Essays
in Honour of H. R. Trevor-Roper* (1981), 212.

III

It is in the nature of commonplaces, of course, that they are slippery things, carrying different meanings for different people, and these were no exception. But we can see some of the new directions in which they might point in Petty's writings, far from commonplace and open to challenge and subsequent ridicule though they were. Just as his Irish enterprises, reconstructed by Dr Barnard, illustrate invention and improvement in not always successful practice, so his papers display in grandiose and uncritical form the kinds of intellectual preoccupation which set the terms for future debate.[72]

'Political arithmetic' is the most famous of them, the term invented by this surveyor-physician in 1672 to describe a method of measurement and diagnosis rather than a conclusion for social investigation. Defined by Davenant as 'the art of reasoning by figures, upon things relating to government', it was, as he said, 'undoubtedly very ancient'.[73] We have seen ample evidence of the taking of censuses and surveys. In 1548 John Hales had compared current with past books of musters and concluded that the population was 'wonderfully diminished'.[74] Plague had been measured by bills of mortality. There had been efforts to collect price statistics in order to have similar warning of dearth. From the 1640s onwards, however, there was a new enthusiasm for the collection of numerical data, not just to get a more 'exact account' of a vital economic indicator like the balance of trade,[75] but to measure social resources and opportunities; and there was an obvious exhilaration in the use of number to provide propaganda for change for the better, for improvement.

The essential method was the employment of what amounted to elementary algebraic equations in order to move by simple arithmetic from the

---

[72] There has been no scholarly life of Petty since E. Strauss, *Sir William Petty: Portrait of a Genius* (1954), but there is important material in L. G. Sharp, 'Sir William Petty and Some Aspects of Seventeenth-Century Natural Philosophy', D.Phil. thesis, Univ. of Oxford, 1976, and on his career in Ireland in the perceptive essays of T. C. Barnard: 'Petty, Irish Landowner'; 'Sir William Petty as Kerry Ironmaster', *Proceedings of the Royal Irish Academy*, 82C (1982), 1–32. He has an acknowledged place in the history of economic thought, though that is not my concern here: M. Bowley, *Studies in the History of Economic Theory before 1870* (1973), 84–6; W. Letwin, *The Origins of Scientific Economics* (New York, 1964), 155–7.

[73] C. Whitworth (ed.), *The Political and Commercial Works of . . . Charles Davenant* (5 vols., 1771), i. 128; Goldie, 'Pett', 267.

[74] BL, Lansdowne MS 238, fo. 309ᵛ. On the use of musters to indicate population totals, see also Vickers, *Bacon*, 397. For early proposals for better registration of vital events, see G. R. Elton, *The Parliament of England 1559–1581* (Cambridge, 1986), 221; J. Strype, *Annals of the Reformation* (4 vols., Oxford, 1824), iv. 62–4; Sharp, 'Petty', 343.

[75] Firth and Rait, *Acts and Ordinances*, ii. 403–6. On the use of figures and numbers more generally, see G. Clark, *Science and Social Welfare in the Age of Newton* (Oxford, 1937), 126–7; J. Hoppit, 'Reforming Britain's Weights and Measures', *Eng. Hist. Rev.*, 108 (1993), 82–104; K. Thomas, 'Numeracy in Early Modern England', *Trans. Roy. Hist. Soc.*, 5th ser., 37 (1987), esp. 131; and on the bills of mortality, J. C. Robertson, 'Reckoning with London: Interpreting the *Bills of Mortality* before John Graunt', *Urban History*, 23 (1996), 325–50.

known to the unknown. It can be illustrated from the two tracts, among those cited at the beginning of this chapter, not written but published by the Hartlib group largely no doubt because of their calculations. *Stanley's Remedy* began with the number of parishes in England—9,725—and the average cost of feeding a pauper—3 pence a day. If two were idle in each parish, their maintenance would cost £88,740 a year; but if there were 80,000 idle, as some thought, £365,000 a year might be saved by their profitable employment. 'Let us admit', says Adam Moore, that there are three million acres of waste, common and marsh: then, given other assumptions about acres per cottage and heads per family, they might if improved support 1,500,000 people.[76] Large numbers opened eyes to large possibilities, despite their shaky foundations, and the method caught on. Leonard Lee used flexible and sometimes unspecified multipliers to move from the 2,800 families not paying taxes in St Olave's, Southwark, to the conclusion that there were more than 40,000 poor in London consuming £160,000 a year unnecessarily.[77] It was not a large step from here to Jonathan Swift's savage satire about the gain to be made for 'the public good' from converting 100,000 Irish infants into a 'new dish . . . on the tables of gentlemen of fortune'.[78]

But number also had the great advantage of permitting measured comparisons across space and time. Petty explained 'how it may be known that the people . . . of London be better than those of Paris'. One should calculate 'what numbers of exposed children' in each city, 'what numbers of murders and manslaughters', of executions and imprisonments, of lawsuits and beggars; how many live by husbandry, how many lawyers and physicians, what quantities of 'liquors' consumed per head; and Petty began to compare the published statistics of the hospitals of the two capitals.[79] He also examined time series, in order to show from the bills of mortality that London had grown faster than Paris; he extrapolated the trend of London's growth forward into the future; and he tried to demonstrate that England would soon be more populous, wealthier, and more powerful than France.[80] There

[76] *Stanley's Remedy* (1646), 2; Moore, *Bread for the Poor*, 14–15. For similar kinds of calculation, see Jenner, *Londons Blame*, 10; R. Haines, *England's Weal and Prosperity* (1681), 11; and for earlier examples: E. A. Lamond (ed.), *A Discourse of the Common Weal of this Realm of England* (Cambridge, 1893), p. xliii; T. E. Hartley (ed.), *Proceedings in the Parliaments of Elizabeth I* (3 vols., Leicester, 1981–95), iii. 144–5.

[77] Lee, *Remonstrance*, 4–5. Hartlib himself was careful in his arithmetic, honestly showing a loss in his calculation of the costs of maintaining poor children in workhouses: *Londons Charity inlarged*, sig. C3^r.　　　　　　　　　　[78] Jonathan Swift, *A Modest Proposal* (1729).

[79] Bodl., MS Film 1953, Petty Papers, Box E, nos. 36, 37; C. H. Hull (ed.), *The Economic Writings of Sir William Petty* (2 vols., Cambridge, 1899), ii. 505–13. As another comparative exercise, Petty wished to calculate the relative life expectations of patients in places with and without 'the best physicians': Lansdowne, *Petty Papers*, ii. 169–70.

[80] Hull, *Economic Writings*, ii. 458–9, 464, 505–6, 517–18; i. 302–5. For similar reasons of policy, he wanted data to be collected of expenditure on the poor over 7 years: Lansdowne, *Petty Papers*, ii. 210.

was the opportunity here for a conception of linear progress, and hence for an alternative to that essentially circular view of corruption and regeneration which Worsley used to justify his saltpetre project, and which George Hakewill had employed in the 1630s to deny the opposite linear assumption of constant decay.[81]

That intellectual revolution was not, of course, so easily achieved. Neither should it be antedated. A more representative reflection of what were still uncertain perspectives in the mid-seventeenth century is the path-breaking exercise in 'shop arithmetic' to which Petty contributed, John Graunt's *Natural and Political Observations* on the London bills of mortality of 1662.[82] There are plenty of linear demonstrations in Graunt: that over time London 'gradually removes westward', that its population was likely to double in the next sixty-four years. There is some optimism: 'my first observation is that few are starved'—only one in 4,000—a major revelation, given the anxieties of the later 1640s.[83] But there is not Petty's overpowering faith in the possibilities of economic growth.

Graunt thought in conventional terms of a fixed amount of trade in the world. In consequence, at the domestic level, he shared some current doubts about whether workhouses might not simply take work away from those already employed, and so 'transfer the want from one hand to another'.[84] He thought similarly in terms of balance when it came to population, with migration explaining and redressing the discrepancies between city and country, those bred in the country dying in town. If some threats to health were waning, others could wax. London was growing 'more unhealthful' as it grew 'more populous'.[85]

[81] Harris, *All Coherence Gone*, 79.

[82] John Graunt, *Natural and Political Observations . . . made upon the Bills of Mortality* (1662). I have used the scholarly edition of the 5th edn. (1676) in Hull, *Economic Writings*, ii. The first edition of 1662 is reprinted in *The Earliest Classics: John Graunt and Gregory King*, introd. by P. Laslett (1973). For the disputed relationship between Petty and Graunt in the authorship of the work, see Hull's introd., esp. pp. xlix–li; Sharp, 'Petty', 367–70; G. Keynes, *A Bibliography of Sir William Petty FRS and of Observations on the Bills of Mortality by John Graunt FRS* (Oxford, 1971), 75–82; T. Aspromourgos, 'The Life of William Petty in Relation to His Economics: A Tercentenary Interpretation', *History of Political Economy*, 20 (1988), 352, n. 15.

[83] Hull, *Economic Writings*, ii. 380, 352, 327.

[84] Ibid. 327–8, 353–4. Graunt was not the first to express doubts about the economic consequences of workhouses: see also Hartlib, *Londons Charitie*, 8; HP, 28/1/11A; [John White,] *The Planter's Plea* (1630), 19–21; C. Jackson, 'The Kendrick Bequests: An Experiment in Municipal Enterprise in the Woollen Industry in Reading and Newbury in the Early Seventeenth Century', *Southern History*, 16 (1994), 55–6 (Reading burgesses on the Kendrick workhouse in the 1630s); and the London orders for the poor of 1579, published in 1582, which tried to ensure that work in Bridewell would not mean the 'overthrow' of tradesmen outside: *Orders appointed to be executed in the Cittie of London* [1582], sig. Biii[r]. For Petty's view that trade might grow 'without increase of people', see Lansdowne, *Petty Papers*, i. 213–14.

[85] Hull, *Economic Writings*, ii. 332, 393–4.

Graunt's text is always equivocal about London, as in its early observation 'that London, the Metropolis of England, is *perhaps* a head too big for the body, and *possibly* too strong'; and Petty's interference in the work seems to me to have compounded, or even caused, that central ambiguity. The data Petty supplied from his home town of Romsey justified some passing, apparently optimistic remarks about the growth of population in the provinces.[86] But Graunt hesitated to conclude categorically, as Petty would have done, that the environment of London might be sufficiently improved to allow city and country both to grow, unimpeded by new threats to health; and Graunt was not alone. There was justified public suspicion in mid-century that the population was in fact falling, which helps to explain contemporary interest in the rights and wrongs of polygamy. It was underlined by Petty's own insistence in 1662 that 'fewness of people is real poverty', and intensified by plague and war soon after.[87] Gregory King and Charles Davenant were not the first to look to political arithmetic to clarify pessimistic preconceptions.[88]

It was anxiety rather than confidence which generated a literature on political economy in the 1670s, therefore, including new tracts on improvement[89] and another clutch of pamphlets on the poor, most of them by the Baptist farmer and projector for 'the public good', Richard Haines.[90] Yet the

[86] Hull, *Economic Writings*, ii. 320–1 (emphasis mine), 372. The latter reference is to ch. 7, parts of which, in range of speculation, seem more like Petty than Graunt: Sharp, 'Petty', 368. For a stimulating analysis of Graunt's assumptions and an argument that his work is more coherent and consistent than I here imply, see P. Kreager, 'New Light on Graunt', *Population Studies*, 42 (1988), 129–40.

[87] Hull, *Economic Writings*, ii. 377–8; L. Miller, *John Milton among the Polygamophiles* (New York, 1974), 28, 49; Lansdowne, *Petty Papers*, ii. 47.

[88] G. S. Holmes, 'Gregory King and the Social Structure of Pre-industrial England', *Trans. Roy. Hist. Soc.*, 5th ser., 27 (1977), 51–3.

[89] W[illiam] C[arter], *England's Interest Asserted, in the Improvement of its Native Commodities* (1669); John Smith, *England's Improvement Revived* (1670); Carew Reynell, *The True English Interest, or An Account of the Chief National Improvements* (1674); Roger Coke, *England's Improvements* (1675); Andrew Yarranton, *England's Improvement by Sea and Land* (1677); A. N[ewbold], *Londons Improvement and the Builder's Security Asserted* (1680); John Houghton, *A Collection of Letters For the Improvement of Husbandry and Trade* (1681). For what it is worth, a computer search of the BL Catalogue shows that the number of holdings including 'improve' or its derivatives in their titles and published at various dates rises from only 9 in the whole period before 1641 to 55 (1641–60), 72 (1661–80), 109 (1681–1700), 139 (1701–20), and 185 (1721–40). The total number of holdings is roughly constant for each 20-year period after 1640, apart from a fall in 1661–80. The totals include some duplicates.

[90] C. S. Nicholls (ed.), *The Dictionary of National Biography: Missing Persons* (Oxford, 1993), *sub* Haines; 'Philo-Anglicus' [probably Haines himself], *Bread for the Poor* (1678), 4. Haines's signed works on the subject were: *The Prevention of Poverty* (1674); *Proposals for building, in every County a Working-Alms-House or Hospital as the best Expedient to perfect the Trade and Manufactory of Linen Cloth* (1677); *Provision for the Poor* (1678); *A Method of Government for such Publick Working Alms-Houses As may be Erected in every County* (1679); *England's Weal and Prosperity Proposed* (1681). Other works on poor relief were *Sir Josiah Child's Proposals for the Relief and Employment of the Poor* (n.d.; Wing dates this

very process of propounding solutions to agricultural and economic depression led some of these writers to an almost Hartlibean confidence in the possibilities of social engineering. Like Chamberlen in 1649, several of them identified prospects for growth in 'employing the poor and making such industrious as are not', and wished to extend what had hitherto been largely urban devices to the countryside. They firmly established in the public mind the assumption that the rural as well as urban poor were a productive resource which could be harnessed, not a rabble to be regulated or edified.[91] From now on it became conventional to criticise the poor law either because it did not encourage training and work or because the Act of Settlement of 1662 kept scarce labour resources where they were not needed.[92] It became standard practice to cite the persuasive figure of £12,000 a year gained long ago by the employment of poor children in godly Norwich,[93] and to set relief of the poor firmly in the context of discussion of the national economy.

Moreover, in that other area of debate of 1662 and the later 1640s, the growth of London, improvement was being embraced as present deliverance as well as looked to for future salvation. The bills of mortality showed that London had, after all, recovered from plague and fire, and its new buildings that linear progress might be possible despite cyclical crises; and the same lesson could be learnt from the urban improvement programme being pursued in Amsterdam, equally despite plague and war, at the same time.[94] Parliament was no more able in the 1670s to reach a clear conclusion about whether or not to ban suburban building than it was about modifying the settlement laws; but there was less conviction now than there had once been that new building should be prevented, and a greater body of opinion that it was 'no nuisance but rather an advantage to the health of the inhabitants'.[95]

?1670, but it cannot be earlier than 1678, as pointed out in Letwin, *Origins of Scientific Economics*, 252); T[homas] F[irmin], *Some Proposals For the imploying of the Poor* (1678); Hale, *Discourse* (1683); Richard Dunning, *A Plain and Easie Method; Shewing How The Office of Overseer of the Poor may be managed* (1685). Child's treatise was incorporated into his *A New Discourse on Trade* (1693), ch. 2.

[91] Chamberlen, *Poore Mans Advocate*, 14; J. O. Appleby, *Economic Thought and Ideology in Seventeenth-Century England* (Princeton, NJ, 1978), ch. 6; E. S. Furniss, *The Position of the Laborer in a System of Nationalism: A Study in the Labor Theories of the Later English Mercantilists* (Boston, Mass., 1920), ch. 6. For interest in the rural poor at the end of the century, see M. Spufford, *Poverty Portrayed: Gregory King and Eccleshall in Staffordshire in the 1690s* (Staffs. Studies, 7, Keele, 1995).

[92] Hale, *Discourse*, 8; Child, *New Discourse*, 62–4; Dudley North, 'Some Notes Concerning the Laws for the Poor', in R. Grassby, *The English Gentleman in Trade: The Life and Works of Sir Dudley North 1641–1691* (Oxford, 1994), 320.

[93] Dunning (*Plain and Easie Method*, sig. A3ᵛ) and others drew the Norwich example from Edward Chamberlayne's *State of England* (e.g. 1671 edn., 150–1), but the citation goes back at least to 1600: J. Thirsk and J. P. Cooper (eds.), *Seventeenth-Century Economic Documents* (Oxford, 1972), 754.

[94] J. I. Israel, *The Dutch Republic: Its Rise, Greatness and Fall 1477–1806* (Oxford, 1995), 863–73; J. I. Israel, 'Innovation in Dutch Cities 1648–1720', *History Today*, 45(3) (Mar. 1995), 14–20.   [95] Edie, 'New Buildings', 47 and *passim*.

The same tune was being learnt elsewhere. After the great Northampton fire of 1675 John Conant not only preached, as Whateley and White had done before him, on the sins which brought such 'public and common calamities'; he also showed that God had turned calamities into blessings. Freed now from fears of 'some epidemical disease' from 'the straitness and inconvenience of poor houses and narrow rooms', Northampton had never been healthier. It was 'in a fair way . . . of being improved, and advanced to a greater degree of lustre and beauty'. Following a conflagration in Caistor in 1681, it was 'observed that every town is bettered exceedingly by being purified by fire'.[96]

This was the frame of mind which sustained Dr Borsay's 'urban renaissance', and its necessary services were also being supplied, whether by private enterprise or public action: fire insurance, fire engines, in vogue in the 1640s and now improved by Dutch hoses, waterworks equally improved by horsepower, beginning in the 1670s with the York Buildings Company for the West End and the Shadwell Waterworks for the East.[97] In the 1680s Sir John Lowther was laying out Whitehaven with the first planned provincial square, taking Hooke's advice on his church, planning a miniature mathematical school like that at Christ's Hospital, and later a workhouse, on which information was naturally sought from Dorchester.[98] Needless to say, Petty incorporated the whole package in his many paper schemes for 'the improvement of London': 'provision for surveyors and pavements and sewers . . for hospitals of several sorts . . . to prevent great plagues . . . a magazine of all commodities; to prevent fires . . . to be well served with waters and fuels'. In such a centre, concentration of trade, industry and

[96] John Conant, *Sermons Preach'd on Several Occasions* (2nd edn., 2 vols., 1699), i. 450, 463–4; Porter, *Great Fire of London*, 157. For the rebuilding of Northampton, and of Warwick after its fire in 1694, see P. Borsay, *The English Urban Renaissance: Culture and Society in the Provincial Town, 1660–1760* (Oxford, 1989), 18–19, 45–6; M. Farr (ed.), *The Great Fire of Warwick 1694* (Dugdale Society, 36, 1992), 33–4. The related Acts of Parliament are 27 Car. II, c. 1, and 6 & 7 Wm & Mary, OA 5.

[97] K. Thomas, *Religion and the Decline of Magic* (1971), 652; G. V. Blackstone, *A History of the British Fire Service* (1957), 26–8, 50–7; H. W. Dickinson, *Water Supply of Greater London* (Newcomen Society, 1954), 47–9. By 1660 at least 60 fire engines had been built in England: E. L. Jones and M. E. Falkus, 'Urban Improvement and the English Economy in the Seventeenth and Eighteenth Centuries', in P. Borsay (ed.), *The Eighteenth-Century Town: A Reader in English Urban History 1688–1820* (1990), 123. For Petty's interest in waterworks, see Hunter, *Establishing the New Science*, 90.

[98] S. Collier and S. Pearson, *Whitehaven 1660–1800* (1991), 10, 31, 33–5; J. V. Beckett, *Coal and Tobacco: The Lowthers and the Economic Development of West Cumberland 1660–1760* (Cambridge, 1981), ch. 7. Sir John Lowther had, as MP, heard parliamentary debates on London's rebuilding, as had another local projector, Sir Robert Paston: P. Gauci, *Politics and Society in Great Yarmouth* (Oxford, 1996), 118–19. William Penn's plans for Philadelphia belong in the same context, and Petty gave him advice on methods of vital registration: M. Girouard, *Cities and People: A Social and Architectural History* (New Haven, Conn., 1985), 247–9; J.H. Cassedy, *Demography in Early America: Beginnings of the Statistical Mind, 1600–1800* (Cambridge, Mass., 1969), 55–7.

consumer emulation would promote economic growth and all the 'arts of delight and ornament'.[99]

One important concomitant of improvement was hence a shift in public attitude towards London, from its representation as parasite to its recognition as stimulus. It had begun under the early Stuarts and had been heralded in Gabriel Plattes's *Macaria*, where it was said to be possible to show 'how great cities, which formerly devoured the fatness of the kingdom, may yearly make a considerable retribution'. On the eve of the Great Fire, William Boghurst could celebrate 'England's great city metropolitan' as 'the glory, life and strength . . . of all the kingdom', and welcome the growth of the West End, with its 'streets and houses uniform and neat'.[100]

The shift of attitude was still incomplete at the end of the century when Davenant noted that some thought London's growth 'pernicious', others 'advantageous', to the kingdom. But Davenant was unable to hide the force of the argument that there was no acre of England which the wealth and trade of London had not 'bettered'. Petty, of course, had no doubt. By the 1680s his numbers had shown him that London was 'the greatest emporium' in the world, bigger than 'Constantinople, Cairo, Agra, Deli, Nanquin'. It was certainly bigger than Paris, wealthier, growing faster, 'the people head for head more amply and commodiously lodged', 'probably the more healthful or with better physicians'.[101]

The modern historian notes that Constantinople was much larger, Paris probably a little larger than London at this point. As Defoe remarked, Petty's calculations 'have since proved absurd and even ridiculous'.[102] But it is persuasive testimony to the power of the ideology of improvement that such a view could be held of a metropolis where mortality was in fact getting worse, to the point where infant mortality rates might soon exceed those of Paris; and it is an equally instructive irony that there should be so unanimous an insistence on the urgent need to make the poor industrious at the very

[99] Bodl., MS Film 1953, Petty Papers, Box E, no. 45; Hull, *Economic Writings*, ii. 474; Lansdowne, *Petty Papers*, i. 33–6, 36–7, 40–2, 255.

[100] Webster, *Hartlib and the Advancement*, 88; William Boghurst, 'Londinologia sive Londini Encomium', BL, Sloane MS 904, fos. 55^r, 57^r.

[101] Thirsk and Cooper, *Seventeenth-Century Economic Documents*, 809–10; Bodl., MS Film 1953, Petty Papers, Box E, no. 37, p. 4; Hull, *Economic Writings*, ii. 505–13, 540. Even Petty thought that London's growth must have a limit, dictated by the capacity of the rural economy to support it, but that limit would not be reached before 1800: ibid. 465.

[102] Beier and Finlay, *London 1500–1700*, 2–3; Daniel Defoe, *A Plan of the English Commerce* (1728), quoted in D. S. Landes, 'What Room for Accident in History?', *Econ. Hist. Rev.*, 47 (1994), 654. By the 1680s Petty was calculating London's population at nearly 700,000, compared with Graunt's 460,000 for 1662: Hull, *Economic Writings*, ii. 331, 456, 464, 532. Others, however, thought it might be 1 m., or even 1.5 m.: Boghurst in Sloane MS 904, fo. 63; Maclean, 'London in 1689–90', 325–6. Gregory King's 530,000 was, of course, more accurate: Thirsk and Cooper, *Seventeenth-Century Economic Documents*, 776.

moment when, if Professor de Vries is right, an 'industrious revolution' was already under way.[103]

IV

Petty's death in 1687 effectively marks the end of the first, pioneering phase of improvement; and it is difficult to escape the conclusion that it had left Rice Bush's joined streams of 1649 dispersed once more into separate channels forty years later. The ideology of improvement for the public good had proved more successful than the absolute power of the early Stuarts in yoking together private and public enterprise in common purpose; but with its second, scandalously speculative phase just around the corner, it is clear that the achievement was neither stable nor permanent. Restoration England had notably failed to produce that 'propitious and wise authority' to which Hartlib and his successors looked for reconciliation, not only between public and private interests but between their goals of decisive public action and the free exchange of information.[104] Richard Haines had probably written first for Shaftesbury's new Council of Trade, itself influenced by Worsley,[105] and then for the Parliaments of the later 1670s; but there had been no new poor law, any more than there had been a general naturalization or any other of the major reforms advocated by political economists. When Matthew Hale's *Discourse Touching Provision for the Poor* was finally published in 1683, maintaining interest in Corporations of the Poor, it was perhaps as much with an eye to a new Parliament as Dudley North's writing of his 'thoughts' about the settlement laws for 'the welfare of the public';[106] but the Parliament of 1685 got no further.

Historical revisionists might argue that a second, packed Parliament of James II could have picked up the challenge, given the king's revival of Shaftesbury's economic programme, Quaker interest in workhouses, and even the Catholic acknowledgement of Hartlib's legacy to be found in a project from Elizabeth Cellier: for a Royal Foundling Hospital and a Corporation of Midwives to reduce the levels of infant and maternal mortality revealed by the London bills.[107] But such a second Jacobean reformation, if

---

[103] J. Landers, *Death and the Metropolis: Studies in the Demographic History of London 1670–1830* (Cambridge, 1993), 136–8, 192–4; J. de Vries, 'Between Purchasing Power and the World of Goods: Understanding the Household Economy in Early Modern Europe', in J. Brewer and R. Porter (eds.), *Consumption and the World of Goods* (1993), 107–21.

[104] HP, 53/36/1. It is indicative of post-Restoration hesitations that Graunt left open the question of whether the fruits of political arithmetic should be available to the many or reserved to 'the sovereign and his chief ministers': Hull, *Economic Writings*, ii. 397.

[105] On the Council of Trade, see P. H. Kelly (ed.), *Locke on Money* (2 vols., Oxford, 1991), 6–8, 11–12.

[106] Grassby, *Dudley North*, 231, n. 5, 313.

[107] Cooper, 'Economic Regulation and the Cloth Industry', pp. 94–5; J. R. Jones, 'James II's Whig Collaborators', *Historical Journal*, 3 (1960), 69; Elizabeth Cellier, *A Scheme for the Foundation of a Royal Hospital* (1687) in *Somers Tracts* (2nd edn., 13 vols., 1809–15), ix. 248–

achieved, would scarcely have satisfied Anglicans, responding to threats from Dissent and Popery with their own revival of 'practical divinity', catechizing and voluntary associations, and thus identifying yet another unresolved issue: how to restore moral and religious purpose to secular improvement, how to reconcile the pursuit of wealth and happiness with the pursuit of holiness.[108]

We must ask in the next chapter whether Parliaments after 1688 could do better than their predecessors and pull together these various strands. For the moment, however, we might take as symptomatic of their continuity and their pedigree the remodelling of the Clerkenwell workhouse, descendant of the first Corporation of the Poor, in 1686. In that year the Middlesex justices agreed to give over a large part of the workhouse to a 'General Nursery', 'College of Infants', or 'Infantory'. It was intended to attract private bene-factions for a public purpose, to join morality with improvement by driving 'wicked and debauched principles' out of pauper children along with ignor-ance and idleness—and all, of course, 'for the public good'. It is probably no more than coincidence that its moving spirit, Thomas Rowe, was a distant relative of Ambassador Roe, one of the first English patrons of Samuel Hartlib.[109]

53. On Cellier, see H. King, 'The Politick Midwife: Models of Midwifery in the Work of Elizabeth Cellier', in H. Marland (ed.), *The Art of Midwifery: Early Modern Midwives in Europe* (1993), 115–30.

[108] See e.g. J. Spurr, 'The Church, the Societies and the Moral Revolution of 1688', in J. Walsh, C. Haydon, and J. Taylor (eds.), *The Church of England c.1689–c.1833* (Cambridge, 1993), esp. 131–40.

[109] *An Account of the General Nursery or Colledg of Infants* (1686), 9, 12; *A Proposal for the Better Education of Infants* (1686); M. Strachan, *Sir Thomas Roe 1581–1644* (Salisbury, Wilts, 1989), genealogical table and p. 222. Rowe's great-grandfather was the uncle of Sir Thomas Roe, the ambassador.

5

THE PARLIAMENT'S REFORMATION

The Parliament's Reformation is the title of a tract which Samuel Hartlib addressed to the Long Parliament in 1646.[1] I have borrowed it for this chapter, however, in order to describe the quarter-century or so after 1688, when Parliament had to respond again to heightened political and religious expectations against a background of war and economic depression; when there were further projects for the reform of public welfare to be put to a new Board of Trade, descendant of the Councils of Worsley and Shaftesbury; and when powerful movements for a reformation of manners and a revival of piety seemed poised once more to yoke religious and secular improvement together in a single channel of endeavour. For a time, particularly in the 1690s, the prospects for a national reformation again seemed to its advocates very real.

Parliament was not, as we shall see, the only focus for reforming aspirations; neither did it give them consistent or unqualified leadership, any more than it had in the 1640s. Now sitting annually, however, it was necessarily the agent if aspirations were to be converted into practical reforms. A glance at the statute book shows some of the consequences, in the shape of an unprecedented volume of legislation on social and economic matters. Between 1689 and 1714 there were 22 statutes for the improvement of harbours and navigable rivers, 30 for the repair of highways, 7 for new urban waterworks.[2] London's streets and fire regulations were again the subject of legislation,[3] and there were Acts for paving and lighting in three other towns.[4] Projects for social and moral reform admittedly occupy rather fewer pages than the enterprises of improvers; but they are there. Courts of

---

[1] Printed in C. Webster (ed.), *Samuel Hartlib and the Advancement of Learning* (Cambridge, 1970), 111–19.

[2] The waterworks were in London (2 Wm & Mary, s. 2, private for York Buildings; 3 Wm & Mary, OA 37); Bristol (7 & 8 Wm III, OA 57); Newcastle (9 & 10 Wm III, OA 91); Deal (13 Wm III, OA 22); Liverpool (8 Anne, OA 46); and Boston (10 Anne, c. 44).

[3] 2 Wm & Mary, s. 2, c. 8; 8 & 9 Wm III, c. 37; 6 Anne, c. 58; 7 Anne, c. 17.

[4] Norwich (11 & 12 Wm III, OA 39; 10 Anne, c. 15), King's Lynn (13 Wm III, OA 15), and Bath (6 Anne, c. 42).

Conscience for small debts were established in four provincial cities;[5] there were two Acts against 'profane cursing' and blasphemy;[6] there was the Marriage Duty Act, with its fiscal penalties for celibacy, born in part, as Dr Brooks has shown, out of political arithmetic.[7] And moral and social reform was as important as civic improvement in shaping the fourteen statutes on whose origins and implications I shall largely concentrate: those which erected new Corporations of the Poor in fourteen provincial towns,[8] and which were accompanied by the revival of the Interregnum Corporation for the City of London.

The Corporations of the Poor constitute a cluster of instances of local reformation of the kind we have observed in previous chapters. Indeed, of the fourteen provincial towns which obtained them, at least nine could claim once to have been godly citadels undertaking similar exercises at some point in the past.[9] By the 1690s the municipal sponsors of new enterprises for the public welfare had changed their language, and often their religious and political sympathies, as intellectual horizons and civic identities shifted. But the bursts of reform which produced Corporations of the Poor between 1696 and 1712 are recognizably the same kind of historical animal as those which gave birth to the first Corporation of the Poor in the 1640s, and to similar projects in the century before that. Linear descendants of those earlier godly enterprises, the Corporations of the Poor tell us a good deal about the impact of improvement on the drive for civic reformation; and they also throw some light on the broader historical questions of why the quest for a national reformation occurred at all, and why it failed.

I

The interplay between continuity and change can be particularly well illustrated in three of the fourteen towns. We can begin with King's Lynn, not because its Corporation of the Poor was the first—the relevant statute did not come until 1701—but because its origins lie before the Revolution of 1688 rather than after it. The decisive and revealing figure in its genesis was

---

[5] Newcastle, Bristol, and Gloucester (1 Wm & Mary, s. 2, private) and Norwich (13 Wm III, OA 16).

[6] 6 & 7 Wm & Mary, c. 11; 9 & 10 Wm III, c. 35.

[7] 6 & 7 Wm & Mary, c. 6; C. Brooks, 'Projecting, Political Arithmetic and the Act of 1695', *Eng. Hist. Rev.*, 97 (1982), 31–53.

[8] Bristol 1696 (7 & 8 Wm III, OA 58); Crediton, Tiverton, Exeter, Hereford, Colchester, Hull, Shaftesbury 1698 (9 & 10 Wm III, OAs 29, 30, 55, 56, 59, 92, 93); King's Lynn 1701 (13 Wm III, OA 15); Sudbury 1702 (1 Anne, s. 1, OA 54); Gloucester 1702 (1 Anne, s. 2, OA 35); Worcester 1703 (2 & 3 Anne, c. 8); Plymouth 1707 (6 Anne, c. 46); Norwich 1712 (10 Anne, c. 15).

[9] The claim would perhaps be stronger for Colchester, Hull, Lynn, Gloucester, Plymouth, and Norwich than for Bristol and Exeter: see Ch. 2 above. For evidence of godly social welfare in early Stuart Sudbury, see P. Slack, *Poverty and Policy in Tudor and Stuart England* (1988), 150–1.

Henry Bell, alderman, merchant, and an architect, as Howard Colvin has demonstrated, of more than welfare projects.[10]

Bell may have first learnt about urban improvement in Northampton, where he was involved in rebuilding after the fire of 1675, and met Robert Hooke. In 1683 he designed what is now the customs house in Lynn, intended as an exchange 'for conference in trade and commerce', 'a building ornamental and of great use and convenience'. But his chief local interest was another echo of Hartlib, the Lynn workhouse in the old St James's chapel, to which he added a classical portico when it was rebuilt to house and train poor children in 1682. After the Revolution of 1688 he was twice mayor, active in schemes for improved navigation and a charity school, and still watching over his workhouse, now governed by a 'Master and Fraternity'.[11] A local Act of 1701 established a Corporation of the Poor to perpetuate that organization, and authorized a scheme for street lamps in order further to 'inlighten' King's Lynn.

Bell's career shows some of the ways in which the new pressures of party politics might alter the context in which local improvement could be pursued. Henry's father, Henry Bell senior, mayor in 1658-9, was much involved in Interregnum projects for the poor, closely allied, for example, to those who planned a copy of Dorchester's brewhouse; and he commissioned a 'topographical draft' of Lynn for the benefit of future mayors, which suggests some sympathy of interest between father and son.[12] Henry Bell junior, however, was educated at the firmly Anglican Caius College of Restoration Cambridge, and by the 1680s he was a Tory, designing the grandest hotel in town, the Duke's Head, for his patron John Turner, and excluded along with Turner when James II purged the corporation of his former supporters in 1688.[13] By 1701 Bell was involved in another political sea-change. Faced with the problems of a depressed urban economy, the now restored Tories looked for powerful allies in the county, and found a political winner. Robert Walpole won his parliamentary spurs by piloting the Act for the Lynn Corporation through the Commons; and in 1702 he took as his reward the parliamentary seat Bell had initially wanted for

[10] H. Colvin, *A Biographical Dictionary of British Architects 1600–1840* (3rd edn., New Haven, Conn., 1995), 118–19; H. M. Colvin and L. M. Wodehouse, 'Henry Bell of King's Lynn', *Architectural History*, 4 (1961), 41–62.

[11] King's Lynn Borough Archives, Hall Book 12, fos. 18v, 132; Norfolk RO, C/GP13/56, St James's hospital book 1682-1742, pp. 1–4; V. Parker, *The Making of Kings Lynn* (1971), 49–52, pl. 39.

[12] King's Lynn Borough Archives, Hall Book 11, fos 7, 34ᵛ, 40ᵛ, 294ʳ. So far as I can tell, Bell was not related to Robert Bell, the Lynn lawyer and hammer of vagrants in the 1570s parliaments (above, p. 38).

[13] Hall Book 12, fo. 65ʳ. On Restoration Caius, see C. Brooke, *A History of Gonville and Caius College* (Woodbridge, Suffolk, 1985), ch. 8.

himself.[14] The Lynn case shows us a declining town seeking salvation in municipal improvement and outside protection, and engaging in a painful retreat from puritanism through Toryism towards Court Whiggery.[15]

Gloucester, my second town, had succumbed to outside pressure much earlier—in 1672, when the gentry marched into the Common Council under a new charter. By the 1690s they were as interested in urban improvement as the surviving representatives of Dissent, and they were especially keen on new schemes for waterworks, from which they might profit as landowners.[16] One of the intruded councillors of 1672, John Powell, now justice of Queen's Bench, was chiefly responsible for the city's Corporation of the Poor, established in 1702. Its purpose was to join a workhouse to the charity school, founded in 1700, the whole being underwritten by a bequest from Timothy Nourse, a landowner at Newent. The trustees of Nourse's benefaction, in addition to Powell, included the bishop, county gentry, and a Presbyterian alderman: one homage at least to the city's past and to the social conscience of what was now a fractured Nonconformity.[17] But the informative figure in all this is Nourse himself, a maverick who tells us as much about the diffusion of Hartlib's legacy as Henry Bell.

Sometime fellow and bursar of University College, Oxford, Nourse had retired to Newent on his conversion to Catholicism in 1673. Thereafter he devoted himself to study and the management of his estates, as a college bursar well might. He also wrote a tract, posthumously published in 1700 as *Campania Foelix, or A Discourse of the Benefits and Improvements of Husbandry*, a work which reveals nothing of his Catholicism but a lot about his other interests. It had appendices attacking the burning of sea-coal in London, showing the lessons to be learnt from study of its bills of mortality, and praising model villages at the gates of parks, 'little towns' such as the Lowthers were erecting at Lowther New Town in Westmorland in the 1680s. The main body of the tract advocated, among other fashionable

[14] J. H. Plumb, *Sir Robert Walpole: The Making of a Statesman* (1956), 98–9, 103–4; B. D. Henning, *The History of Parliament: The House of Commons 1660–1690* (3 vols., 1983), iii. 613.

[15] Cf. the similarly complicated shifts in Great Yarmouth, with different political alignments but the same combination of local self-interest with grand improvement schemes: P. Gauci, *Politics and Society in Great Yarmouth* (Oxford, 1996), 206–16, 237–48.

[16] *VCH Gloucestershire*, iv. 113, 149; A. R. Warmington, '"Madd, bedlam Madd": An Incident in Gloucester's 17th Century Municipal History Reconsidered', *Transactions of the Bristol and Gloucestershire Archaeological Society*, 111 (1993), 171–2; Glos. RO, GBR, B3/7, fos. 57ᵛ, 86ᵛ, 141; B8/12/16-20.

[17] Henning, *House of Commons 1660–90*, iii. 268–9; Glos. RO, GBR, B3/8, pp. 51, 69, 75; P. Ripley, 'Poverty in Gloucester and Its Alleviation 1690–1740', *Transactions of the Bristol and Gloucestershire Archaeological Society*, 103 (1985), 194–5. James Forbes noted in 1712 that there had been 'a visible decay in the power of godliness' in Gloucester since 1687: 'a going into factions and parties and not the former success of ordinances &c': W. Lloyd, *Bicentenary, 1899: A Brief Account of the Foundation and History of the Protestant Dissenting Meeting-House in Barton Street, Gloucester, 1699* (Gloucester, 1899), 29–30.

improvements, uniformity of measures, pawnshops, and, of course, 'colleges' to employ the poor. These workhouses would draw together 'the scattered currents of charity' (which sounds like Rice Bush) and make useful subjects out of the riffraff who were 'the corrupt and excrementitious parts of the body politic' (which sounds like Benjamin Worsley). But Nourse thought such enterprises could no longer be entrusted to town councils full of Dissenters, 'chambers' of a 'sacrilegious disposition'. Though the Gloucester Corporation of 1702 did not achieve it, he would have preferred management to be in the safe hands of landed 'trustees' and gentry 'visitors'.[18]

In obtaining their statutory Corporations, both Lynn and Gloucester were jumping on a bandwagon which was already moving. It had been set in motion in the much larger and much more independent city of Bristol, my third town, where circumstances were very different. There the leading figure was the 'great projector', linen-draper, merchant, and Whig, John Cary.[19] His papers show his interest in works of political arithmetic; and his own *Essay on the State of England* of 1695 marks him firmly as an economic improver for 'the public good'. It also announced some of the motives which inspired the creation of the Bristol Corporation of the Poor in 1696: the need to set the poor profitably to work, and for a larger unit for welfare purposes than the parish. In 1700 further tracts by Cary celebrated the success of the Bristol workhouse and suggested, as Matthew Hale and Josiah Child had done before him, that incorporated unions might be adopted by country parishes as well as towns.[20]

Cary sent a copy of his 1695 *Essay* to John Locke, who replied that he would 'employ the first leisure I have to read it over with attention'; and unlike most of us in such circumstances, Locke did so. The correspondence connected Cary to the Board of Trade, which in 1696 was considering Locke's own scheme for working schools, and hence to Thomas Firmin and others shortly to be involved in reviving the London Corporation of the Poor.[21] Cary's allies in Bristol provided other links with the past: notably the

---

[18] *DNB sub* Nourse; Timothy Nourse, *Campania Foelix* (1700), 228, 234, 236–8, 294, 331–2, 349–50. On Lowther New Town, see N. Pevsner, *The Buildings of England: Cumberland and Westmorland* (Harmondsworth, Middx., 1967), 274.

[19] For Cary and the Corporation's history, see E. E. Butcher, *Bristol Corporation of the Poor 1696–1898* (Bristol, 1972); E. E. Butcher (ed.), *Bristol Corporation of the Poor: Selected Records 1696–1834* (Bristol Record Society, 3, 1932); J. Barry and K. Morgan (eds.), *Reformation and Revival in Eighteenth-Century Bristol* (Bristol Record Society, 45, 1994), 10. Cary is styled 'the great projector' in *Some Considerations Offer'd to the Citizens of Bristol Relating to the Corporation of the Poor* (1711), 12.

[20] BL, Add. MS 5540, fos. 22, 59–62; John Cary, *An Essay on the State of England in Relation to its Trade* (Bristol, 1695), 151–2, 156, 167; John Cary, *An Account of the Proceedings of the Corporation of Bristol . . . for the better Employing and Maintaining the Poor of that City* (1700); John Cary, *A Proposal Offered to the Committee of the Honourable House of Commons* [1700].

[21] BL, Add. MS 5540, fo. 68; S. Macfarlane, 'Social Policy and the Poor in the Later Seventeenth Century', in A. L. Beier and R. Finlay (eds.), *London 1500–1700: The Making of*

Quakers, who were busy organizing their own workhouse in Bristol at this time, who provided three of the first four treasurers of the Corporation of the Poor, and whose interest in workhouses has a pedigree going back through John Bellers to Thomas Laurence of Marlborough and so to Hartlib.[22] Support also came from the two Whig MPs in 1696, one of them Robert Yate, whose father had been involved in a workhouse scheme in the 1650s; and from Nathaniel Wade, Rye-House plotter and supporter of Monmouth, who had been brought onto the council with Cary in 1688, when James II's charter turned Bristol politics upside down.[23] One or two of Cary's supporters were undoubted Anglicans. The critics they castigated as opponents of 'anything that offers for the public good' seem only to have included High Tories at this stage.[24] But the broad alliance which gave a Corporation to Bristol—unlike those in the smaller towns of Lynn and Gloucester—was wholly civic and predominantly, though by no means exclusively, old Whig.

The political alignments evident in these three towns covered the whole of the political spectrum which had been alternately smashed and recast by the events of the 1680s; and the same variety was manifested among the other towns which acquired statutory Corporations. It must be confessed that something like the Bristol scenario is the most common. It comes as no surprise to find that Hull acquired a Corporation of the Poor in 1698 whose backers included several Presbyterians, an Independent, Daniel Hoare, whose father had been involved in poor relief reform in 1675, and possibly some of the Quakers.[25] There was a still greater bias in Colchester,

the Metropolis (1986), 261; H. R. Fox Bourne, *The Life of John Locke* (2 vols., 1876), ii. 377–90; M. G. Mason, 'John Locke's Proposals on Work-House Schools', *Durham Research Review*, 13 (1962), 8-16.

[22] M. M. Tomkins, 'The Two Workhouses of Bristol 1696–1735', MA thesis, Univ. of Nottingham, 1962, 21–2; R. Mortimer (ed.), *Minute Book of Men's Meeting of the Society of Friends 1686–1704* (Bristol Record Society, 30, 1977), pp. xxviii-xxx, xxxviii, 109.

[23] Bristol AO, Common Council Proceedings 1649-59, p. 99; P. McGrath (ed.), *Merchants and Merchandise in Seventeenth-Century Bristol* (Bristol Record Society, 19, 1955), 161–3; Barry and Morgan, *Reformation and Revival*, 8–9.

[24] BL, Add. MS 5540, fo. 100. The Anglican supporters included John Bachelor, Sir John Duddleston, and even Arthur Bedford and Edward Colston, and the High Tory opponents were led by Sir John Knight: Barry and Morgan, *Reformation and Revival*, 8, 11. In 1706, Matthew Tindal thought 'High Church' men were 'not fond of Corporations for employing the poor' in general, because their management fell to 'the sober and industrious, whom they despair to bring over to their interest': ibid. 53.

[25] J. Tickell, *The History of the Town and County of Kingston upon Hull* (1796), 776–7; Hull City RO, Incorporation of the Poor Minute Book 1698–1746, 1698 entries; Bench Book 7, pp. 424–5; Bench Book 8, pp. 441–5; *VCH East Riding*, i. (1969), 119–20, 164, 348; W. Whitaker, *One Line of the Puritan Tradition in Hull: Bowl Alley Lane Chapel* (1910), 87–9. Quakers are difficult to identify, but Robert Nettleton, mayor in 1697–8, apparently belonged to a Quaker family: *VCH East Riding*, i. 311. It should also be said that the incumbents of the two Hull churches were among the Corporation's supporters and benefactors: Tickell, *Hull*, 776–7.

where the supporters of the 1698 Corporation were either Quakers or representatives of old Dissent, and in Exeter, also a beneficiary in 1698, where the Corporation of the Poor was protected against a hostile Tory town council by Dissenters and two Whig MPs.[26] The chief power behind the revival of the London Corporation, also in 1698, was the Whig grandee Sir Robert Clayton, and the Corporation's Assistants, who included Bellers and Firmin's nephew, were almost to a man his allies: 'Dissenters and divers . . . Quakers', said a critic.[27]

There is no doubt, therefore, that in several towns Corporations of the Poor represented an opportunity, eagerly seized, for a revival in the municipal involvement of old Dissent. That was the overt purpose of the clause in the Bristol Act and in all those of 1698 exempting the Governors, Assistants, or Guardians[28] of Corporations of the Poor from the penalties of the Test Act. Yet the Test Act clause was not common to all the Acts establishing Corporations after 1698, when national and local political kaleidoscopes shifted, but Corporations of the Poor remained in fashion. It was included in the statutes for the strong Dissenting centres of Sudbury in 1702 and Plymouth in 1707, though the first Governor of the Plymouth Corporation was in fact a Tory, James Yonge.[29] But the clause was not part of the statute for Bell's King's Lynn in 1701 or Nourse's Gloucester in 1702. It was not thought necessary for Worcester's Corporation of 1703, which was backed by a Tory MP and by local 'country gentlemen'.[30] Neither was it sought by once godly Norwich, the last town granted a Corporation in 1712, which was by then still more firmly in Tory hands.[31]

Corporations of the Poor were not always potential Trojan horses for municipal Dissent, therefore, any more than their recipients were any longer

[26] Slack, *Poverty and Policy*, p. 197.

[27] Macfarlane, 'Social Policy and the Poor', 261–6; *Reasons Humbly Offered to this Honourable House, why a Bill Pretended to give further Powers to the Corporation for setting the Poor of the City of London . . . to Work, should not pass into a Law* [1700]. The London Quakers, like those in Bristol, were soon to have their own workhouse: it was in the part of the Clerkenwell premises once occupied by Thomas Rowe's nursery: T. V. Hitchcock (ed.), *Richard Hutton's Complaints Book* (London Record Society, 24, 1987), p. xiv; above, p. 101. Lady Clayton had a statue of Firmin in her garden: [Stephen Nye,] *The Life of Mr Thomas Firmin* (1698), 85.

[28] The term 'Guardian', which was to recur in the later history of English poor relief, had been used in 1596 in Sir Richard Martin's proposals for Bridewell: one of the governors was to be a resident Guardian: Huntington Library, Ellesmere MS 2522, fo. 13[r]. The governors of the London Corporation of the Poor of the 1640s had been Assistants, not Guardians.

[29] Slack, *Poverty and Policy*, 203, n. 43, 198. Cf. J. M. Triffitt, 'Believing and Belonging: Church Behaviour in Plymouth and Dartmouth 1710–30', in S. Wright (ed.), *Parish, Church and People: Local Studies in Lay Religion 1350–1750* (1988), 191–2.

[30] Worcs RO, Worcester Chamber Order Book 1669–1721, p. 26; *Commons Journal*, xiv. 244. The MP was Samuel Swift: R. Sedgwick, *The House of Commons 1715–1754* (2 vols.), ii. 459.

[31] Slack, *Poverty and Policy*, 197; N. Rogers, *Whigs and Cities: Popular Politics in the Age of Walpole and Pitt* (Oxford, 1989), 308–12.

unanimously Calvinist citadels. Their local contexts testify to diversity, not, it would seem, to any powerful grass-roots impetus springing from a common religious or political commitment. If we are to explain their proliferation, we must look elsewhere: to trends in opinion and new political opportunities at the centre, which seemed to offer the prospect of a genuine —if not in the end a very robust—reforming consensus.

II

As Cary's example shows, the Board of Trade was one stimulus. The Board's report to the king in 1697 on the need to employ and train the poor prompted tracts advertising workhouses as the ideal means to 'improve' the labouring population; and its great inquiry into the national cost of poor relief in 1696 stirred up local interest in mounting expenditure which seemed only to subsidize idleness.[32] The Board's conclusion that parish poor rates amounted to £400,000 a year was curiously little publicized, but that was perhaps because larger numbers were preferred to accurate ones; the estimates put forward in contemporary pamphlets, ranging up to the £1 million a year suggested by Cary himself, did more to underline the size of the burden which it was one purpose of Corporations of the Poor to reduce.[33]

Parliament itself could provide the same kind of encouragement, once local interests learnt from experience not only how to manipulate it but what kinds of initiative might get the fairest wind from back-bench opinion. By 1700 a major city like Norwich, promoting bills for a Court of Conscience, for cleaning and lighting its streets and for new waterworks, was well used to the parliamentary machinations necessary to get its own way. Different parties in Bristol and King's Lynn produced printed broadsheets for and against their Corporations of the Poor for distribution to MPs, a method of lobbying already familiar to Edward Odling petitioning Interregnum Parliaments on behalf of their London predecessor.[34] The council of Hereford employed its own parliamentary solicitor in 1695 in order to promote a bill for improving the navigation of the Wye and the Lugg, a

---

[32] Macfarlane, 'Social Policy and the Poor', 256, 261; Slack, *Poverty and Policy*, 170–1; M.D., *A Present Remedy for the Poor* (1700), 8. The 1697 report is in PRO, CO 389/14/127–38.

[33] J. C[ary], *Reasons For Passing the Bill for Relieving and Employing the Poor of this Kingdom* [c.1699]; M.D., *Present Remedy*, 7; S. Webb and B. Webb, *English Local Government. English Poor Law History*, i: *The Old Poor Law* (1927), 152. The £1 m. figure was still being cited in 1731: John Asgill, *An Essay upon Charity* (1731), 11. A 1680 tract had, however, guessed rightly at £400,000: [W. Petyt,] *Britannia Languens, or A Discourse of Trade* (1680), 132. Davenant estimated that the total had been £665,362 c.1685: J. Thirsk and J. P. Cooper (eds.), *Seventeenth-Century Economic Documents* (Oxford, 1972), 803.

[34] Norfolk RO, Norwich Assembly Book 7, 1683–1714, fos. 111–14, 120ᵛ, 122ᵛ; *The Case of the Poor within the City of Bristol* [c.1714]; *The Case of the Work-house and Hospital of the City of Bristol* [c.1718]; *Reasons humbly Offer'd against Lynn Poor-Bill* [c.1701]; *Reasons for Passing the Bill for Better Employing the Poor of Lynn* [c.1701]. For Odling, see above, p. 86; BL, 669.f.19(48).

project which was obviously of more immediate concern to it than the Corporation of the Poor proposed three years later.[35]

But a Corporation of the Poor was what Hereford got in 1698, perhaps at the suggestion of Paul Foley, the Speaker. In the same year the mayor of Hull was firmly advised by one of the town's MPs about the sort of work-house he must promise if he wanted a Corporation of the Poor: the old Charity Hall must engage in 'some manufacture'. Thus instructed, the mayor sought the help of Gloucester's Justice Powell when the Hull bill was held up longer than that for Hereford.[36] Add to this Parliament's suspension of the normal fees charged for private legislation in the case of poor relief bills, and we can see why Nottingham's council thought in 1701 that there was 'now . . . great encouragement given by . . . Parliament' to Corporations, and why Dorchester and Halifax tried unsuccessfully to obtain them as additional protection for already well-established workhouses.[37] Only parliamentary orchestration of this kind can explain why other small towns —Crediton, Tiverton, and Shaftesbury—ended up with Corporation Acts plainly designed for large cities with several parishes needing centralization. Their promoters were men with larger than local fish to fry, like Sir Matthew Andrews, Shaftesbury's MP and member of the committees on the Crediton and Tiverton bills, but also a governor of Christ's Hospital and friend of Foley.[38]

For many MPs, as Dr Hayton has demonstrated, the largest fish was moral reform. The campaign for a national reformation of manners had as many roots as the Corporations of the Poor which were one weapon in its armoury. The character of some of them will be familiar from previous chapters, as with the popular scare about divine punishments to come elicited by an earthquake in 1692, the 'trembling year', or William III's famous letter to Bishop Compton of 1689 urging 'a general reformation of manners of all our subjects', which adopted the stance common to monarchs

[35] Herefords. RO, HLC/A/1, pp. 24, 27, 51–2.

[36] Hull City RO, L1178, 1182, 1184.

[37] P. Langford, *Public Life and the Propertied Englishman 1689–1798* (Oxford, 1991), 164; W. H. Stevenson et al. (eds.), *Records of the Borough of Nottingham*, v. 404; *Commons Journal*, xiii. 793; J. Watson, *The History and Antiquities of the Parish of Halifax* (1775), 628–9. In Dorchester, despite the failure of the bill, the governors of the old hospital/workhouse of John White's day nevertheless styled themselves 'the Corporation of the Guardians of the Freeschool and Almshouse': Dorset RO, DC/DOB/16/6, 5 May 1707. Other places attempting, and failing, to gain Corporations were Ashford, Tower Hamlets, St Martin-in-the-Fields (Westminster), and Leicester: *Commons Journal*, xiii. 413, 415, xvi. 45; M. Bateson et al. (eds.), *Records of the Borough of Leicester*, v. 39, 53–4, 56.

[38] Henning, *House of Commons 1660–90*, i. 534–6; *Commons Journal*, xii. 102, 118. The group of West Country members involved with these bills also included Thomas Bere (Tiverton), Thomas Foley (Weobley), John Hoblyn (Bodmin), and Edward Seaward (Exeter), all interested in the pursuit of a national reformation: ibid. 102, 118, 268; D. Hayton, 'Moral Reform and Country Politics in the Late Seventeenth-Century House of Commons', *P&P*, 128 (1990), 90–1.

at the start of a reign.[39] The latter also inaugurated something more specific to the 1690s in the shape of the propaganda of 'courtly reformation', which Tony Claydon has shown to have been vital to the king's efforts to mould political consensus and 'ride the tiger' of party.[40]

The real novelty, and the underlying resilience of the campaign, however, lay in the Societies for the Reformation of Manners which pursued it, and they were modelled on what one of their publicists called 'religious societies of another kind'.[41] They owed their organization to the Anglican associations in London of the 1670s and 1680s, whose own origins—extending from English Puritanism to German pietism—are currently being investigated, but whose effect in reinvigorating the established Church is now indisputable.[42] A crucial figure in their genesis was Anthony Horneck, who in himself draws together strands discussed earlier in this book, having works of economic improvement and political arithmetic in his library, and preaching as happily as any early Stuart divine on the text of 'a city set upon a hill' from the pulpit of the old Savoy.[43] One aim of the Reformation Societies was to harness the Anglican revival he had helped to stimulate to an even broader Protestant enterprise; and one part of the enterprise was a set of Corporations of the Poor designed, as the preambles of the relevant statutes said, to repress 'idleness and debauchery'.

In Bristol, therefore, the Society for the Reformation of Manners, founded in 1700, cooperated closely with the Corporation. Through its leaders, John Duddleston and John Bachelor, it had a slightly more Anglican tinge to it; but it met weekly in the Corporation workhouse, and its members substantially overlapped with the Corporation Guardians: not only Duddleston and Bachelor, but Whigs like Yate and Wade and even the Quaker Charles

[39] Ibid. 48–91; Thomas Doolittle, *Earthquakes Explained and Practically Improved* (1693), 140; C. Rose, 'Providence, Protestant Union and Godly Reformation in the 1690s', *Trans. Roy. Hist. Soc.*, 6th ser., 3 (1993), 152-4; D. W. R. Bahlman, *The Moral Revolution of 1688* (New Haven, Conn., 1957), 15–16.

[40] T. Claydon, *William III and the Godly Revolution* (Cambridge, 1996), 3, 111, 115, 177, 191, 203, 235.

[41] *A Brief Account of the Nature, Rise and Progress of the Societies for Reformation of Manners* (Edinburgh, 1700), 39. For an account of the history of the Reformation Societies in London, see R. B. Shoemaker, 'Reforming the City: The Reformation of Manners Campaign in London, 1690–1738', in L. Davison, T. Hitchcock, T. Keim, and R. B. Shoemaker (eds.), *Stilling the Grumbling Hive: The Response to Social and Economic Problems in England 1689-1750* (Stroud, Glos., 1992); R. B. Shoemaker, *Prosecution and Punishment: Petty Crime and the Law in London and Rural Middlesex c. 1660-1725* (Cambridge, 1991), ch. 9.

[42] J. Spurr, 'The Church, the Societies and the Moral Revolution of 1688', and C. Rose 'The Origins and Ideals of the SPCK 1699–1716', both in J. Walsh, C. Haydon, and J. Taylor (eds.), *The Church of England c.1689–c.1833* (Cambridge, 1993), 127–42, 172–90; E. Duffy, 'Primitive Christianity Revived, Religion Renewed in Augustan England', in D. Baker (ed.), *Renaissance and Renewal in Christian History* (Studies in Church History, 14, Oxford, 1977), 291–8.

[43] *Bibliotheca Hornecciana* (1697); A. Horneck, *Several Sermons* (2 vols., 1698), i, sermon 15.

Harford were active in both.[44] The complexion of the Reformation Society in Hull seems to have been very similar; and if the one in Gloucester was rather more Anglican (though still eirenic) in tone—as it may have been since the lead seems to have come from Bishop Fowler, a close friend of Thomas Firmin—then that again ensured harmony between the movement for moral reform and the local Corporation of the Poor.[45]

In other actual or would-be Corporation towns, campaigns for a reformation of manners occurred without organized societies: in Dorchester in 1705, Norwich in 1707, and Plymouth in 1708, and in Hereford, where the Grand Jury, styling themselves 'the representatives as well of the inferior, better and capital citizens', presented the constables for not prosecuting 'vice and ill manners' from 1691 through to 1706.[46] All these activists would have backed the plea for Protestant union against the vices of 'a corrupted and profligate age' made to the Nottingham Reformation Society in 1701: 'surely doing good ought not to be made an enclosure. . . . Every good man has a right in religion and good manners.'[47]

As Dissenters and Quakers moved out of their enclosure and met Anglicans equally interested in a 'practical divinity' springing from primitive Christianity,[48] it is not surprising that there was some exchange of clothes and tactics. If the charity schools of the SPCK borrowed elementary instruction from earlier institutions, like Halifax's Bluecoat Hospital of 1645,[49] in Anne's reign the London Corporation of the Poor moved deliberately to meet them, advertising its own success in catechizing as well as in educating and employing poor children.[50] It seems the merest chance that there was no

[44] Barry and Morgan, *Reformation and Revival*, 3–62.

[45] Whitaker, *Puritan Tradition in Hull*, 87–90. The Gloucester Society is badly documented, but for some hints, see J. B. T. Homfray, 'George Bull, D.D., 1634–1710', *Transactions of the Bristol and Gloucestershire Archaeological Soc.*, 92 (1973), 134; *DNB sub* Edward Fowler; T. Isaacs, 'The Anglican Hierarchy and the Reformation of Manners 1688–1738', *Journal of Ecclesiastical History*, 33 (1982), 399; Bodl., Rawlinson MS D.129, fos. 7–8. One would very much like to know whether James Forbes, preacher in the cathedral in the Interregnum and thereafter pillar of Gloucester Dissent until 1712, was involved.

[46] Dorset RO, B2/8/2, Dorchester Offenders Book 1696–1716, 1704–5; Norfolk RO, Norwich Quarter Sessions Minute Book 1702–13, 18 Jan. 1706/7, articles to constables; West Devon RO, Plymouth Records, W330, Examinations and Informations,1708; HMC *Rye and Hereford*, 351–2; Herefords. RO, Hereford City Sessions 1704–6.

[47] John Ellis, *The Necessity of a National Reformation of Manners* (2nd edn., 1701), sig. A7ᵛ.

[48] See e.g. J. Spurr, *The Restoration Church of England 1646–1689* (New Haven, Conn., 1991), ch. 6; Horneck, *Several Sermons*, i. 14; Josiah Woodward, *An Account of the Rise and Progress of the Religious Societies* (2nd edn., 1698), 26, 143–4; John Bellers, 'Proposals for Raising a Colledge of Industry' (1695), in G. Clarke (ed.), *John Bellers: His Life, Times and Writings* (1987), 62.

[49] Watson, *Halifax*, 609–27. From 1680 efforts were made to teach children to read and write in Hull's Charity Hall: Hull City RO, Bench Book 7, p. 659, Bench Book 8, p. 264.

[50] *A Short State and Representation of the Proceedings of the President and Governors for the Poor of London* (1702); *London Workhouse, A True Report* [1704]. For arguments on the form of catechism to be used in the Bristol Corporation workhouse, see Barry and Morgan,

Corporation of the Poor in Chester, where there was a Society for the Reformation of Manners and where, in 1700, bishop and gentry set up one of the earliest provincial charity schools in the country: in the old St John's hospital, next to the house of correction, so that all kinds of 'vice and debauchery . . . especially among the poorer sort' could be combated together. That was the aim of the London Corporation, according to a broadsheet of 1702, and it was work tending 'to the reformation, happiness and welfare of succeeding generations'—a nicely Hartlibean trio of goals.[51]

Associated philanthropy, as it was later termed, was equally too useful a tool to neglect. Regular subscriptions had long been known as a charitable mechanism: according to John Howes, the mid-Tudor London hospitals issued printed tickets with blanks to be filled in for the purpose. But the tactic flourished after the success of the Corporation of the Sons of the Clergy of 1678. Henry Bell's new workhouse in King's Lynn in 1682 was supported by charitable 'subscribers';[52] and almost all the statutes for Corporations of the Poor sought to attract benefactors by stipulating that donors of £50 or £100 could be coopted as Guardians. Wealth and benevolence, irrespective of religious or party affiliation, were prima facie qualifications for the management of welfare. Preaching in Worcester cathedral in 1703, Thomas Cooke proclaimed that there was 'no one act the wisdom of man can invent' that would do more than a Corporation to bring about 'what the nation seems industriously at this time to aim at', 'a general reformation of manners'; and one of its chief virtues was the fact that it gave 'the charity of every private man . . . room to centre and unite for the public good'.[53]

For a moment, for a few years around 1700, the hopes of reformers such as Josiah Woodward that the Societies for the Reformation of Manners would 'discountenance strife and restore unity' in one grand endeavour looked more plausible than usual.[54] While the SPCK heard approving noises about the Corporation workhouses from its correspondents, Arthur Bedford, writing from Bristol, hoped their Quaker supporters might be brought back into the bosom of the Church. Bristol's eccentric High Tory, Sir John Knight, kept his distance from the Reformation Society as he had from the

Reformation and Revival, 45, n. 73; and for the catechizing of poor children in Hull: Hull City RO, Incorporation of the Poor Minute Book 1698–1746, 22 Aug. 1715.

[51] R. Hewitt-Jones, 'The Background, Origins and Development of the Blue Coat Schools of Chester and Liverpool 1700–1834: A Study in Educational Philanthropy', MA thesis Univ. of Liverpool 1974, i. 2–3, 11, 106; Bahlman, *Moral Revolution,* 38–9; *Short State and Representation.*
[52] R. H. Tawney and E. Power, *Tudor Economic Documents* (3 vols. 1924), iii. 419; E. H. Pearce, *The Sons of the Clergy* (2nd edn., 1928), 77; Norfolk RO, C/GP13/56, St James's hospital book, pp. 1–4. For subscriptions for a Kent almshouse in 1605, see W. K. Jordan, *Social Institutions in Kent 1480–1660* (Archaeologia Cantiana, 75, 1961), 50.
[53] Thomas Cooke, *Workhouses the best Charity: A Sermon* (1702), 4, 23.
[54] *Brief Account . . . of the Societies for Reformation of Manners,* 29.

Corporation of the Poor, but in 1690 as mayor he had inaugurated a campaign for moral reform which would have pleased his Dissenting father.[55] The quest for municipal improvement could easily be brought under the same umbrella, as it had been in the past. Petitioning in 1700 for a lighting and street-cleaning Act, Norwich councillors pointed to the 'lewd and disorderly persons' who took advantage of dark nights, as well as to 'great quantities of filth' in the streets; while Charles Brent, preaching before the Bristol Corporation of the Poor in 1704, noted how much the 'face of poverty' in the city had changed, so that it now looked 'neat and wholesome'.[56]

The potential scope of this appeal is perfectly illustrated by the 'Charitable Fund', which sought incorporation and advertised for subscribers 'for the public good' in 1704. It proposed to set up pawnshops, hospitals, workhouses, free schools, and a fund for poor prisoners in London; and it intended to employ paupers 'to sweep and clean the streets . . . make convenient walks, and repair the highways', which would 'very much contribute to the health of the inhabitants'. Its chief supporters were Josiah Woodward and members of the SPCK, but the sixty-one Anglican divines and fourteen Dissenting ministers listed among the subscribers ranged across a broad spectrum, from Isaac Watts through Benjamin Hoadly to Francis Atterbury.[57] The literature they proposed to reprint in their campaign was equally eclectic: Woodward on the Reformation Societies, of course, White Kennett on charity schools, and Brent on the Bristol Corporation; *Pietas Hallensis* on the great pietist orphanage, hospital, and school at Glaucha in Saxony;[58] but also Hale, Child, and Firmin on the poor, William Whateley of Banbury on Dives and Lazarus, and even the Book of Orders of Charles I. Here at least improvement and reformation, public cleanliness and varieties of godliness, private charity and the public good marched together.

[55] E. McClure (ed.), *The Minutes of the Society for Promoting Christian Knowledge 1698–1704* (1888), 272; Barry and Morgan, *Reformation and Revival*, 45–7; Hayton, 'Moral Reform and Country Politics', 64, 75. On the complex allegiances of the Knight family, see also J. Barry, 'The Politics of Religion in Restoration Bristol', in T. Harris, P. Seaward, and M. Goldie (eds.), *The Politics of Religion in Restoration England* (Oxford, 1990), 169–75.

[56] Norfolk RO, Norwich Assembly Book 7, fo. 114; Charles Brent, *Persuasions to a Publick Spirit: A Sermon* (1704), 22. Cf. J. Beattie in Davison et al., *Stilling the Grumbling Hive*, 53–4, for concern about violent crime in the 1690s.

[57] *Proposals for Establishing a Charitable Fund in the City of London . . .* (2nd edn., 1706), title-page, 17; *Advertisement From the Charitable Fund intended to be established in London . . .* [1708], 1, 3.

[58] August Francke's achievements in Halle were publicized by the SPCK in 3 volumes of *Pietas Hallensis* (1706–16). On the 'Protestant international' of which this was an example, see W. R. Ward, *The Protestant Evangelical Awakening* (Cambridge, 1992), ch. 8, and on Halle, R. L. Gawthrop, *Pietism and the Making of Eighteenth-Century Prussia* (Cambridge, 1993), chs 7, 8.

III

They did not march together for very long, of course. The Charitable Fund failed to get off the ground, and the more general prospect of philanthropic union which it reflected proved too fragile to be more than a pipedream. The immediate and obvious reason for that was the renewed polarization of denominational and party divisions in the latter part of Anne's reign, when High Tories, excluded from what had seemed an emerging consensus, followed Sacheverell and moved onto the attack.[59] Catching the same tide in Bristol in 1711, a pamphleteer rewrote the history of the local Corporation of the Poor. Although he admitted that it had originally been supported by 'some of the church party, nay even pinnacle-men', it was now plain that its driving force—and that of 'all such new corporations about the kingdom'— had been the 'factious designs', the 'itch of government and dominion', of 'Whigs and Dissenters'.[60] After 1714 the Whigs took revenge in their turn, particularly, as Dr Rose has shown, against charity schools and the Tory vestries which sustained them. Nothing could have been more factious than the extraordinary fracas in Chislehurst church in 1718, which led to collectors for London charity schools being prosecuted as vagrants soliciting money for seditious, i.e. Jacobite, purposes.[61]

The vulnerability of the reformation campaign to the squalls and squabbles of party points to much more fundamental weaknesses, however. Despite the many links of location and family connection between civic reformers and their Puritan predecessors, they did not command anything like the same authority. Henry Bell was not Henry Sherfield of Salisbury, any more than Thomas Cooke of Worcester could be another John White of Dorchester. Even if they had had the same single-minded purpose—and their wider cultural horizons prevented that[62]—they could not dominate towns now firmly dependent on gentry support. The mayor of Hereford, Bridstock Harford, third in a dynasty of once parliamentarian civic worthies, put together an alliance behind the city's statute for a Corporation of the Poor. His purpose was to prise a bequest for a workhouse out of the hands

[59] There were some local exceptions to this pattern, as in Yarmouth, where there was continuing accommodation between various religious and political interests: Gauci, *Politics and Society*, 237–43, 260–1.

[60] *Some Considerations Offer'd to the Citizens of Bristol Relating to the Corporation for the Poor* (n.p., 1711), 8; Barry and Morgan, *Reformation and Revival*, 11–12.

[61] C. Rose, '"Seminarys of Faction and Rebellion": Jacobites, Whigs and the London Charity Schools, 1716–1724', *Historical Journal*, 34 (1991), 831–55; *DNB sub* William Hendley.

[62] Bell's interest in the history of painting gave him a sense of cultural and historical relativism which would have been quite foreign to Sherfield: Henry Bell, *An Historical Essay on the Original of Painting* (1728), 10, 48, 120. He owned works by Rembrandt and Holbein: Colvin and Wodehouse, 'Henry Bell', 62. Cf. the interest in the history of music of Arthur Bedford of Bristol: J. Barry, 'Cultural Patronage and the Anglican Crisis in Bristol c.1689– 1775', in Walsh et al., *Church of England*, 196, 204–6.

of landed trustees, the chief of them Lord Chandos, resident in the deanery. But he depended heavily on Chandos's enemies in the county, and when their disputes were patched up in Anne's reign, the town effectively surrendered. Chandos retained the spoils and the Corporation never became a reality.[63]

Yet civic independence was no longer any guarantee of coherent civic reform either. Cary's Corporation in Bristol was deliberately designed to circumvent a municipal corporation which he had seen too often purged and mismanaged in the 1680s.[64] The forty-eight Guardians, who joined the mayor and aldermen on its governing body, were directly elected by special assemblies of ratepayers. But that semi-autonomy, copied in most later Corporations, made it a pressure group among others, and as obvious a symptom of division as the separate Quaker workhouse. In one way or another most of the statutory Corporations of the Poor were testimony to a lack of confidence in chartered civic authorities discredited and disoriented in the 1680s. The principal and predictable exception was Tory Norwich, where the Corporation of the Poor was firmly under the municipality's thumb, all its Guardians being chosen by the aldermen and Common Council.[65]

Religious denominations were no more easily held together than civic power groups, however convergent their expressed interest in 'practical holiness'. There was nothing new in the incompatibility between High Tories, keen to maintain a clerical monopoly of moral reform, and civic reformers looking for the same purpose to the civil magistrate. But there had now moved into the breach between them a number of voluntary associations trespassing on the territory of each of them, raising subscriptions for a host of philanthropic purposes, and treading on one another's toes, as the SPG did those of Robert Clayton's New England Company, originally founded in 1649.[66] The Reformation Societies might try to span the whole of

[63] Herefords. RO, HLC/A/1, pp. 51–2, 85, 110, 180, 192; A. Harford, 'The Harfords of Bosbury', *Archaeologia Cambrensis*, 6th ser., 9 (1909), 294–7; G. Davies, 'The Election at Hereford in 1702', *Huntington Library Quarterly*, 12 (1948–9), 322–7. Some of the political and personal background, including an elopement, is described in Henning, *House of Commons 1660–1690*, iii. 408–9.

[64] Cf. Barry and Morgan, *Reformation and Revival*, 10.

[65] The Norwich arrangements to safeguard municipal control were deliberate insertions in the bill by the Norwich Assembly: Norfolk RO, Norwich Assembly Book 7, fo. 200ᵛ. The other exception to open election of Guardians was in Crediton, where they were chosen by the vestry.

[66] Hayton, 'Moral Reform and Country Politics', 66–7; G. S. De Krey, *A Fractured Society: The Politics of London in the First Age of Party, 1688–1717* (Oxford, 1985), 83–4. In addition to Clayton, important figures in the New England Company who have been referred to above were William Steele, Recorder of London, its first President, and Sir John Maynard, grandfather of Maynard Colchester, pillar of the reformation of manners movement: above, pp. 86, n. 38, 85, 89. Another earlier association undermined by religious particularism in the 1680s was the Welsh Trust, founded in 1674 to promote religious education in Wales: N. E. Key, 'Comprehension and the Breakdown of Consensus in Restoration Herefordshire', in Harris et al., *Politics of Religion*, 203–4.

the gap, but they could not for long keep Dissenters in harness with zealous Anglicans. Neither could they restrain that distinctive Anglican piety which is reflected, for example, in the home-made crucifix attached to the final pages of the Bodleian copy of one of Woodward's reformation tracts.[67] Like Puritanism before it, the revived Anglicanism drew much of its vitality from the very fact of its being in contention, now fighting both Dissent and the values of a commercial society as vigorously as it had earlier fought Popery in the West End. There were simply too many contenders for the high moral ground for any comfortable joint occupation of it.

While Parliament was well placed to ventilate contentions of this kind, and in individual cases could reach some sort of accommodation between rival interest groups, it was ill-equipped to override them all in the interests of a consistent national policy. The Corporations of the Poor are excellent examples of parliamentary success in orchestrating some kinds of local effort. They suggest that the term 'reactive state', which has been coined to describe the formation of domestic policy after 1688, underestimates Parliament's creativity.[68] But it does not understate it by very much. Parliament notably failed in the one area where success seemed most likely, in the reform of the poor law itself. Despite general acknowledgement of its inadequacies, despite Commons debates on its reform on at least thirteen occasions between 1694 and 1704, the poor law of Elizabeth was not replaced by the poor law of Anne. The enormous bill sponsored by a stalwart of the SPCK, Humphrey Mackworth, seemed to have all that was necessary to do the trick. It consolidated existing statutes and strengthened their employment provisions. It paid modest tribute to the reforming ideas of the past half-century, permitting parishes to appoint salaried assistant overseers and to combine to employ the poor; and it incorporated churchwardens and the benefactors of charity schools, in order to encourage bequests for such good works. The bill passed all its stages in the Commons and then failed in the Lords in 1705.[69]

The failure of so complex a piece of legislation late in a session, when the peers were preoccupied with other issues,[70] is perhaps understandable. But now that there were regular sessions, that kind of accident ought not to have been the permanent death sentence it had often proved before 1689. More

---

[67] Woodward, *Account . . . of the Religious Societies*, 203 (Bodl., Vet. A3, fo. 987).

[68] Davison et al., *Stilling the Grumbling Hive*, introd.

[69] Macfarlane, 'Social Policy and the Poor', 252; M. Ransome, 'The Parliamentary Career of Sir Humphrey Mackworth', *University of Birmingham Historical Journal*, 1 (1948), 244–6; HMC *House of Lords*, vi. 273–87.

[70] Notably the Case of the Aylesbury Men. Joanna Innes suggests that the peers were also opposed to new local machinery for the supervision of charities which would encroach on Chancery's powers: 'The "Mixed Economy of Welfare" in Early Modern England: Assessments of the Options from Hale to Malthus (c.1683–1803)', in M. Daunton (ed.), *Charity, Self-Interest and Welfare in the English Past* (1996), 174, n. 45.

decisive in the failure of successive bills were Parliament's suspicion of major legislation—'too long, unintelligible and impracticable' said one critic of the poor-law bill; its worries about general Acts which might occasion who knew what local difficulty; and its preference for the local option, as with the Corporations.[71] There are obvious parallels with Parliament's painfully piecemeal steps towards commercial protection, in which some of the same individuals and interests were involved, and with earlier experiments with industrial regulation which led J. P. Cooper to conclude that the English state was 'both too strong and too weak' to pursue either *laissez-faire* or centralized regulation in its economic and social policies.[72]

There were, moreover, real issues at stake, broadcast in a free press and exploited by vested interests, which could amply justify failures of legislative nerve. Defoe's great diatribe against workhouses in *Giving Alms no Charity* (1704), which the Webbs thought helped to kill Mackworth's bill, returned to the point Graunt had toyed with in 1662 and which others had echoed since: that subsidized employment of the idle impoverished those already in work, 'enriching one poor man to starve another'.[73] Its force was virtually conceded in the provision in Worcester's Corporation Act that any cloth made in the workhouse should not be sold within the city in competition with other local products, and in the Gloucester council's insistence that the industries in its workhouse should not compete with those of freemen outside.[74]

Workhouses were also vulnerable to the accusation that they increased rather than reduced the charge of the poor, with their huge capital outlays and heavy running costs. There was no money to be made from the common workhouse occupations of beating hemp and picking oakum, that is to say, literally from old rope. Defending the Norwich Corporation in 1720, John Fransham analysed poor relief expenditure in the city over the past 100 years in order to show that recent increases were due to 'the stagnation of trade'.

---

[71] Richard Cocks in Bodl., MS Eng.hist.b.209, fo. 81ʳ (reversed); Langford, *Public Life and the Propertied Englishman*, 156–7. Cf. J. Innes, 'Parliament and the Shaping of Eighteenth-Century English Social Policy', *Trans. Roy. Hist. Soc.*, 5th ser., 40 (1990), 83; J. Hoppit, 'Patterns of Parliamentary Legislation, 1660–1800', *Historical Journal*, 39 (1996),109–31.

[72] J. O. Appleby, *Economic Thought and Ideology in Seventeenth-Century England* (Princeton, NJ, 1978), 248–50; P. O'Brien, T. Griffiths, and P. Hunt, 'Political Components of the Industrial Revolution: Parliament and the English Cotton Textile Industry, 1660–1774', *Econ. Hist. Rev.*, 44 (1991),402–5; J. P. Cooper, 'Economic Regulation and the Cloth Industry in Seventeenth-Century England', *Trans. Roy. Hist. Soc.*, 5th ser., 20 (1970), 98–9.

[73] Webb and Webb, *Old Poor Law*, 114; Daniel Defoe, *The Shortest Way with the Dissenters and Other Pamphlets* (Oxford, 1927), 173; above, p. 95. Cf. A. W. Secord (ed.), *Defoe's Review* (New York, 1938), i. 349–50, and for a similar view, Cocks, cited in Innes, 'Mixed Economy of Welfare', 174, n. 45.

[74] 2 & 3 Anne, c. 8; Ripley, 'Poverty in Gloucester', 197. For an attempt to answer the case made by Graunt, before Defoe wrote, see Cooke, *Workhouses the best Charity*, 23 (1702), and for efforts to answer Defoe: *Proposals For Establishing a Charitable Fund*, 23; [Laurence Braddon,] *The Regular-Government and Judicious-Employment of the Poor* (1721), 20.

But he also had to identify a second line of defence, to which advocates of workhouses increasingly retreated: the need to restore 'the former spirit of frugality' which had once kept the poor from claiming exorbitant doles. Like charity schools, expensive workhouses would produce a future pay-off by educating 'a virtuous and laborious generation'—in other words, by reforming manners.[75]

Yet the utility and legitimacy of attempts at moral and educational improvement were themselves the subject of dispute in a society where social as well as commercial relationships were becoming more complicated. The intrusions of the Reformation Societies—their use of lay informers, printed blank warrants and summary committals—ran counter to developing notions of privacy and liberty[76] and drew widespread opprobrium, with Defoe again in the van. He could see their historical roots: they were 'a natural consequence' of the Protestant Reformation. But that did not excuse their evident hypocrisy in a city where 'some cry religion up, some cry it down', and where corruption began at the top:

> Magistrates who should reform the town
> Punish the poor men's faults and hide their own.[77]

Defoe did not go as far as Bernard Mandeville in his savage scepticism about reform. He welcomed charity schools, for example, partly because they might be a vehicle for social mobility—one of the features which led Mandeville to join Cato in the great two-pronged attack against them in 1723.[78] But the various critics of reformation threw down intellectual challenges which did as much as the rage of party to undermine any public consensus there might have been behind it.

[75] J[ohn] F[ransham], *An Exact Account of the Charge for Supporting the Poor of the City of Norwich* (1720), 9, 11, 24–31; Cary, *Account of the Proceedings of the Corporation of Bristol*, 20.

[76] Shoemaker, *Prosecution and Punishment*, 252–72. Cf. M. Ingram, 'Reformation of Manners in Early Modern England', in P. Griffiths, A. Fox, and S. Hindle (eds.), *The Experience of Authority in Early Modern England* (1996), 51; P. Collinson, 'The Cohabitation of the Faithful with the Unfaithful', in O. P. Grell, J. I. Israel, and N. Tyacke (eds.), *From Persecution to Toleration: The Glorious Revolution and Religion in England* (Oxford, 1991), 74; and for the changing focus of reformation campaigns as attitudes changed, see F. N. Dabhoiwala, 'Prostitution and Police in London, c.1660–c.1760', D.Phil. thesis, Univ. of Oxford, 1995.

[77] [Daniel Defoe,] *The Poor Man's Plea To all the Proclamations, Declarations, Acts of Parliament etc. . . . for a Reformation of Manners* (2nd edn., 1698), 2; [Daniel Defoe,] *Reformation of Manners, A Satyr* (1702), 15, 19. Sir Richard Cocks responded with a call to those enforcing the law to be themselves 'very circumspect in our lives and conversation': *A Charge Given to the Grand-Jury of the County of Gloucester* (1723), 19.

[78] P. Earle, *The World of Defoe* (1976), 219; H. Monro, *The Ambivalence of Bernard Mandeville* (Oxford, 1975), 92–7; T. A. Horne, *The Social Thought of Bernard Mandeville: Virtue and Commerce in Early Eighteenth-Century England* (1975), 68. On Mandeville's much-debated thought, see also M. M. Goldsmith, *Private Vices, Public Benefits: Bernard Mandeville's Social and Political Thought* (Cambridge, 1985); E. G. Hundert, *The Enlightenment's Fable: Bernard Mandeville and the Discovery of Society* (Cambridge, 1994).

The acute anxiety, almost paranoia, which Mandeville in particular aroused among reformers seems to me persuasive evidence of their own lack of confidence in their case. Lethal though Mandeville's surgical knife was, honed by his peculiar combination of skills in behavioural physiology and the Augustinian analysis of the emotions, it would not have done such damage had it not struck patients conscious of their own frailty.[79] The 1723 edition of *The Fable of the Bees* articulated doubts which were already current in unfocussed form; and they were doubts which called into question two assumptions which had been almost axiomatic in much previous writing about improvement and social reform: first, that private interests and the public good must necessarily coincide, if each were properly perceived; and secondly, that the public good was a good, that is to say that it was consistent with some religious or ethical ideal.

Part of the damage was done once it became obvious that charity and good works were not only self-interested — that was part of the axiom — but might be misdirected, corrupted, by motives of personal pride or profit. Suspicion of the 'vain magnificence of buildings' evident at Bedlam, Chelsea, and Greenwich, which can be detected in some writers on workhouses and hospitals after 1700, suggests some appreciation of the point.[80] It could scarcely be missed once promoters of charities borrowed the methods of joint-stock companies and found themselves in the new world of stock-jobbery and speculation that came with war finance and the financial revolution.

The rise, fall, and amalgamation of fire insurance companies from the 1680s showed something of what was in store.[81] Charles Davenant tried to defend a scheme for a joint stock for poor relief, put to Parliament without result in 1698: the subscribers of the initial £300,000 were to receive only a 'moderate' return, with 'just and reasonable restraints upon it'. But moral ambivalence cried out for attention in the activities of the Charitable Corporation, initially projected in 1699, which opened pawnshops for the poor in 1719. Over the next decade it amassed a capital of almost £500,000, tried

---

[79] Hundert, *Enlightenment's Fable*, 23, 35–50. Its title was not the least provocative feature of *The Fable of the Bees*, given the common use of the beehive as a positive image of an industrious society (e.g. H[umphrey] M[ackworth], *England's Glory; or, The Great Improvement of Trade in General* (1694), 20–1) and its employment on the seal of the Bristol Corporation of the Poor (Barry and Morgan, *Reformation and Revival*, 51).

[80] *Proposals For Establishing a Charitable Fund*, 21; D. T. Andrew, *Philanthropy and Police: London Charity in the Eighteenth Century* (Princeton, NJ, 1989), 27 n., 33. Aske's Hospital at Hoxton, built by the Haberdashers in 1691–3 and designed (like Bethlem) by Robert Hooke, provided another recent example: I. W. Archer, *The History of the Haberdashers' Company* (Chichester, 1991), 104–9.

[81] P. G. M. Dickson, *The Sun Insurance Office 1710–1960* (1960), 6–14. Cf. W. R. Scott, *The Constitution and Finance of English, Scottish and Irish Joint-Stock Companies to 1720* (3 vols., Cambridge, 1912), i, chs. 15–17; C. MacLeod, *Inventing the Industrial Revolution: The English Patent System 1660–1800* (Cambridge, 1988), 151–2.

to ensure a certain dividend for its subscribers, and was discredited by speculation, mismanagement, and embezzlement.[82] That kind of questionable charity was as effective as the South Sea Bubble in exposing the raw nerve which Mandeville struck so accurately in 1723. From then onwards, all philanthropic projectors were aware, as one of them said, that 'in the most virtuous schemes we observe men act upon principles of corruption'.

> Corruption poisons with a general taint
> And even the applause of virtue is but faint,

lamented the Corporation's obituarist in 1732.[83]

Still more damaging to old certainties, however, was growing suspicion of a much more dangerous possibility: that corrupt private interests might in fact confer public advantages, even if they could not be defined as moral goods; that Mandeville was right to take previous arguments about the public utility of the profit motive to their logical conclusion and equate 'private vices' with 'public benefits'. Davenant had hinted as much: defending the proposed joint stock of 1698, he accepted that—in an age 'leaning towards corruption'—'the prospect of some honest gain' might be necessary to persuade 'people to do the public faithful service'. For Mandeville, however, corruption should be positively embraced for what it was. It must be welcomed by policy, not—as Worsley had argued—transformed and transmuted by it.[84]

This was more than a debating point once the competitive, consumer society which some improvers thought essential for economic growth began to materialize in reality. Humphrey Mackworth, urging greater 'industriousness' as the means to 'improve' *England's Glory* in 1694, had included among national blessings 'London: so great and glorious, that it invites all people to come over and stay here'.[85] Defoe and Mandeville appreciated, though Mackworth did not, that Petty's London, now that it had arrived, was scarcely consistent with Societies for the Reformation of Manners, prosecuting 3,000 people a year for offences which included trading on Sundays,[86] or with public subsidies to employment which perturbed the market and suppressed

---

[82] C. Whitworth (ed.), *The Political and Commercial Works of . . . Charles Davenant* (5 vols., 1771), ii. 206–15; *A Short History of the Charitable Corporation* (1732), 5–6, 10, 22, 25; John Innes, *The Charitable Corporation Vindicated* (1745), 1; Scott, *Joint-Stock Companies*, i. 364, iii. 380; S. Lambert (ed.), *House of Commons Sessional Papers of the Eighteenth Century* (145 vols., Wilmington, Dela., 1975–6), xiv: *Charitable Corporation 1732–1734*, 189; below, pp. 130,142.

[83] Charles Chambres, *A Sermon Preach'd at Dartford in Kent, At the Opening of the New Workhouse there* (1729), 12; *Short History of the Charitable Corporation*, title-page. Cf. Robert Nelson, *An Address to Persons of Quality and Estate* (1715), xxv–xxvi.

[84] Whitworth, *Works of Davenant*, ii. 214; above, pp. 24, 84.

[85] Mackworth, *England's Glory*, sig. A3. The report of the Board of Trade to William III had stressed the economic virtue of consumption in order to achieve full employment: PRO CO 389/14/137–8.

[86] Shoemaker, 'Reforming the City', 105.

initiative and ambition. Economic and moral improvement might be incompatible goals.

Dudley North had noted dismissively that 'countries which have sumptuary laws are generally poor'.[87] Mandeville extended almost indefinitely the list of morally improving obstacles to the pursuit of wealth. 'The road that leads to virtue' was paved not only by sumptuary laws, but by charity schools, almshouses, new churches, and press censorship. All these would have the splendid effect of returning artificers to the plough, turning merchants back into farmers, emptying 'sinful over-grown Jerusalem' of 'the covetous, the discontented, the restless and ambitious', and would finally produce 'an harmless, innocent and well-meaning people, that would never dispute the doctrine of passive obedience'.[88] That sneer was a nail in the coffin of much that previous chapters have surveyed, from the carefully balanced common weal to the ordered cities of the godly and the political economy regulated by absolute power.

IV

What Dr Hayton has called the 'moral panic of post-Revolution England' had therefore not held its victims together for very long, and it had been dissipated by more than the natural evaporation which afflicted similar episodes, local or national, in the past. Professor Burtt has argued with some force that the Anglican and Reformation societies had given a large part of their game away by underlining the secular benefits of their activities at least as much as the religious, promising that charity schools, for example, would make 'the meaner sort of people useful in their generation'. When the promised secular benefits were disputed, as either unlikely to materialize or undesirable, their advocates were left high and dry.[89] But that weakness put them in good historic company. What was new was the exposure of their Achilles' heel to public dissection and attack from a variety of directions, some of them novel; and that was their misfortune, scarcely their fault.

Some reformers reacted to the failure of national reformation as the godly

---

[87] [D. North,] *Discourses upon Trade* (1691), 15. For the accurate observation that 'all sumptuary laws are vanished by the mixture of gentry with the plebs in corporations', see Edward Waterhouse (1665), quoted in L. Manley, *Literature and Culture in Early Modern London* (Cambridge, 1995), 516.

[88] Monro, *Ambivalence of Mandeville*, 19.

[89] Hayton, 'Moral Reform and Country Politics', 89; S. Burtt, *Virtue Transformed: Political Argument in England, 1688–1740* (Cambridge, 1992), 44, 57, 63; Josiah Woodward, *The Great Charity of Instructing Poor Children: A Sermon . . .* (3rd edn., 1703), 17. The Societies claimed, of course, that 'the deluge of public wickedness is visibly abated', but without evidence: *Brief Account of the Societies for Reformation of Manners*, 14. The modern historian, noting from his statistics a decline in beer consumption in the 1690s and a slight drop in the bastardy rate in the 1700s, might attribute the first to economic depression and the second to the effects of military service abroad: B. R. Mitchell and P. Deane, *Abstract of British Historical Statistics* (Cambridge, 1971), 251; P. Laslett, K. Oosterveen, and R. Smith (eds.), *Bastardy and Its Comparative History* (1980), 14.

had earlier done, seeking refuge once more in enclosure, pursuing their ideal in cloisters and Utopian communities, as Edward Stephens and Sir Richard Bulkeley did.[90] Many more refused to throw in the towel and continued to try to hold piety and national progress in harness. William Hendley, veteran of the Chislehurst dispute, represented much contemporary opinion when he defended charity schools against Cato and Mandeville in 1725. He still insisted that they were 'useful', that they promoted 'felicity' and the 'trade that makes a nation opulent and flourishing'. But he thought it wise to assert, not entirely consistently, that 'the end and design of them are purely religious'. For Mandeville had already pointed out that 'religion is one thing and trade is another'.[91] Marriages between moralism and national improvement, which remained a feature of British public life well into the twentieth century, had henceforth to live with that probing and provocative scepticism.

In effect, commerce, war finance, and the free press which allowed debate about their consequences had given birth to those intellectual obstacles to any agreed notion of public or civic virtue which Professors Pocock[92] and Burtt have in somewhat different ways sought to elucidate. Civic humanism and the godly quest for moral reform might hang together harmoniously enough, as they did in the intellectual make-up of a Country Whig like Sir Richard Cocks.[93] They could be vociferous allies against 'corruption' and its advance with commerce and a mobile moneyed society. But both were undermined when money, commerce, and corruption bit back, not only through the political strength of the 'interests' which they supported but through their involvement in charitable projects and their delivery of secular improvements, social goods. There had been predictable failure in the political arena. After 1688, courtly reformation was bound to be powerless and hence artificial; and a Parliament of citizens had more immediate and divisive issues to worry about. But Mandeville's articulation of unresolved (and perhaps unresolvable) intellectual issues, which were to occupy political and moral philosophers for a generation,[94] had done as much as political

---

[90] Duffy, 'Primitive Christianity', 294, 298; T. V. Hitchcock, '"In True Imitation of Christ": The Tradition of Mystical Communitarianism in Early Eighteenth-Century England', in M. Gidley and K. Bowles (eds.), *Locating the Shakers* (Exeter, 1990), 20.

[91] W. Hendley, *A Defence of the Charity-Schools* (1725), 28–31, 58; Andrew, *Philanthropy and Police*, 35.

[92] J. G. A. Pocock, *The Machiavellian Moment: Florentine Political Thought and the Atlantic Republican Tradition* (Princeton, NJ, 1975), ch. 13.

[93] D. W. Hayton (ed.), *The Parliamentary Diary of Sir Richard Cocks 1698–1702* (Oxford, 1996), p. xv.

[94] See e.g. J. G. A. Pocock, *Virtue, Commerce and History* (Cambridge, 1985); J. Robertson, 'The Scottish Enlightenment and the Limits of the Civic Tradition', in I. Hont and M. Ignatieff (eds.), *Wealth and Virtue: The Shaping of Political Economy in the Scottish Enlightenment* (Cambridge, 1983), 137–78; M. M. Goldsmith, 'Regulating Anew the Moral and Political Sentiments of Mankind: Bernard Mandeville and the Scottish Enlightenment', *Journal of the History of Ideas*, 49 (1988), 587–606; J. P. Greene, 'The Concept of Virtue in Late Colonial British America', in R. K. Matthews (ed.), *Virtue, Corruption and Self-Interest:*

circumstances to destroy any possibility of an unquestioned public policy for wholesale social reform. It could have no reliable foundation once the pluralism of a complex society dethroned a single public virtue.[95]

The demise of a consensual public virtue did not, however, spell the end of civic consciousness—far from it. It simply scattered the various elements which might have been put together in a coherent programme, like seeds from a particularly fragile pod, far and wide. There were still evident gaps in welfare provision, and there was ample benevolence, energy, and wealth to be harnessed in a public still fully persuaded of the obligations of charity. Ignoring or suppressing any philosophical doubts, projectors and philanthropists competed to fill the vacuum.

At one end of the spectrum of opinion was the once reckless but now ageing Whig lawyer, Laurence Braddon, borrowing the clothes of the Charitable Corporation in 1720 in a new proposal to raise a £10 million fund by subscription: its purpose was to employ the nation's poor, many of them in newly planned 'Collegiate cities', to lend money on pawns and erect public granaries, all—since he drew on the techniques of political arithmetic —for 'the public good'.[96] From a very different stable came the posthumous *Address* of 1715 by the Non-Juror and pillar of the SPCK Robert Nelson, setting out a long agenda for 'Christian beneficence'. It included the whole Anglican shopping-list—charity schools, the SPG, 'books of practical divinity for youth', the reformation of manners; it embraced new items which were to be picked up later on, like hospitals for foundlings and prostitutes as well as those which Petty had wanted where 'improvements' could be 'made in the art of curing' for 'the good of the public'; and it applauded the Corporations of the Poor in Exeter, Plymouth, Tiverton, Bristol, Worcester, all of which were 'capable of further improvements'.[97]

Both these authors looked to some degree to Parliament to facilitate their projects, Braddon hoping for a statute in addition to a royal charter in order to encourage investors in his corporation, Nelson tacitly acknowledging past statutes for Corporations of the Poor. But Parliament had plainly failed, and disinterested patriotism proved inadequate, as Braddon acknowledged:

By the costly experience of near forty years past, Great Britain hath found that the generality of Whigs and Tories, High-Church and Low-Church moneyed-men, are not to be moved by the love of their country, or the public good.

Political Values in the Eighteenth Century (1994), 27–54; A. O. Hirschman, *The Passions and the Interests: Political Arguments for Capitalism before its Triumph* (Princeton, NJ, 1981).

    [95] Burtt, *Virtue Transformed*, 158.
    [96] [Laurence Braddon,] *A Corporation Humbly Propos'd For Relieving, Reforming, and Employing the Poor* (1720); Braddon, *Regular-Government*; [idem,] *Particular Answers to the most Material Objections made to the Proposal . . . (1722).
    [97] Nelson, *Address*, pp. xv, 100–87, 211.

The driving power of Braddon's scheme therefore came from 'the private gain to the subscribers'—'in this proposal, private gain shall advance the public good'—just as surely as Nelson's programme depended upon appeals to older notions of stewardship and duty, and on the charity of persons of quality 'giving what is your own and . . . giving without any prospect of advantage'.[98] A pluralist society produced not only a variety of recipes to advance the public welfare but a variety of agents to assemble and deliver the goods.

With his usual acumen, Defoe quickly took the point when he defended Hendley's charity school collection at Chislehurst. If vice was to be combated, virtue must be allowed its multiple heads. Not only was it folly to think that the state could provide for all: 'parish provisions for the poor' could never 'answer all the ends of necessary charity in a commonwealth'. More important, exclusive reliance on public provision for public welfare amounted to saying 'that men shall not be virtuous'.[99] The multiple agencies of virtue and welfare must be the theme of the next chapter.

[98] Braddon, *Regular-Government*, 22–3; Nelson, *Address*, 220–1.
[99] [Daniel Defoe,] *Charity Still a Christian Virtue* (1719), 14–15.

6

BODIES POLITIC

An examination of welfare activity in the final decades covered by this study—the quarter-century from 1714 to 1740—brings into sharper focus a topic which has been implicit, if not always at the forefront of attention, in previous chapters: the subject of agency. Thus far, most of my clusters of reforming activity have depended upon some authority willing and able to impose a reformation: godly magistrates, would-be absolute monarchs or their ministers, or a Parliament informed for a time by a moral consensus. Each of these proved wanting in one way or another. But they left behind them a multitude of what might be termed residuary bodies, survivors from the various efforts at reformation considered earlier in this book, all of them armed for action. Some were agents of local government, from county quarter sessions down to the vestries of the civil parish. Some were corporations, old or new, chartered or statutory, whether municipal or otherwise. Some were formally charitable trusts and others less formal voluntary associations.

Not all of them were strictly speaking 'bodies politic' incorporated in law. But they were all in a more general sense 'political bodies'. That was the term Josiah Woodward applied to the voluntary religious societies, which he thought 'not only requisite but even natural' in a world 'where considerable bodies of men of contrary inclinations join together to oppose them.'[1] These contending associations included many of the subsidiary bodies run by men of property which Dr Langford's Ford Lectures showed us shaping the competitive public world of Hanoverian England;[2] and they necessarily determined much of the quality and quantity of its welfare activity. When there was no single authority able to impose reformation in the name of a single public good, several lesser agents pursued improvement in a number of them.

---

[1] Josiah Woodward, *An Account of the Rise and Progress of the Religious Societies* (2nd edn., 1698), 24–5.
[2] P. Langford, *Public Life and the Propertied Englishman 1689-1798* (Oxford, 1991).

I

The importance of lesser agents can be illustrated from the fate of the Corporations of the Poor whose origins were examined in the previous chapter. The Corporations were themselves, of course, as much subsidiary bodies as their predecessors, the chartered boards of governors of the London hospitals and some of their provincial copies. Like them, they often found themselves at odds with other bodies: with municipal corporations, as in Exeter, where mayor and justices had to be forced by King's Bench to confirm the Corporation's poor rates;[3] and, more often still, with the parishes, whose powers they threatened more directly. The parishes generally won, and nowhere quite so spectacularly as in Bristol, where a contentious pair of statutes in 1714 and 1718 removed the Corporation's earlier control of parochial charities and made churchwardens *ex officio* Guardians of the Poor. From then on, the Bristol Corporation was the champion of parochialism against any further centralization, precisely the opposite of what John Cary had intended.[4]

In the later 1720s when interest in municipal Corporations of the Poor temporarily revived, similar conflicts were re-enacted, sometimes with additional players. Gloucester's Corporation was resuscitated in 1727 after being in abeyance for twenty years, having been judged 'impracticable'. But it was restored only after long debate and in the teeth of opposition from the trustees of the charity school—'gentlemen of undoubted character and reputation'—who feared that the Guardians would again be 'insignificant fellows' elected by ratepayers and the town council, a sentiment Timothy Nourse would have endorsed. In the event, a ratepayer franchise was reintroduced, but with a high property threshold.[5] In Worcester the controversy which broke out in 1729, which lasted for a generation and which spawned a Chancery case and two Acts of Parliament, was so complicated as to be almost unintelligible to the later observer. The Corporation workhouse had been closed down in 1711 and leased by the Guardians to a group of trustees. They in turn leased part of it to the Chamber of the city for use as a hop-market. The question of who should have the profits, and for what purpose, led to a five-cornered fight between Chamber, Guardians, work-

---

[3] Devon RO, Exeter Corporation of the Poor Court Book 1698–1702, fos. 27ʳ, 35–6, 40ᵛ.
[4] 13 Anne, c. 32; 4 Geo. I, OA 17; J. Barry, 'The Parish in Civic Life: Bristol and Its Churches, 1640–1750', in S. Wright (ed.), *Parish, Church and People: Local Studies in Lay Religion 1350–1750* (1988), 169. The issue of parochial authority was raised in discussion of Nottingham's proposed Corporation in 1701, and it hampered the Canterbury Corporation of the Poor erected in 1728: *Records of Nottingham*, v. 405; Canterbury Cathedral Library, CC/Q/GB/A/1, Guardians of the Poor Minute Book 1728–32, p. 151.
[5] Glos. RO, GBR, B3/9, fos. 142ᵛ–143; R. Sedgwick, *The House of Commons 1715–54* (2 vols., 1970), i. 246; 13 Geo. I, c. 19. Guardians were also to be elected to serve for 6 years rather than one, in order further to prevent the dangers of popular elections. These issues were fought out again in 1764: *VCH Gloucestershire*, iv. 147–8.

house trustees, parish vestries, and finally Nonconformist parishioners and ratepayers excluded from all these bodies. Much the most interesting noise in the battle came from the excluded parishioners. Castigated by the rest as 'Jacobites . . . Dissenters, beggars, populace', they turned on the church-wardens and overseers with an even more resonant accusation: under the provisions of the Poor Relief Act of 43 Elizabeth, these officers had excluded 'the other inhabitants of their parishes' and 'taken upon themselves an absolute power'.[6]

The charge tells us something about the executive authority of the civil parish, that now well-established creation of Tudor statutes which, from the Poor Law of 1536 onwards, appropriated and adapted ecclesiastical units for the purposes of the state.[7] Henry Sherfield's brewhouse bill of 1626 would have given the institution a final statutory seal of approval. One of his clauses incorporated every set of churchwardens and overseers in the coun-try; another declared that parish priests, officers, and 'the most substantial inhabitants' were 'bodies politic' in law.[8] Neither clause proved essential in practice. Ministers and churchwardens were already being construed as corporations for charitable purposes.[9] Select and close vestries were equally well established by the 1650s, sometimes given coherence in the early seven-teenth century by Puritan élites, as in parts of Essex, but resting on very much older foundations like the parish councils of the 'five' or the 'eight' in some Devon parishes or the 'sixteen men' or ' four-and-twenty' in parts of Westmorland.[10]

Parishes were hence well practised in resisting encroachments on their autonomy by the time they faced the Corporations of the 1690s and their

---

[6] Worcs. RO, Worcester Chamber Order Book 1722–42, pp. 97, 105, 111, 135; Shelf C.2, box 4, workhouse papers, especially *The Case of the Ministers, Churchwardens . . . within the city of Worcester* [1729]; Shelf B.3, box 4A, petition 'for re-election of guardians and overseers of the poor and to have more power' [n.d., ?1731], 1.

[7] B. Kümin, *The Shaping of a Community: The Rise and Reformation of the English Parish c.1400–1560* (Aldershot, Hants, 1996), 246–8, 263–4.

[8] Hants RO, J. L. Jervoise, Herriard Collection, M69/S6/xxi.4; above, p. 43. Sherfield was no doubt looking back to 39 Eliz. I, c. 5 (1598), which provided for the incorporation of houses of correction and hospitals as bodies 'corporate and politic'.

[9] G. Jones, *History of the Law of Charity 1532–1827* (Cambridge, 1969), 66–8; John Herne, *The Law of Charitable Uses* (2nd edn., 1663), 122; William Sheppard, *Of Corpor-ations, Fraternities and Guilds* (1659), 3.

[10] J R. Kent, 'The Centre and the Localities: State Formation and Parish Government in England c. 1640–1740', *Historical Journal*, 38 (1995), 392, 403–4; W. Hunt, *The Puritan Moment: The Coming of Revolution in an English County* (Cambridge, Mass., 1983), 82–3; Kümin, *Shaping of a Community*, 240; C. M. L. Bouch and G. P. Jones, *A Short Economic and Social History of the Lake Counties 1500–1830* (Manchester, 1961), 150–1; J. Campbell 'The Late Anglo-Saxon State: A Maximum View', *Proceedings of the British Academy*, 87 (1995), 50–1. More than half of London's parishes had select vestries by the 1630s: I. W. Archer, *The Pursuit of Stability: Social Relations in Elizabethan London* (Cambridge, 1991), 69.

successors.[11] Their entrenched oligarchies were also themselves open to attack, and not only in metropolitan London, where they had become Tory strongholds. In the 1720s pamphleteers complained that the 'corruption of parish officers has long been a matter of complaint': unrepresentative vestries had raised exorbitant rates for highways, sewers, watch and ward, scavengers and the poor, and used the cry of 'reformation' — now a 'poor stale pretence' — for 'the basest purposes'. Defoe, always an accurate barometer of shifts in opinion, famously christened all this *Parochial Tyranny*.[12]

As the Worcester and Gloucester cases indicate, however, it was a tyranny mitigated by the presence of other bodies, corporate or unincorporated. They included chartered bodies, like Hull's Trinity House which came into conflict with the Corporation of the Poor; groups of municipal feoffees and trustees in places like Bury St Edmunds, which had filled much of the vacuum left behind by the Dissolution; and the thousands of charitable trusts which had been created since then.[13] W. K. Jordan's figures suggest that testamentary bequests had created at least 10,000 charitable trusts in England by 1660. The Gilbert Survey of the 1780s shows that by 1740 the number had certainly doubled, and may well have grown more than three-fold. Some of the endowments — nearly a fifth of the number in 1660 — were vested in the bodies politic of parishes. Another fifth or more in 1660 were in the hands of municipal or other corporations, including the chartered livery companies of London.[14] But the rest were controlled by self-perpetuating groups of individuals; and some of them, to complicate matters further, were acting for unincorporated craft guilds and companies, whose

[11] See e.g. the disputes in Interregnum Salisbury described by John Ivie: P. Slack, *Poverty in Early-Stuart Salisbury* (Wilts. Record Society, 31, 1975), 109–34.

[12] [John Marryott,] *A Representation of Some Mismanagements By Parish-Officers in the Method at present followed for Maintaining the Poor* (1726), pp. iv, 7–9; A.B., *A Dialogue betwixt John Hu–tt and Edward An–on of Ch[else]a* (1723),12; 'Andrew Moreton' [Daniel Defoe,] *Parochial Tyranny: or, the House-Keeper's Complaint against the insupportable Exactions and partial Assessments of Select Vestries* [1727]. *A Representation* was essentially a puff for Matthew Marryott, on whom see below, pp. 133–5. John Marryott, its possible author, and a relation, was keeper of St Giles-in-the-Fields workhouse, itself criticized in *The Workhouse Cruelty, Workhouses turn'd Gaols, And Gaolers Executioners* [c.1730].

[13] J. Innes, 'The "Mixed Economy of Welfare" in Early Modern England: Assessments of the Options from Hale to Malthus (c.1683–1803)', in M. Daunton (ed.), *Charity, Self-Interest and Welfare in the English Past* (1996), 152; R. Tittler, *Architecture and Power: The Town Hall and the English Urban Community c.1500–1640* (Oxford, 1991), 87.

[14] These estimates, as fallible as the sources from which they derive, are based on reworkings of data in: W. K. Jordan, *Philanthropy in England 1480–1660* (1959), 29, 118–23; C. Wilson, 'The Other Face of Mercantilism', in D. C. Coleman (ed.), *Revisions in Mercantilism* (1969), 130; D. Owen, *English Philanthropy 1660–1960* (Cambridge, Mass., 1964), 73–4. Wilson's total of 60–70,000 trusts returned to the Gilbert survey seems to me, from inspection of the *Abstract (Parliamentary Papers* (1816), xvi), too large, but the returns are in any case partial, as Wilson makes clear. See also C. Wilson, 'Poverty and Philanthropy in Early Modern England', in T. Riis (ed.), *Aspects of Poverty in Early Modern Europe* (Florence, 1981), 253–79.

charitable activities were often expanding in the later seventeenth century as their narrowly economic functions withered away.[15]

In order to complete the picture, moreover, we must add in the new voluntary associations which multiplied in the century after 1660. Some were subscription charities, sometimes originating in meetings in London coffee-houses like Garraway's, where in the 1680s Firmin and his friends discussed designs 'relating to the public good'; sometimes they had roots in the regular 'county' meetings of provincial merchants in London, of which the earliest known example is a Devon society in the 1630s.[16] Others were Benefit Societies, the earliest perhaps founded in Bethnal Green in 1687; there were 49 of them, with 2,000 members, in Norwich alone by 1750.[17] A few were friendly societies developing out of craft associations: the Newcastle keelmen, for instance, who were able to fund from 1701 a 'very capacious, beautiful and useful hospital' for their old and disabled members. Defoe, who jumped to the defence of the keelmen in their struggles with the Newcastle hostmen, naturally welcomed such embodiments of self-help, wished to see their wide extension, to widows as well as seamen, to the funding of 'pension-offices' as well as hospitals, and thought them immune from every kind of corruption.[18]

As we saw in the last chapter, however, there was no great gulf fixed between these various kinds of associated activity and the murkier world of insurance, annuities and joint-stock speculation; and corporations and trusts, with the attractions of legal permanence and some protection at law against the dangers of unlimited liability, were very much involved in it.[19] The most

---

[15] See e.g. R. M. Berger, *The Most Necessary Luxuries: The Mercers' Company of Coventry 1550-1680* (University Park, Pa., 1993), 196 n., 209, and *passim*. For the popularity of trusts for various purposes in the 18th c., see F. W. Maitland, 'Trusts and Corporations', in H. A. L. Fisher (ed.), *The Collected Papers of F. W. Maitland* (Cambridge, 1911), 398-400.

[16] [Stephen Nye,] *The Life of Mr Thomas Firmin* (1698), 39; N. E. Key, 'The Political Culture and Political Rhetoric of County Feasts and Feast Sermons, 1654-1714', *Journal of British Studies*, 33 (1994), 230, 233-4; John Shawe, *Memoirs of the Life of John Shawe* (Hull, 1824), 12.

[17] G. Finlayson, *Citizen, State, and Social Welfare in Britain 1830-1990* (Oxford, 1994), 24; P. Clark, *Sociability and Urbanity: Clubs and Societies in the Eighteenth-Century City* (Dyos Memorial Lecture, Leicester, 1988). See also Prof. Clark's forthcoming book, *The Rise of British Clubs and Societies* (Oxford, 1999), and for 'box clubs' in London, W. Maitland, *The History of London* (1739), 682-3.

[18] J. Ellis, 'A Dynamic Society: Social Relations in Newcastle-upon-Tyne 1660-1760' in P. Clark (ed.), *The Transformation of English Provincial Towns* (1984), 200, 211; E. W. Dendy, *Extracts from the Records of the Company of Hostmen of Newcastle-upon-Tyne* (Surtees Society, 105, 1901), pp. lii, 172-7 (pamphlets probably by Defoe); Daniel Defoe, *An Essay upon Projects* (1697), pp. iv-v, 128, 132, 146-8.

[19] M. J. Daunton, *Progress and Poverty: An Economic and Social History of Britain 1700-1850* (Oxford, 1995), 239-40, points to the effect of a legal decision in 1673 that assets held on trust could not be claimed by a trustee's creditors. For examples of early projects for the poor indebted to the new speculative ethos, see Dixey Kent, *To the Honourable the House of Commons . . . Proposals humbly offered for a Provision for the Poor* [1694], and John Cole, *An humble proposal to . . . Parliament . . . for Employing and Maintaining the*

prominent example of the interconnections was the York Buildings Company, which Professor Larry Stewart has shown to have been at the centre of a web of financial and technological ventures ostensibly for the public good. Founded in 1675 and incorporated by statute in 1690, originally to provide water for the West End, by the 1720s the Company was connected via life annuity ventures to the Royal Exchange Assurance, and via lotteries to the Charitable Corporation. Contemporaries hailed the Company's 'dragon' — its great water-tower erected beside the Thames in 1721—as an icon of corruption; and we might well take it as the symbol of a burgeoning enterprise culture, the first of its kind, which linked improvement to welfare and blurred distinctions between private and public as effectively as any of its successors.[20]

One result was that some kinds of provision for social welfare and municipal improvement came to be undertaken either by private speculators or by subsidiary bodies. In today's jargon they were part privatized, part put out to new agencies. While voluntary societies and life insurance companies both proposed to build homes—almshouses in effect—for their elderly members, fire insurance companies were setting up fire brigades, and other London companies exploiting patents for new methods of lighting streets and laying on piped water supplies.[21] It should be stressed that there was no consistent public policy here. Statutes from the 1690s to the 1720s authorized particular municipalities or justices of the peace in general to raise rates for purposes such as cleaning, paving, and lighting: they seem, on the face of it, to be bringing under public management services which had once been the responsibility of private citizens.[22] At the same time, however, responsibilities were also being shifted in other and novel directions.

Some services—particularly piped water—were simply too expensive for

Poor [1700], which wanted all or part of the nation's poor rates to be managed by trustees or undertakers. The attempt to 'fuse private profit and social benefaction' in early insurance companies is discussed in G. Clark, 'Life Insurance in the Society and Culture of London, 1700–75', *Urban History*, 24 (1997), 23.

[20] A. J. G. Cummings and L. Stewart, 'The Case of the Eighteenth-Century Projector: Entrepreneurs, Engineers, and Legitimacy at the Hanoverian Court in Britain', in B. T. Moran (ed.), *Patronage and Institutions: Science, Technology, and Medicine at the European Court 1500–1750* (Woodbridge, Suffolk, 1991), 245–8; L. Stewart, *The Rise of Public Science: Rhetoric, Technology, and Natural Philosophy in Newtonian Britain, 1660-1750* (Cambridge, 1992), 337–59.

[21] P. G. M. Dickson, *The Sun Insurance Office 1710–1960* (1960), 12, 15, 21–3; W. R. Scott, *The Constitution and Finance of English, Scottish and Irish Joint-Stock Companies to 1720* (3 vols., Cambridge, 1912), iii. 11–17, 32–6, 52–60.

[22] E. L. Jones and M. E. Falkus, 'Urban Improvement and the English Economy in the Seventeenth and Eighteenth Centuries', in P. Borsay (ed.), *The Eighteenth-Century Town: A Reader in English Urban History 1688–1820* (1990), 134–6; M. Falkus, 'Lighting in the Dark Ages of English Economic History: Town Streets before the Industrial Revolution', in D. C. Coleman and A. H. John (eds.), *Trade, Government and Economy in Pre-Industrial England: Essays presented to F. J. Fisher* (1976), 257, 259–60.

public authorities to undertake alone, and had to be financed, as they were stimulated, by the private sector. But other services were thought too important to be left to hidebound municipal corporations, hostile, Thomas Short alleged, to a town's 'welfare' and to 'ingenuity and improvements'.[23] The historical researches of Robert Brady and Thomas Madox demonstrated what the *quo warranto* proceedings of the later seventeenth century had already proved in harsh reality: that municipal privileges — 'absurd rights', Brady thought — were an artificial creation of Crown or aristocratic favour, not the time-honoured defences of long-independent communities.[24] Now lacking confidence in themselves, 'untrusted because untrustworthy, untrustworthy because untrusted', in Maitland's phrase, few municipalities were engaging by 1740 in the kind of enterprises they had once undertaken, not only under godly magistrates, but in the later Middle Ages.[25]

It was not only poor relief which was taken away from them by new organizations. The Turnpike Trust for Bath got cleaning and lighting powers in 1707, and the Corporation of the Poor lit the streets of Gloucester after 1764. The Tiverton Guardians of the Poor, with their rating powers, were the obvious body to be obliged, in 1732, to provide a fire-engine.[26] The first provincial improvement commission, erected for Salisbury in 1737, was closely modelled on the Corporations of the Poor; and its 'Directors and Trustees', as they were instructively termed, brought together, as the town council could not, the most public-spirited citizens, from the urban cartographer William Naish to an assiduous Archdeacon who got himself elected by one of the vestries.[27]

These new, multipurpose, and to a degree representative bodies were in some respects the fulfilment of seventeenth-century aspirations, if we remember Hartlib's hopes for the first London Corporation of the Poor. But if we add to them the activities of voluntary associations, trusts, and corporations, we are reminded instead of an older world in which public welfare had been managed by a variety of agencies. In the fifteenth century,

[23] Thomas Short, *New Observations on City, Town and Country Bills of Mortality* (1750), 79.

[24] Robert Brady, *An Historical Treatise of Cities and Burghs or Boroughs* (2nd edn., 1704), p. i; Thomas Madox, *Firma Burgi* (1726).

[25] F. W. Maitland, *Township and Borough* (Cambridge, 1898), 95. For comparison with late medieval activity, see J. Campbell, 'Norwich', in M. D. Lobel (ed.), *Historic Towns*, ii (1975), 21–2, and for examples elsewhere: *VCH Gloucestershire*, iv. 262, 265; *VCH Wiltshire*, vi. 100; *VCH Warwickshire*, viii. 271; *Coventry Leet Book*, iii. 586–7.

[26] R. S. Neale, *Bath: A Social History 1680–1850* (1981), 177; 4 Geo. III, c. 60; Falkus, 'Lighting in the Dark Ages', 259. The Act erecting a Corporation of the Poor in Canterbury in 1728 included lighting powers, but they appear to have been exercised by the justices in session: I Geo. II, c. 20; Canterbury Cathedral Library, CC/J/Q/O/18, 22 Aug. 1728.

[27] 10 Geo. II, c. 6; Wilts. RO, Salisbury Corporation records, G.23/1/85, Minutes of the Directors of the Highways 1737–72. For a similar project in Colchester at the same time, see Langford, *Public Life and the Propertied Englishman*, 168–9; *Commons Journal*, xxxii. 738, 789.

public services had been provided by a dense network of subsidiary bodies and voluntary associations, not least, of course, by guilds and fraternities — 30,000 of them, Dr Rosser estimates — which might maintain almshouses, schools, or even water conduits.[28] Before we pursue the implications of that analogy, however, we should look at the re-emergence in early Hanoverian England of two other kinds of public service which have appeared in various forms in previous chapters, and which similarly cast comparative light back on the past: workhouses and hospitals. These were the targets to which the SPCK turned its energies when charity schools were discredited after 1715.

II

In 1722 Henry Newman, secretary of the SPCK, noted that 'twenty-four years of experience' had shown 'that a working school is in all respects preferable to one without labour, and more in keeping with the present trend of public opinion'. He was not only thinking of working charity schools, like the influential Grey Coat Hospital in St Margaret's, Westminster. He was reflecting also on the parish workhouses which he had visited in Essex, and which Dr Hitchcock has shown to have been part of a whole wave of new foundations in south-eastern England in the years around 1710, many of them inspired by an energetic entrepreneur 'for the public good', Matthew Marryott.[29] Further foundations were encouraged by Knatchbull's Act, otherwise known as the Workhouse Test Act, of 1723, which permitted parishes to hire or erect workhouses, contract for the employment of the poor there, and combine for these purposes. The SPCK gave its full backing to the Act, publicized the early results in its first *Account of Several Workhouses* published in 1725, and learnt from its correspondents that charity schools were falling out of favour and parish workhouses taking their place. Dr Hitchcock calculates that by the 1740s there were at least 600 workhouses in England, housing and employing almost 30,000 people.[30]

This might seem simply the culmination of a long-running saga, but the

---

[28] G. Rosser, 'Going to the Fraternity Feast: Commensality and Social Relations in Late Medieval England', *Journal of British Studies*, 33 (1994), 431, 444; *VCH Staffordshire*, xiv. 96.

[29] L. W. Cowie, *Henry Newman: An American in London 1708–43* (1956), 96; C. Rose, 'Evangelical Philanthropy and Anglican Revival: The Charity Schools of Augustan London, 1648–1740', *London Journal*, 16 (1991), 41; *Methods Used for Erecting Charity-Schools* (1717), 5; J. Simon, 'From Charity School to Workhouse in the 1720s: The SPCK and Mr. Marriott's Solution', *History of Education*, 17 (1988), 114, 120–1; T. Hitchcock, 'Paupers and Preachers: The SPCK and the Parochial Workhouse Movement', in L. Davison, T. Hitchcock, T. Keim, and R. B. Shoemaker (eds.), *Stilling the Grumbling Hive: The Response to Social and Economic Problems in England 1689–1750* (Stroud, Glos., 1992), 155–9; [? Marryott,] *Representation of Some Mismanagements*, 16. For a full account of Marryott, see T. Hitchcock, 'The English Workhouse: A Study in Institutional Poor Relief in Selected Counties 1696–1750', D.Phil. thesis, Univ. of Oxford, 1985, ch. 2.

[30] 9 Geo. I, c. 7; M. Clement (ed.), *Correspondence of the SPCK Relating to Wales 1699–1740* (Board of Celtic Studies, History and Law Series, 10, Cardiff, 1952), 131, 136, 209, 226; Hitchcock, 'Paupers and Preachers', 160.

movement was different in two significant respects from previous bursts of enthusiasm for 'houses of occupations' and 'Colleges of Industry'.[31] In the first place, the vast majority of the new workhouses were not grand civic institutions but literally parochial affairs, usually in small premises, often managed by private contractors, some of them, like Marryott, running more than one house at a time. In small towns and villages they were a response to rising costs, as the parish relief system became universal. But their popularity even in large cities shows that they were also testimony to the autonomy of the civil parish. There were new parish workhouses in Nottingham in 1725 and 1726, for example, Lancaster and Chester in 1730, Liverpool in 1732, Hereford in 1738.[32]

Secondly, the primary purpose of the new institutions was not the profitable employment or moral reform of their inmates, but deterrence for those outside. Expenditure on outdoor relief was to be cut, and might even be abolished altogether, by denying pensions to those who refused to enter the workhouse. It is not entirely clear where this mechanism—the workhouse test—first originated. For workhouse enthusiasts, it may have been the result of experience triumphing over hope, since the poor failed to flock willingly into the new institutions built by the Corporations to train and educate them. For sceptics like Richard Cocks, it was probably an obvious point of principle that workhouses should exist only 'to employ the impotent in some measure, and to terrify those of ability'.[33] Deterrence was certainly being widely attempted in the decade or so before the 1723 Act. A model workhouse at Strood in Kent was designed to ensure that 'a great many will take care to maintain themselves rather than come into the house'. The 'advantage' of the house erected in Romford in 1719 was similarly said to arise 'from the apprehensions the poor have of it' which 'prompt them to . . . do their utmost to keep themselves off the parish'.[34]

In practice it was rarely possible to maintain a rigid workhouse test for very long, least of all in the larger towns. In Hull, for example, outdoor relief

---

[31] For Bellers's interest in Colleges of Industry, see G. Clarke (ed.), *John Bellers: His Life, Times and Writings* (1987), 47 (1695).

[32] *Records of Nottingham*, vi. 101, 107, 108; R. Hewitt-Jones, 'The Background, Origins and Development of the Blue Coat Schools of Chester and Liverpool 1700–1834: A Study in Educational Philanthropy', MA thesis, Univ. of Liverpool, 1974, i. 41; S. Handley, 'Local Legislative Initiatives for Economic and Social Development in Lancashire 1689–1731', *Parliamentary History*, 9 (1990), 31; Herefords. RO, St Nicholas Parish, Hereford, AG 81/25, 11 Oct. 1738.

[33] Bodl., MS. Eng.Hist.b.209, fo. 81ᵛ (reversed). For similar notions, see *To the Honourable the House of Commons: A Proposal for the setting the Poor to Work* [1700].

[34] [Caleb Parfect,] *Proposals made in the year 1720 to the Parishioners of Stroud . . . for Building a Work-House there* (1729), 6; *An Account of Several Workhouses* (1725), 53; *VCH Essex*, vii. 77. Cf. *An Account of Several Workhouses* (2nd edn., 1732), p. vii; F. G. Emmison, *The Relief of the Poor at Eaton Socon 1706–1834* (Bedfordshire Historical Record Society, 14, 1933), 21–3; E. M. Hampson, *The Treatment of Poverty in Cambridgeshire* (Cambridge, 1934), 72–5.

was 'discontinued' in 1728, perhaps on Marryott's advice, but it was fully functioning again within a decade. Whether successful or not, however, this 'improved new method of relieving the poor', as it was described in Dartford in 1729, was indeed novel.[35] Abandoning seventeenth-century ambitions to build a positive reformation of the labouring poor on the back of an expensively embellished poor law, it resorted instead to negative incentives to self-sufficiency in the interests of economy. That perhaps explains why Knatchbull's bill succeeded, when Mackworth's had not. Its aim was not the 'great confinement' of large numbers of paupers; it was the exclusion of as many people as possible from the net of the poor law altogether.

The second new target of the SPCK—the voluntary hospital—was very different. The voluntary hospital, funded by subscription, looked outward, to embrace that broad segment of humanity which the parochial workhouse was rejecting, and to harness private benevolence while the public sector was, it was hoped, being cut down to size. Beginning in London with the Westminster Hospital of 1720, and in the provinces with the Winchester County Hospital of 1736, hospitals and infirmaries became the main focus of associated philanthropy in the mid-eighteenth century: there were five voluntary hospitals in London and nine in the provinces by 1750. Their appeal lay in a persistent and powerful ideal: 'charity universal', in the words of the motto of the Bristol Infirmary, founded in 1737.[36]

The universal charity of the SPCK undoubtedly inspired the founders of the Westminster, like the pious banker Henry Hoare, and Samuel Wesley the younger, usher at Westminster School; but they did not at first visualize its realization in an institution. They were members of a 'Charitable Society' set up in 1715 for 'the more easy and effectual relief of the sick and needy' by other means. Meeting weekly, their intention was to engage in the traditional works of mercy towards the 'poor wretch' who was 'a representative of Jesus Christ': to relieve poor strangers, visit prisoners, provide nurses for poor women in labour, and above all visit the sick and supply them with medicines and medical care. Their purpose was partly utilitarian: to make inroads into the surplus mortality recorded in the London bills, where

---

[35] Hull City RO, Incorporation of the Poor Minute Book 1698–1746, 3 Oct. 1726, 1 Apr. 1728, 1738 entries; G. Jackson, *Hull in the Eighteenth Century: A Study in Economic and Social History* (Oxford, 1972), 322; Charles Chambres, *A Sermon Preach'd at Dartford in Kent, At the Opening of the New Workhouse there* (1729), 3. In Canterbury also, outdoor relief was stopped in 1728 and then in operation again by the 1770s at the latest: Canterbury Cathedral Library, CC/Q/GB/A/1, pp. 17–19; CC/Q/GB/A/2. For other cases, see W. L. Blease, 'The Poor Law in Liverpool 1681–1834', *Transactions of the Lancashire and Cheshire Historical Society*, 61 (1909), 121; P. Anderson, 'The Leeds Workhouse under the Old Poor Law 1726–1834', *Thoresby Miscellany*, vii (Thoresby Society, 56, 1981), 88; Emmison, *Eaton Socon*, 27.

[36] J. Woodward, *To Do the Sick No Harm: A Study of the British Voluntary Hospital System to 1875* (1974), 147; M. E. Fissell, *Patients, Power, and the Poor in Eighteenth-Century Bristol* (Cambridge, 1991), 85.

18,000 or so deaths a year were supposedly attributable to a lack of medical attention. More fundamental, however, was a religious purpose: 'to take care of the souls of those who are sick and needy, as well as of their bodies', and ensure that they received 'the things which are necessary to their salvation'.[37]

Both these intentions plainly owed something to the German pietism of Protestant Halle. But they owed even more to philanthropic winds now blowing in from the Catholic south. The first publication of the Charitable Society drew heavily upon a French original, describing the Daughters and Sisters of Charity, 'servants of the sick poor', who were active in much of France from the 1680s.[38] The proposed 'sisters' of the Charitable Society, who were to visit the sick, were exactly like the Dames de la Miséricorde in Montpellier, and they were similar to the lay fraternities of Turin, publicized in an Italian tract by the Jesuit Andrea Guevarre, who had been active in founding such associations in southern France. Guevarre's work was also translated, by the SPCK, in 1726.[39]

Between 1715 and 1719, however, the Charitable Society had turned away from the provision of community care by its members and proposed to found instead an 'infirmary' for the 'sick and needy' of Westminster. Brothers and sisters willing to visit the sick were no doubt thinner on the ground in London than in Montpellier or Turin; and hospitals were anyway coming back into fashion. The London Huguenots—a French connection

[37] J. G. Humble and P. Hansell, *Westminster Hospital 1716–1966* (1966), 5, 9–12; C. Rose, 'The Origins and Ideals of the SPCK 1699–1716', in J. Walsh, C. Haydon, and J. Taylor (eds.), *The Church of England c.1689–c.1833* (Cambridge, 1993), 185; *The Charitable Society: Or, A Proposal For the More Easy and Effectual Relief of the Sick and Needy* (1715), sigs. A2ᵛ, A3ᵛ, p. 26; *A Charitable Proposal For Relieving the Sick and Needy, And other Distressed Persons* (1719), 5, 6–8. The latter was first published in 1716, and may have been by the Revd Patrick Cockburn: L. W. Hanson, *Contemporary Printed Sources for British and Irish Economic History 1701–1750* (Cambridge, 1963), 237, no. 2263. On the origins of the Westminster Hospital, see also A. Wilson, 'The Politics of Medical Improvement in Early Hanoverian London', in A. Cunningham and R. French (eds.), *The Medical Enlightenment of the Eighteenth Century* (Cambridge, 1990), 10–24.

[38] *The Charitable Society*, 22–3, refers to a French author and the Bodleian copy (Bodl. 24768 e. 13) has an MS note on the dorse of the title-page (of post-1736 date to judge by its content) describing a 'French sermon' as the original text; see also Hanson, *Printed Sources*, 229, no. 2194. I have been unable to identify the French original. Might it have been by Pierre Vigne? See D. Hickey, 'Preaching and Teaching: Pierre Vigne and the Sisters of the Holy Sacrament; The Grass Roots of the Catholic Reformation', *Proceedings of the Western Society for French History*, 19 (1992), 29–38.

[39] C. Jones, *Charity and Bienfaisance: The Treatment of the Poor in the Montpellier Region 1700–1815* (Cambridge, 1982), 49–50, 54; C. Jones, *The Charitable Imperative: Hospitals and Nursing in Ancien Regime and Revolutionary France* (1989), pp. 89–90, 105, and *passim*; [Andrea Guevarre,] *Ways and Means For Suppressing Beggary And Relieving the Poor By Erecting General Hospitals and Charitable Corporations* (1726), pt. iii; Hitchcock, 'Paupers and Preachers', 166, n. 54. On Guevarre's activities, see also J. P. Gutton, *La Société et les pauvres: l'exemple de la généralité de Lyon 1534–1789* (Paris, 1970), 395–6; C. C. Fairchilds, *Poverty and Charity in Aix-en-Provence 1640–1789* (Baltimore, 1976), 95, 168–9, n. 86; S. Cavallo, *Charity and Power in Early Modern Italy: Benefactors and Their Motives in Turin, 1541–1789* (Cambridge, 1995), 183–4, 194.

closer to home—founded one of their own, La Providence, chartered in 1718 and built close to the old pesthouse in St Giles Cripplegate. John Bellers, the Quaker philanthropist, turned at much the same time from promoting workhouses to advocating the 'improvement of physic' by means of hospitals for incurables, infirmaries for 'every capital distemper', and teaching hospitals, particularly in the university towns.[40] Thomas Guy, benefactor of a largely rebuilt St Thomas's, was planning another grand hospital by 1721, in order to surpass 'the endowment of kings', i.e. Chelsea and Greenwich. The Westminster Hospital was part of a general resurgence of public interest in the medical contribution to metropolitan welfare, of which Hartlib and Petty would have thoroughly approved.[41]

Bellers's reference to the universities tempts one to add to the list John Addenbrooke, who died in 1719, and John Radcliffe, who died in 1714, the richest physician in London, but victim, it was said, 'to the ingratitude of a thankless world, and the fury of the gout'. While Addenbrooke's will provided for 'a small physical hospital for poor people' in Cambridge, however, Radcliffe's made no reference to a hospital in Oxford at all. His Infirmary must be attributed to a later vice-chancellor and some responsive Radcliffe trustees. The first patients were not admitted to the Radcliffe until 1770, or indeed to Addenbrooke's until 1766.[42] There was also a conspicuous gap of nearly twenty years between the Westminster Hospital of 1720 and its first provincial copies, thanks partly to a decline in subscription and joint-stock activity after the South Sea Bubble, partly perhaps to that suspicion of benefactions like Guy's—'so many monuments of ill-gotten riches, attended with late repentance'—which lay behind the Mortmain Act of 1736.[43] The Corporations of the Poor in Lynn and Norwich added small infirmaries to their workhouses in 1725 and 1726, and the opening of the Edinburgh

[40] A. G. Browning, 'On the Origin and Early History of the French Protestant Hospital (La Providence)', *Proceedings of the Huguenot Society of London,* 6 (1898-1901), 43–53; C. F. A. Marmoy, 'The "Pest House" 1681–1717: Predecessor of the French Hospital', ibid. 25 (1992), 385–99; Clarke, *Bellers,* 177–203. Bellers's list was substantially replicated in Robert Nelson's 1715 account of Anglican charitable endeavours: *An Address to Persons of Quality and Estate* (1715), 210–12.

[41] Woodward, *To Do the Sick No Harm,* 14–15. Cf. also the activities of the two branches of the London dispensary for the poor founded in 1696: A. Rosenberg, 'The London Dispensary for the Sick Poor', *Journal of the History of Medicine,* 14 (1959), 41–56.

[42] A. Rook, M. Carlton, and W. Graham Cannon, *The History of Addenbrooke's Hospital Cambridge* (Cambridge, 1991), 1–2; H. D. Rolleston, *The Cambridge Medical School* (Cambridge, 1932), 161–2; [W. Pittis,] *Dr Radcliffe's Life and Letters* (4th edn., Dublin, 1724), 111, 122–8; C. R. Hone, *The Life of Dr. John Radcliffe* (1951), 123–4; I. Guest, *Dr John Radcliffe and His Trust* (1991), 209. Joanna Innes reminds me that Radcliffe's father was keeper of the house of correction at Wakefield during the Interregnum.

[43] D. T. Andrew, *Philanthropy and Police: London Charity in the Eighteenth Century* (Princeton, NJ, 1989), 46–7, 27, n. 42; D. Solkin, 'Samaritan or Scrooge? The Contested Image of Thomas Guy in Eighteenth-Century England', *Art Bulletin,* 78 (1996), 467–84. For Mandeville's comparable criticism of Radcliffe, see *The Fable of the Bees,* ed. F. B. Kaye (2 vols., Oxford, 1924), i. 262–4; and on the Mortmain Act, see further below, p. 143.

hospital in 1729 must have stimulated interest south of the border.[44] But the first new county hospitals came only in the later 1730s and 1740s and by then, as Donna Andrew has shown, there were new inputs from anxieties about the nation's health and manpower in time of war to prompt subscriptions.[45] Nevertheless, the seeds of that later evolution of the hospital had been sown earlier, in the years around 1720, by an SPCK looking for new outlets for benevolence, and by charitable physicians finding a social role commensurate with their new wealth and professional status: John Colbatch, for instance, who perhaps first proposed the Westminster infirmary, or Richard Mead, heir to Radcliffe's practice, who was instrumental in the erection of Guy's.[46]

Quite as striking as the novel elements in the eighteenth-century hospital, however, are echoes of older themes in English social welfare. It is not just that the last time when physicians in any number contributed to the formation of social policy had been in the early sixteenth century. The Charitable Society's wish to minister to the poor representatives of Christ takes us back to Bishop Ridley in 1552. Guy's Hospital, intended initially for incurables, had exactly the same purpose as its neighbour, St Thomas's, when that was refounded in the 1540s.[47] More striking still was the Foundling Hospital, not erected until 1739 but first planned by Thomas Coram in 1722 as a joint-stock venture, and supported by Richard Mead and Thomas Bray of the SPCK. That was a straight replacement for the original Christ's Hospital, whose doors had been firmly closed to foundlings by parish-settlement regulations after 1662.[48] In searching for charitable objects not covered by legislation, as Alured Clarke, founder of the Winchester and Exeter hospitals, did, or for targets 'which the charity of others had not reached', as did Thomas Guy, the promoters of eighteenth-century hospitals were rediscovering the past.[49]

[44] King's Lynn Borough Archives, Hall Book 12, 1684–1731, fo. 471ᵛ; Norfolk RO, Norwich Assembly Book 8, 1714–31, p. 240; G. B. Risse, *Hospital Life in Enlightenment Scotland* (Cambridge, 1986), 20, 25–9. Glasgow's hospital opened in 1733: *A Short History of the Town's Hospital in Glasgow* (3rd edn., Edinburgh, 1738), 6. For the charitable activities of the SPCK in Edinburgh, see Andrew Gairdner, *An Historical Account of the Old People's Hospital commonly called the Trinity Hospital in Edinburgh* (Edinburgh, 1734), 3–4.

[45] Andrew, *Philanthropy and Police*, 54–7. Cf. the parallel development of naval hospitals: J. G. Coad, *The Royal Dockyards 1690–1850: Architecture and Engineering Works of the Sailing Navy* (1989), 194–8.

[46] Humble and Hansell, *Westminster Hospital*, 9; H. C. Cameron, *Mr. Guy's Hospital 1726–1948* (1954), 12, 49; G. Holmes, *Augustan England: Professions, State and Society, 1680–1730* (1982), 206–35.

[47] Above, p. 20; Cameron, *Guy's Hospital*, p. 41.

[48] R. K. McClure, *Coram's Children: The London Foundling Hospital in the Eighteenth Century* (New Haven, Conn., 1981), 8–9, 19, 21–2.

[49] Woodward, *To Do the Sick No Harm*, 12–13, 15. Innes, 'Mixed Economy of Welfare', 145, 172, points out that infirmaries (like schools) were favourite objects of voluntary charity because they could not be funded from poor rates, and perhaps remained outside the law because charity funded them in other ways.

Like the Charitable Society, the Foundling Hospital also suggests that they were led to that discovery through the French connection. Its promoters circulated an account of the Foundling Hospital of Paris to drum up support, and proposed to imitate 'the Dames and Sisters of Charity' there in a London 'confraternity' of gentlewomen who would raise funds for the scheme.[50] This was another lay fraternity which never quite got off the ground; but along with references to the mechanism of fraternities came some of the attitudes now necessarily associated with them: echoes in fact of the Counter-Reformation philanthropy of southern Europe, which Professor Pullan has sensitively dissected. Part of the new sensibility was a sentimentality concerning very young children, which Pullan detects as early as the fifteenth century in the founding of the Innocenti in Florence. It had been evident in some of Hartlib's writings and in pietist Halle, and it was voiced by visitors to the Quaker workhouse in London in the 1720s who 'held up their hands saying, "Oh! poor little creatures!"' at the sight of children working, a prospect which had drawn Pepys's admiration sixty years before.[51] Still more striking, however, are the hints in early Hanoverian England of what Professor Pullan terms 'redemptive charity': a quest for self-sanctification through saving the souls of others, for example, and a deliberate seeking out of social and moral outcasts to be reclaimed and embraced with humility.[52]

The Charitable Society wished to edify its members at least as much as its targets, to inculcate in them, it said, the virtues of 'patience and humility, tenderness and compassion, mortification and self-denial'. That quotation is from the translated part of the Society's first publication; and it might seem a wholly foreign cuckoo in the English nest, were it not for the fact that mortification of a kind was to be demonstrated in some other mid-eighteenth-century philanthropic enterprises: the Lock Hospital of 1746 for sufferers from venereal disease, for example, or the Magdalen House of 1758 for penitent prostitutes.[53] There were certainly wartime anxieties and utilitarian purposes involved here. But there was also an elevation of the quality of mercy above that of justice within the broad spectrum of traditional charity which seems to me to jar with what had for long been the

[50] McClure, *Coram's Children*, 21, 258. Cf. *An Account of the Foundation and Government of the Hospital for Foundlings in Paris drawn up at the command of her late Majesty Queen Caroline* (1739).

[51] B. Pullan, *Orphans and Foundlings in Early Modern Europe* (Stenton Lecture 1988, Reading, 1989), 17; above, pp. 82, 90; T. V. Hitchcock (ed.), *Richard Hutton's Complaints Book* (London Record Society, 24, 1987), 78.

[52] B. Pullan, 'Charity and Poor Relief in Italian Cities', *Continuity and Change*, 3 (1988), 193–5.

[53] *The Charitable Society*, 24; Andrew, *Philanthropy and Police*, 69–71, 119–27. Cf. earlier English astonishment at 'persons of quality' visiting the sick and tolerating their 'offensive smell' in the Hôtel Dieu of Paris: M. H. Nicolson (ed.), *The Conway Letters* (rev. edn., Oxford, 1992), 59–60.

mainstream of English moral and social reform. It was not quite in symmetry with the correction and discrimination expressed in English institutions from Bridewell through the enclosed Protestant almshouse to the Corporations of the Poor.

Of course, new kinds of sensibility did not divert or obliterate older native impulses. They simply added one more layer to the multi-layered cake of eighteenth-century attitudes to the poor, and this particular layer was never a very thick one.[54] In 1737 Alured Clarke reasserted an older English perspective in arguing that mortification and humiliation would be the effect of hospitals on their inmates, not on their patrons and benefactors: 'Great numbers of the poor must be insensibly reclaimed from their vices', he asserted, 'by the daily spectacles of misery which they will have before their eyes.' The voluntary hospitals remained very English creations, designed, Clarke said, to turn their patients into 'useful members of the public'. Like the Corporations of the Poor, they could still be thought 'a means conducive towards a national reformation in the common peoples'.[55]

Voluntary hospitals also resembled the Corporations in reflecting and sometimes perpetuating local divisions and rival corporate identities, while claiming, again like the Corporations, that they were consensual undertakings, healing social as well as physical wounds, spanning 'every denomination and party'.[56] Trying to raise funds for the Northampton Infirmary in the 1740s, Philip Doddridge found the clergy backward: 'For among some men even charity grows odious when recommended by a Dissenter.' In Exeter two rival hospitals were founded in 1741, one by the city council, the other—the Devon and Exeter—by cathedral clergy and county gentry. Three years later Rocque's engraving of the city deliberately displayed the town hospital in pleasant pastures graced by a dairy maid, while the county

---

[54] For a sensitive analysis of the different layers, see S. Lloyd, 'Perceptions of Poverty in England, 1680–1770', D.Phil. thesis, Univ. of Oxford, 1991, chs. 1 and 2. John Spurr's comment on the 'low-key' note of Anglican piety when compared with that of the Counter-Reformation applies to the 18th c. as much as to the later 17th c.: *The Restoration Church of England 1646–1689* (New Haven, Conn., 1991), 372–3.

[55] Alured Clarke, A *Sermon Preached in the Cathedral Church of Winchester Before the Governors of the County-Hospital* (2nd edn., 1737), 12–13; Fissell, *Patients, Power and the Poor*, 84. Cf. R. Porter, 'The Gift Relation: Philanthropy and Provincial Hospitals in Eighteenth-Century England', in L. Granshaw and R. Porter (eds.), *The Hospital in History* (1989), 167; A. Digby, *Making a Medical Living: Doctors and Patients in the English Market for Medicine, 1720–1911* (Cambridge, 1994), 234.

[56] Clarke, *Sermon*, p. vii; A. Borsay, 'Cash and Conscience: Financing the General Hospital at Bath *c.*1738-50', *Social History of Medicine*, 4 (1991), 219–20. A. Wilson, 'Conflict, Consensus and Charity: Politics and the Provincial Voluntary Hospitals in the Eighteenth Century', *Eng. Hist. Rev.*, 111 (1996), 599–619, overstates the political links of the hospitals, but demonstrates that in many situations they aimed at and sometimes achieved their 'eirenic' purpose.

hospital was pictured next to a graveyard and behind a funeral procession.[57]

Yet even so, despite these continuities, the voluntary hospitals could claim with greater justice than any of their recent predecessors to be for 'the good of mankind in general'.[58] Their long, socially heterogeneous subscription lists might be counterbalanced by much more exclusive boards of directors, but their voluntary organization gave them an unusually wide base of benevolence, broadly reflecting the commercial or landed interest groups of their different localities.[59] They might seem 'the most general, as well as unexceptionable' of all charities even to their patients. As Dr Fissell has shown, the poor were able to manipulate short stays in hospitals to their own purposes, just as they were able to do in some eighteenth-century workhouses.[60] Voluntary hospitals were to some degree a responsive, flexible facility, closer in character to the original Savoy Hospital and some of its medieval predecessors than to the reformed almshouses or the bridewells of the later sixteenth and seventeenth centuries. In these respects they seem to take us back 200 years before 1740, to a point not very distant from that at which this book began.

III

The proliferation of charitable agencies in the first half of the eighteenth century had not, of course, resolved all the doubts and difficulties of the past. If it had stimulated and manipulated civic consciences, it also left them far from untroubled. We have already seen the continuing sensitivity to charges of 'corruption' in any seemingly benevolent activity, which had been provoked by Mandeville's intellectual challenge on the one hand and by the development of new forms of public and private finance on the other. No less perplexing and equally persistent was the related problem of accountability.

The Crown, and more recently municipal corporations and parish

---

[57] G. F. Nuttall, *Calendar of the Correspondence of Philip Doddridge DD (1702-1751)* (HMC, JP 26, 1979), 190; Porter, 'Gift Relation', 154-5; P. M. G. Russell, A *History of the Exeter Hospitals 1170-1948* (Exeter, 1977), 18.

[58] Borsay, 'Cash and Conscience', 216.

[59] Porter, 'Gift Relation', 158-61; K. Wilson, 'Urban Culture and Political Activism in Hanoverian England', in E. Hellmuth (ed.), *The Transformation of Political Culture in England and Germany in the Late Eighteenth Century* (1990), 164-84. For the Bristol Infirmary, where Quakers were once again important managers, see Fissell, *Patients, Power, and the Poor*, 110-14; and for a thorough analysis of subscribers to the Bristol, Devon and Exeter, and Northampton institutions after 1750, see A. Berry, 'Patronage, Funding and the Hospital Patient c. 1750-1815: Three English Regional Case Studies', D.Phil. thesis, Univ. of Oxford, 1995.

[60] Woodward, *To Do the Sick No Harm*, 149; Fissell, *Patients, Power, and the Poor*, 94-109. For movement of the poor, especially children and young adults, in and out of the Hull workhouse, see Hull City RO, Workhouse Admittance and Discharge Book 1729-1759; Jackson, *Hull*, 323.

oligarchies, had all been found wanting on that score; and the various new vehicles we have surveyed had been nothing if not attempts to provide a remedy. From 1649 onwards most Corporations of the Poor had their governing assistants elected rather than nominated, and from the 1690s generous benefactors were added to their number so that they could watch over their own investment in the public good. Subscription charities in their turn were preferred to chartered and incorporated ones, because their managers could more easily be called to account. The various parts of that amalgam of voluntary societies, joint-stock projects, and trusts which might, among other things, run parish workhouses and hospitals were all intended to ensure that funds could not be 'misapplied', to bring integrity to public and semi-public administration, and to guarantee the 'consent' of those most involved, i.e. the public-spirited and the propertied.[61]

From the 1730s, however, the efficacy of these new devices seemed increasingly open to question. Criticism of the once model workhouse of St Giles in the Fields in 1730 began a process which culminated in the 1770s with widespread agreement that principles of deterrence, the use of managers, and contracting out had made parish workhouses 'a dreadful engine of oppression' from whose 'sordid tyranny there is no appeal'.[62] In 1731 a bill for an incorporated workhouse in Manchester provoked all the usual political and religious infighting which had impeded earlier Corporations of the Poor, but also some newly fashioned statements of principle. 'New government corporations against the consent of the people', one critic asserted, would 'as naturally corrupt as a stagnating pool', unless fair elections preserved them 'clean and sweet like running water'.[63] The bugbear in Manchester was a body of twenty-four self-coopting trustees who were to run the operation, and within a year there were indisputable 'breaches of trust' for public attention to focus on: in the Charitable Corporation, whose committee had acted without reference to the general body of the subscribers, and the York Buildings Company, where joint-stock organization had been no protection against gross mismanagement.[64] When similar doubts

---

[61] *Account of Several Workhouses* (1732 edn.), pp. iv–vii; Clarke, *Sermon*, p. vii; Woodward, *To Do the Sick No Harm*, 150. Langford, *Public Life and the Propertied Englishman*, ch. 4, 'Qualified Rule', and pp. 490–500, explores and illustrates this theme.

[62] *Workhouse Cruelty*; Hanson, *Printed Sources*, 442, no. 4143; S. Webb and B. Webb, *English Local Government: English Poor Law History*, i: *The Old Poor Law* (1927), 279; D. Marshall, *The English Poor in the Eighteenth Century* (1926), 138. Cf. Hampson, *Treatment of Poverty*, 85–6, for criticism of parish workhouses in 1751.

[63] R. Parkinson (ed.), *The Private Journal and Literary Remains of John Byrom*, i, pt. 2 (Chetham Society, 34, 1855), 483. On the background, see Handley, 'Local Legislative Initiatives', 21–2, 33; K. Kondo, 'The Workhouse Issue at Manchester: Selected Documents, 1729–35, Part One', *Kenkyu Ronshu: Bulletin of the Faculty of Letters, Nagoya University*, 33 (1987), 1–96.

[64] P. G. M. Dickson, *The Financial Revolution in England: A Study in the Development of Public Credit 1688–1756* (1967), 155; S. Lambert (ed.), *House of Commons Sessional Papers*

were extended even to voluntary hospitals, as they were in the House of Lords debates on the Mortmain Bill in 1736, no part of eighteenth-century charitable endeavour could rest secure.

The roots of the Mortmain Act have still to be properly investigated. It was partly prompted by fears for the landed interest and the supposed threats to it posed by benefactions like Thomas Guy's. It was partly an expression of anticlericalism, aroused by debates over Queen Anne's Bounty. It can scarcely have been directed at charitable activity in general, since its proposer, Joseph Jekyll, was a governor of city hospitals and president of the Westminster infirmary.[65] Dictated though they may have been by the immediate pressures of parliamentary debate and party warfare, the remarks made in the Lords about charitable institutions are nevertheless instructive. One opponent of the bill defended death-bed bequests proceeding 'from a sincere regard to the public good', and—taking Mandeville on board—thought them acceptable even if they came 'from the pride and vanity of the donor'. Speakers for the bill, however, argued that too many landed estates were in the hands of 'charitable foundations', whether they were 'incorporate bodies' or 'corporations or bodies politic'. They threatened to 'become too numerous'. Hospitals in particular had 'increased prodigiously within the last century', and were run by governors who were not 'answerable to any for their conduct'. Patronage and jobbery and the establishing of an 'interest' were 'the true source of that spirit which has been lately raised for erecting and endowing hospitals'.[66]

Though doubtless a minority voice, this scepticism about voluntary activity was probably one element in the revival of debate about public provision for the poor through the law, and how that could be made accountable. It began in 1735 with William Hay's proposals, drawing on Hale, Child, and Cary, for new Corporations of the Poor in each county, to fund workhouses, hospitals for children and the impotent, houses of correction, and even outdoor relief. The House of Commons voted in favour of the main principles of the scheme, but got no further. The Manchester débâcle was still too recent, and in the aftermath of the Excise Crisis there were revived anxieties about new magistracies, 'unknown heretofore', 'dangers to our constitution'. Perhaps in response, Hay revised his scheme in 1747, intending

of the Eighteenth Century (145 vols., Wilmington, Dela., 1975–6), xiv: *Charitable Corporation 1732–34*, 190,192; [Samuel Horsey,] *Answer of Samuel Horsey, Esq., Governor of the York Buildings Company, to the Misrepresentations of his Conduct* (1733), 3.

[65] Owen, *Philanthropy*, 87; Jones, *Law of Charity*, 109–13; L. Colley, *In Defiance of Oligarchy: The Tory Party 1714-60* (Cambridge, 1982),107–10; Langford, *Public Life and the Propertied Englishman*, 492. On Jekyll, see P. Clark, 'The "Mother Gin" Controversy in the Early Eighteenth Century', *Trans. Roy. Hist. Soc.*, 5th ser., 38 (1988), 75. I am indebted to Joanna Innes for her advice on the Mortmain debates.

[66] W. Cobbett (ed.), *Parliamentary History of England* (36 vols., 1806–20), ix, cols. 1122, 1125, 1132, 1136, 1146–8, 1156.

new corporations now for the relief of the poor 'by voluntary charities' and providing that they be run by 'men of great credit' (and estates worth £300 or more).[67] Within a year, however, new poor law incorporations were being set up again by local Act, for Bury St Edmunds in 1748 and six other towns by 1780, and then from 1756 for groups of rural parishes in East Anglia, most of which had been incorporated by 1785. They formed the background to William Gilbert's career as the promoter of various kinds of organization for public poor relief between the 1760s and 1780s.[68]

Joanna Innes has illuminated the multiple strands in later eighteenth-century debates about the poor law, many of which lie beyond the boundaries of this book. There was controversy about the relative merits of indoor as against outdoor relief, as well as over the proper balance between public and voluntary activity; there was a new appreciation of the problem of rural as against urban poverty; and there were efforts once more, as in the 1690s, to gather accurate information about the resources being transferred to the indigent and impotent. All this owed something to the social and economic problems which came first with war and then with the return of population growth and inflation after mid-century.[69] What is interesting for our purposes, however, is the persistence of the terms in which debate was conducted. It was still about the ways in which men should associate, who they should be, and to whom they should account. They might be incorporated, 'one body politic in law', as the Commons resolved in 1735, or be 'district committees' of 'gentlemen respectable for their character and fortune in the county', as Gilbert proposed in the 1780s.[70] But in either case they were local and multiple bodies. Whatever doubts and difficulties they might involve, and however much the balance between voluntary and public activity might move backwards and forwards, there was no going back on that. There might be proposals for regular reports by public agencies to Parliament, but there was no serious prospect and little suggestion that there could be a single national road to welfare paved by central authority.

It is true that the balance between central and local initiative could also shift from time to time, even before 1740. When circumstances seemed to

---

[67] [William Hay,] *Remarks on the Laws Relating to the Poor* [1735], 17, 33–4, 39; [William Hay,] *Remarks on the Laws relating to the Poor* (1751), 24; Innes, 'Mixed Economy of Welfare', 154–5; Andrew, *Philanthropy and Police*, 45.

[68] Innes, 'Mixed Economy of Welfare', 161–3; Webb and Webb, *Old Poor Law*, 121, 126–30; J. Innes, 'Parliament and the Shaping of Eighteenth-Century English Social Policy', *Trans. Roy. Hist. Soc.*, 5th ser., 40 (1990), 88–9.

[69] In addition to the works cited above, see J. Innes, 'The Domestic Face of the Military-Fiscal State: Government and Society in Eighteenth-Century Britain', in L. Stone (ed.), *An Imperial State at War: Britain from 1689 to 1815* (1994), 96–127; J. Innes, 'The Invention of Rural Poverty in Later Eighteenth-Century England' (forthcoming).

[70] Hay, *Remarks* (1751 edn.), 24; [William Gilbert,] *A Plan of Police, exhibiting the Causes of the Present Increase of the Poor* (1786), 32–3; William Gilbert, *Considerations on the Bills for the better Relief and Employment of the Poor* (1787), 22.

demand it, the direction and agency of policy could change, apparently against the political and cultural grain of Hanoverian England. Old-style crises could still call forth determined conciliar intervention, as with the threat of plague in 1713 and the early 1720s, when suspect shipping was identified, isolated, and on occasion destroyed.[71] We have learned from recent work that the flexibility and creativity of Hanoverian government should not be underrated, however disengaged from domestic affairs it might appear when compared with continental regimes. It could respond quickly and powerfully to challenges, as for example in Scotland before and after the '15. Its campaigns against cattle plague, in 1714 and 1745–8, involving the compulsory slaughter and quarantining of animals, are excellent examples of ruthless action when it was necessary.[72]

Yet Scotland was not England, and cattle were not men, though they were certainly property. The outcry occasioned by the Quarantine Act of 1721, which threatened the imposition of military *cordons sanitaires* if plague arrived, suggests that, in some respects, early Stuart governments had more room for executive manoeuvre than their eighteenth-century successors.[73] As for the modified crises still caused by dearth, when exports of grain were banned under the royal prerogative in 1766, the enabling statute having recently expired, the government had to fight hard to overcome resistance to 'an extraordinary exertion of royal power'.[74] Past events had created a political culture in early Hanoverian England which, if it did not entirely close off some avenues of policy, at least made them more difficult to pursue.

That culture was the stronger because it was not rooted only in politics, in the rhetoric of liberty and property, and in party and denominational allegiances, but in the social fabric which nourished innovation and improvement for the public good. As Professor Stewart has demonstrated, science had not become the beacon of enlightened rulers which Bacon and the elderly Petty wanted; it had become 'public' at the level of the coffee-house and local gentlemen's society, and been a matter of contention between rival projects, experiments, patents, and joint-stocks.[75] Political arithmetic had similarly been fragmented, losing any contact, it has been said, with econometrics, surviving as the collection of statistics for a variety of sometimes

[71] P. Slack, *The Impact of Plague in Tudor and Stuart England* (1985), 324–5. Conciliar action was based on a statute of 1710: 9 Anne, c. 2.

[72] Innes, 'Domestic Face', 104, 106, 117–18; J. Broad, 'Cattle Plague in Eighteenth-Century England', *Agricultural History Review*, 31 (1983), 104–15. It is possible that English reactions were influenced by measures taken in Italy: L. Wilkinson, *Animals and Disease: An Introduction to the History of Comparative Medicine* (Cambridge, 1992), 51.

[73] Slack, *Impact of Plague*, 326–35.

[74] P. Lawson, 'Parliament, the Constitution and Corn: The Embargo Crisis of 1766', *Parliamentary History*, 5 (1986), 24. For earlier delays in parliamentary and government responses to dearth, see R. B. Outhwaite, *Dearth, Public Policy and Social Disturbance in England, 1550–1800* (1991), 37–9.

[75] Stewart, *Rise of Public Science*.

unadventurous purposes. Local bills of mortality were newly compiled, as in Northampton, or further refined, as in London and Norwich; but there was no national census, which when proposed in 1753 was thought 'totally subversive of the last remains of English liberty'.[76] Instead there was work like Thomas Short's, beginning in the 1730s, on local variations in mortality. That itself rested on a tradition of inquiry into correlations between the weather, locality, and disease which went back to Sydenham and Locke as well as Graunt, and it expressed and reinforced an environmental approach to disease which was entirely in tune with localist and voluntarist sentiment.[77]

Medical environmentalism was to have positive results in encouraging better sanitation and environmental improvement in general.[78] It was not inherently hostile to government initiative and direction. But in early Hanoverian England it offered no support to government intervention and public health campaigns on the grand scale, which were anyway thought inimical to trade, local autonomy, and individual liberty. It is striking that no analogies with human epidemics were drawn from the campaign against cattle plague.[79] Inoculation against smallpox, introduced in the early 1720s, was welcomed by several medical men as 'a most beneficial improvement in the practice of physic'. It was an obvious subject for early statistical study and for experimental investigation by the Royal Society, and the practice was gradually adopted in fashionable circles.[80] General inoculations at parish

[76] J. Hoppit, 'Political Arithmetic in Eighteenth-Century England', *Econ. Hist. Rev.*, 49 (1996), 516–40; P. Buck, 'People Who Counted: Political Arithmetic in the Eighteenth Century', *Isis*, 73 (1982), 32, 36; D. V. Glass, *Numbering the People: The Eighteenth-Century Population Controversy and the Development of Censuses and Vital Statistics in Britain* (Farnborough, Hants, 1973), 16, 20; J. K. Edwards, 'Norwich Bills of Mortality 1707–1830', *Yorkshire Bulletin of Economic and Social Research*, 21 (1969), 110–12. John Fransham was a compiler of the Norwich bills, which helps to account for his interest in collecting, and his access to, data on poor-relief expenditure: above, p. 118.

[77] J. C. Riley, *The Eighteenth-Century Campaign to Avoid Disease* (1987), 5–29; Short, *New Observations;* [Thomas Short,] *A General Chronological History of the Air, Weather Seasons, Meteors &c* (1749). For later 17th-c. interest, see K. Dewhurst, *John Locke: Physician and Philosopher* (1963), 18–19, 300–2; K. Dewhurst, *Dr. Thomas Sydenham (1624–1689)* (1966), 60–1; L. Mulligan, 'Self-Scrutiny and the Study of Nature: Robert Hooke's Diary as Natural History', *Journal of British Studies*, 35 (1996), 311–42.

[78] Riley, *Eighteenth-Century Campaign.* Progress was slow and piecemeal, however, and, in London at least, not evident before the second half of the 18th c.: R. Porter, 'Cleaning up the Great Wen: Public Health in Eighteenth-Century London', in W. F. Bynum and R. Porter, *Living and Dying in London (Medical History,* suppl. 11, 1991), 63–9; A. Hardy, 'Water and the Search for Public Health in London in the Eighteenth and Nineteenth Centuries', *Medical History,* 28 (1984), 256–8; J. Landers, *Death and the Metropolis: Studies in the Demographic History of London 1670–1830* (Cambridge, 1993), 353–7.

[79] Slack, *Impact of Plague,* 326, 329–31; A. Hardy, 'The Medical Response to Epidemic Disease during the Long Eighteenth Century', in J. A. I. Champion (ed.), *Epidemic Disease in London* (Centre for Metropolitan History, Working Paper 1, 1993), 66.

[80] Philip Rose, *An Essay on the Small-pox; Whether Natural or Inoculated* (1724), 5; G. Miller, *The Adoption of Inoculation for Smallpox in England and France* (Philadelphia, 1957); Wilson, 'Politics of Medical Improvement', 24–34.

expense became common only after 1750, however, and there was little hint that smallpox cases might be isolated as plague cases had been until the founding of the London Smallpox Hospital in 1746.[81] The adoption of inoculation certainly depended on rebutting weighty theological and practical arguments, since it was a clear case of 'tempting providence' and of ends justifying means (which made its advocates sound like Mandeville);[82] but earlier campaigns against plague had been similarly vulnerable. In the early eighteenth century the ravages of infectious disease, which could readily be seen in the bills of mortality, were not used, as they might have been and as they sometimes were in other countries, to justify moves towards some centralized model of 'medical police'.[83]

Later in the century, and still more after 1830, much of this was to change, though in ways more complicated and involving a less decisive break with the past than has sometimes been supposed.[84] The same might be said about changes in the methods of regulating the poor, with which public health was, as ever, intimately connected. The Poor Law Amendment Act of 1834 and the other parliamentary reforms to local government in the 1830s and 1840s made less of a difference than disciples of Jeremy Bentham or Edwin Chadwick imagined. Though they destroyed parochial autonomy once and for all, centralizing tendencies were counterbalanced by a new civic confidence in reformed municipal corporations. As for voluntary activity, that became more rather than less important. Dr Finlayson's conclusion about the century after 1834 is instructive:

The Poor Law of 1834 was the product of a society which saw the state in minimal terms: as an agency which was primarily designed to enable and encourage voluntary initiatives to proceed. . . . That could not be said of the society which produced the Welfare State in the twentieth century.[85]

---

[81] P. Razzell, *The Conquest of Smallpox* (Firle, Sussex, 1977), 46; J. R. Smith, *The Speckled Monster: Smallpox in England 1670–1970, with particular reference to Essex* (Chelmsford, 1987), 38, 47–8. Isaac Maddox, Bishop of Worcester and founder of the infirmary there, was instrumental in the origin of the Smallpox Hospital.

[82] Cf. e.g. Rose, *Essay on the Small-pox*, 9–10, and T. A. Horne, *The Social Thought of Bernard Mandeville: Virtue and Commerce in Early Eighteenth-Century England* (1978), 75. Some of the arguments in debate were the same as in the controversy over quarantine against plague in 1720–2, and involved the same writers, e.g. Mead and Edmund Massey.

[83] Cf. G. Rosen, 'Cameralism and the Concept of Medical Police', *Bulletin of the History of Medicine*, 27 (1953), 21–42; and L. Brockliss and C. Jones, *The Medical World of Early Modern France* (Oxford, 1997), 734–8, 750–60, for environmentalism and aspirations towards medical police in relatively close harmony in mid-18th-c. France.

[84] See e.g. J. V. Pickstone, 'Dearth, Dirt and Fever Epidemics: Rewriting the History of British "Public Health", 1780–1850', in T. Ranger and P. Slack (eds.), *Epidemics and Ideas: Essays on the Historical Perception of Pestilence* (Cambridge, 1992), 125–48.

[85] D. Eastwood, *Governing Rural England: Tradition and Transformation in Local Government 1780–1840* (Oxford, 1994), 261–5; G. Finlayson, *Citizen, State, and Social Welfare in Britain 1830–1990* (Oxford, 1994), 413, and cf. p. 83. See also J. Harris, 'Political Thought and the Welfare State 1870–1940', *P&P*, 135 (1992),116–17; J. Harris, 'Enterprise

Pursuing our earlier analogy, we might plausibly suggest that that could have been said, with only slight adjustment, of the society of the later Middle Ages: the society which produced guilds, fraternities, and feoffees as well as parishes and municipal corporations, all of them to some degree involved in public welfare. The 'mixed economy of welfare'[86] which had been firmly established by 1740 not only persisted for another two centuries. It restored and refurbished a pre-Reformation achievement.[87]

IV

The reminders of the fifteenth century which have recurred through this chapter underline how profound was the social damage done by the Tudor Reformation; and much of the story told in this book has been about attempts to put some of the pieces back together again, just as Trinity Houses replaced seamen's fraternities, and Christ's Hospital, Abingdon, incorporated in 1553, perpetuated in different and attenuated form the great guild of the Holy Cross.[88] It would obviously be false to argue that there was a complete hiatus in associated and voluntary activity in England for a century and more after the 1540s. Corporations, trusts, trading companies, parish vestries, not to mention religious combinations, all did something to fill the gap. But in the later seventeenth and early eighteenth centuries, with the invention of new means of stimulating private interest and private investment in public welfare, there was undoubtedly a renaissance. It was a significant choice of phrase when an Anglican writer in 1680 advocated the formation of 'fraternities or friendly societies', on the eve of their proliferation.[89]

In 1698 Josiah Woodward still had to defend the Reformation Societies against the charge that each of them was 'a society within a society', by which he meant a sect within the larger whole of the Church. Another of their advocates made the persuasive point, however, that only tyrannies

---

and Welfare States: A Comparative Perspective', *Trans. Roy. Hist. Soc*, 5th ser., 40 (1990), 193–4 and n. 62; and Prof. Harris's forthcoming Ford Lectures: 'A Land of Lost Content? Visions of Civic Virtue from Ruskin to Rawls'.

[86] The term is discussed in Finlayson, *Citizen, State, and Social Welfare*, 6.

[87] The comparison between the 15th c. and 18th c. is nicely pointed by G. Rosser, 'Solidarités et changement social: les fraternités urbaines anglaises à la fin du Moyen Âge', and J. Barry, 'Identité urbaine et classes moyennes dans l'Angleterre moderne', both in *Annales: Économies Sociétés, Civilisations*, 48 (1993), 1127–43 and 853–83. For the later Middle Ages, see also M. K. McIntosh, 'Local Responses to the Poor in Late Medieval and Tudor England', *Continuity and Change*, 3 (1988), 213–25; above, pp. 132–3; below, pp. 151–4.

[88] G. G. Harris, *The Trinity House of Deptford 1514–1660* (1969), 19–22; Rosser, 'Solidarités', 1140–1.

[89] *The Country Parson's Advice*, quoted in J. Spurr, 'The Church, the Societies and the Moral Revolution of 1688', in Walsh et al., *Church of England*, 137. On this general theme see J. Barry, 'Bourgeois Collectivism? Urban Association and the Middling Sort', in J. Barry and C. Brooks (eds.), *The Middling Sort of People: Culture, Society and Politics in England 1550–1800* (1994), 108–9.

would object to such 'occasions of concourse', which were as legitimate as any associations 'meeting to consider of useful projects and inventions'.[90] In essence, this was a replaying of the arguments which had been advanced in defence of separatism in the 1640s, when new gathered churches had been compared to old companies of merchants: they were all 'particular societies' or 'corporations' which posed no conceivable threat to 'civil peace'.[91]

By the 1720s that argument for rights of association had plainly been won, thanks among other things to suspicion of the arbitrary powers of Crown, municipal corporations and even finally parish vestries. The problems of accountability remained, as much with the new kinds of political body as with the old, and they occasioned debate in the 1730s and beyond. But there was no denying what had been rediscovered: the public advantages of competing and overlapping societies within societies. Writing in 1699, another defender of associations for the reformation of manners called these units 'civil societies'.[92] We would nowadays apply the term also to the wider polity of which they had become a fundamental and characteristic part.

[90] Woodward, *Account . . . of the Religious Societies*, 142; *A Letter to a Minister of the Church of England Concerning the Societies for Reformation of Manners* (1710), 8.
[91] Roger Williams (1644), in A. S. P. Woodhouse, *Puritanism and Liberty* (1938), 267.
[92] *An Account of the Societies For Reformation of Manners in London and Westminster And other Parts of the Kingdom* (1699), 100.

7

CIVIL SOCIETIES

Current interest in the concept and reality of 'civil society' springs largely from political events at the end of the twentieth century. It has been prompted on the one hand by the collapse of communist regimes in central and eastern Europe and the consequent interest in what can and should fill the vacuum and, on the other, by arguments in the West about the proper limits of state activity and the costs of an ever-expanding public sector (not least in the realm of social welfare). For a variety of reasons attention has been directed to forms of association below and outside the apparatus of the state: to the 'little platoons', from churches to families, which fill the much-contested gap between public and private spheres and which seem vital to social cohesion. The stronger and more active these building-blocks, it is argued, the healthier the desirable end, a civil society.[1]

Though currently particularly fashionable, the theme and the term have, of course, a history. When Sir Thomas Smith referred to a 'society civil', he appears to have meant one ordered by government and law, equivalent to a 'common wealth'; and to the extent that a 'common wealth' involved, as we saw in the first chapter, normative connotations to do with well-being and (to some extent) participation, the theme as well as the term may be thought to go back, in embryo, at least as far as the sixteenth century. By the early eighteenth century Mandeville and at least one of his critics were using 'civil society' in much the same sense: it was the entity which, properly governed, might—or might not—benefit from public and private virtue.[2] It is only in the later eighteenth century, however, that discussion of the relationship between civil society and the state in something like their modern senses can

[1] R. Dahrendorf, 'Prosperity, Civility and Liberty', *Proceedings of the British Academy*, 90 (1996), 234; D. Winch, *Riches and Poverty: An Intellectual History of Political Economy in Britain, 1750–1834* (Cambridge, 1996), 11–12. For introductions to an expanding literature see J. L. Cohen and A. Arato, *Civil Society and Political Theory* (Cambridge, Mass., 1992); J. Hall (ed.), *Civil Society: Theory, History, Comparison* (Cambridge, 1995).

[2] N. Wood, 'Foundations of Political Economy: The New Moral Philosophy of Sir Thomas Smith', in P. A. Fideler and T. F. Mayer (eds.), *Political Thought and the Tudor Commonwealth* (1992), 159; above, pp. 6, 12–13; H. Monro, *The Ambivalence of Bernard Mandeville* (Oxford, 1975), 188-9; Bernard Mandeville, *The Fable of the Bees*, ed. F. B. Kaye (2 vols, Oxford, 1924), i. 3, 347–9; ii, title-page opp. p. 392; Robert Burrow, *Civil Society and Government vindicated . . . in a Sermon* (1723), 1-11.

be identified with any confidence. It is possible to trace a continuity of discourse from Adam Ferguson's *Essay on the History of Civil Society* of 1767 onwards, and its intricacies are beginning to attract attention.[3] It may well be that a study of the modern history of both concept and reality could contribute to a better understanding of what is still, it must be said, an ill-defined piece of political and sociological shorthand.

My own concern nevertheless lies further in the past: in the two-and-a-half centuries before 1740, rather than in the two-and-a-half centuries since then. It may readily be granted that eighteenth-century England was a civil society, in most current senses of the term as well as in contemporary parlance. But if, as was suggested in the last chapter, something very like it existed also in the fifteenth century—at least in its multiple ways of delivering public welfare—the parallel may help to explain why the story told in this book turned out as it did: why some potential avenues of development in the interim between the fifteenth and eighteenth centuries proved fruitful, and why others proved to be dead ends.

We might also expect to find a comparison with other parts of western Europe instructive. By the eighteenth century, and often long before, some of them had at least as valid a claim to be civil societies as did Britain; and they shared many of the same inputs into their approaches to public welfare. If the outcome in other countries was sometimes different, as the previous chapter hinted, we need to ask why that was if we are properly to understand English developments. We might even find our attention diverted away from civil society and back towards the state, or rather perhaps towards questions which focus on the importance of the relationship between the two.

I

We might usefully begin with the fifteenth century, and with the recent work of Ronald Hutton on the rituals of 'Merry England'. The proliferation of religious and secular festivals which he finds in the century before 1500, and which he links with contemporaneous investment in parish churches, chantries, guilds, and other local institutions, leaves no room for doubt that the later Middle Ages were at least as fertile and creative a period for

---

[3] M. B. Becker, *The Emergence of Civil Society in the Eighteenth Century* (Bloomington Ind., 1994), p. xi and *passim*; F. Oz-Salzberger, *Translating the Enlightenment: Scottish Civic Discourse in Eighteenth-Century Germany* (Oxford, 1995), 142–53. There is also relevant information in A. Black, *Guilds and Civil Society in European Political Thought from the Twelfth Century to the Present* (1984). Black, however, was writing before late 20th-c. events led political theorists to define civil society (in part at least) in terms of associations. He draws a distinction between what he terms 'guild' values, of a corporate kind, and those of 'civil society', by which he means liberal values of personal freedom and ultimately individualism. It will be clear that in this chapter I prefer to think of civil society and guilds as intimately related. In his conclusion Black accepts 'cross-fertilization' between the two, particularly in urban societies, until the end of the 17th c. (p. 237); I would see it as continuing until at least the French Revolution.

associative activity as the eighteenth century.[4] When Hutton discusses the reasons for the late medieval creativity, therefore, he raises issues germane to the present inquiry. He asks in particular whether the root causes were economic or ideological. Was it a matter of 'surplus wealth seeking investment' in a period of demographic decline and economic stagnation? Or was it a matter of religious aspirations, of a late medieval piety which sought salvation through individual and collective acts of penance of various kinds?

As Hutton recognizes, the two explanations are not mutually exclusive. Penance involved what might be termed 'the purchase of paradise' and hence had to be afforded; and the economic explanation also has its complexities. The historical demographer might argue that a decline in transmission of property between generations in the post-Black Death period was responsible for 'surplus wealth'.[5] Keith Wrightson, a social historian, suggests that the pressures arising from a late medieval shortage of labour might have encouraged neighbourly cooperation and collective activities of all kinds, and hence the competitive expressions of local identity which are particularly notable in fifteenth-century parishes. Having investigated the various possibilities, Professor Hutton concludes nevertheless that the 'independent power of ideology' was more important than social and economic circumstances.[6]

The issue merits further consideration here, not only because it needs to be raised with respect to the eighteenth century when ideology had clearly changed but economic conditions were in many respects similar, but also because it has particular relevance to the theme of public welfare throughout our period. We might expect economic circumstances to have had some connection with perceptions of the kinds of social problem and opportunity considered in this book. Little has been said so far, perhaps surprisingly, about possible links between policies and attitudes on the one hand and social and economic circumstances on the other. Before we conclude, we must ask whether there were causal connections of this kind and whether, for example, the multiple purposes and means of delivery of social and public services in the fifteenth and eighteenth centuries were in any way connected with the economic background which, superficially at least, they also shared: that is to say, relatively stable populations, relatively high popular standards of living, a generally 'low-pressure' socio-economic regime.

[4] R. Hutton, *The Rise and Fall of Merry England: The Ritual Year 1400–1700* (Oxford, 1994). A subsequent work provides evidence that some of his rituals, like parish wakes and dedication festivals, may have revived in the later 17th and early 18th cs., which would reinforce the parallel: R. Hutton, *The Stations of the Sun: A History of the Ritual Year in Britain* (Oxford, 1996), 352–3. Cf. pp. 422, 426.

[5] The same might perhaps be argued with respect to the period 1660–1760.

[6] Hutton, *Merry England*, 62–7; K. Wrightson, review in *Times Literary Supplement*, 14 Oct. 1994, 6; Hutton, *Stations of the Sun*, 413–14.

There is certainly something to be said for inferring such a link between economic cycles and policy or welfare cycles. It seems unlikely to be entirely accidental that the 'high-pressure' regime, which we may take to have been at its most severe between roughly 1570 and 1630, coincided with the period when the monarchy on the one hand and godly magistrates on the other strove to invent and impose new schemes for public welfare by diktat. By contrast, the fifteenth and early eighteenth centuries, when pluralist provision was not only tolerated but even welcomed with some enthusiasm, were periods when a broadly based associated philanthropy could be afforded, and when social problems were not grave enough to make more centralized coercive alternatives palatable. When one looks at the position more closely, however, this kind of economic determinism turns out to suffer from the same weaknesses when applied to the general picture as it did when applied to the specific case of Puritan reformers. That is to say, it tells us something about an undoubtedly relevant background, but little about activities in the foreground where many other forces were in play.

At first sight, the later Middle Ages seem to confirm the determinist case. High pressure in the 1290s and famine in 1315–16 produced the aggressive attitudes towards the poor and vehement government attacks on grain-hoarders and speculators which were to recur in the 1590s, and which were unlike anything to be found in the low-pressure regime which followed the Black Death.[7] Yet when we turn to the period after 1350, we find that local responses to economic conditions had more than one strand and no uniform predetermined consistency. On the one hand there was, as one might expect, a general increase in the number of fraternities. In Salisbury's three parishes alone there were twenty-two of them, and Dr Brown attributes their multiplication across the whole diocese to increased opportunities to acquire property. On the other hand, there seems to have been nothing like the same investment in another form of collective endeavour, hospitals. In Norwich their decay was unusually pronounced, and Dr Rawcliffe finds the 'decades of stagnation' after 1350 producing not only that, but also a shift in the management of poor relief to 'the stricter confines of the parish'—well before the harsher conditions of the later sixteenth century which might be supposed to have dictated it.[8] Choices were being

---

[7] The forthcoming work of Phillipp Schofield, cited in *Local Population Studies, 57* (autumn 1996), 11; W. C. Jordan, *The Great Famine: Northern Europe in the Early Fourteenth Century* (Princeton, NJ, 1996), 172.

[8] A. D. Brown, *Popular Piety in Late Medieval England: The Diocese of Salisbury 1250–1550* (Oxford, 1995), 137, 177; C. Rawcliffe, *The Hospitals of Medieval Norwich* (Norwich, 1995), 10–11. Brown also finds a decline in bequests to hospitals and some increasing involvement of parishes, although his interpretation of these phenomena is rather different from Rawcliffe's: *Popular Piety*, ch. 8. The issue is related to the still unresolved question of whether there was tension or cooperation between parish and fraternity in the later Middle Ages, on which see G. Rosser, 'Communities of Parish and Guild in the Late Middle Ages', in

made between various welfare options, as they were to be again in godly cities.

Furthermore, a narrowing of focus to the parish is not the only feature of welfare attitudes and practices which can be found in periods dominated by different kinds of social and economic pressure. A public insistence on work and labour discipline is there consistently from the Black Death onwards, for example, in both low- and high-pressure regimes. Still more fundamentally, much the same might be said about associative and collective activity in general, in the Middle Ages at least. Contrary to what has perhaps so far been implied, it was far from new in the fifteenth century, and Susan Reynolds attributes its increasingly various forms between 900 and 1300 to the *growth* of population and economy, not to their stagnation or decline.[9] It would appear that none of the more striking features of English public welfare in our period—the dominance of the parish, an insistence on labour, and a strong voluntary sector—can be consistently tied to a particular set of economic circumstances.

If we look in more detail at the episodes described in this book, it seems clear also that long phases of high or low pressure were less important in producing new or particularly intense responses than short periods of crisis of no more than a decade: the 1520s, 1540s, and 1590s, for example, or, as it happens, the 1620s, 1640s, and 1690s. Moreover, the degree of reforming zeal or policy creativity with which these crises were met seems to have had little to do with their comparative severity, as measured on some kind of historical Richter scale, of grain prices, for example; and it had a good deal to do with more densely textured contemporary perceptions of what were in each case extremely complicated conjunctures of war, dearth, disease, and sometimes currency problems and political upheavals. Indeed, the circumstances which provoked most contemporary debate seem often to have been economic perturbations which did not produce the extreme scarcities which might have been expected, as in the 1540s, later 1620s, and 1690s.[10]

It cannot be said either that perceptions of crisis suddenly disappeared in the early eighteenth century, least of all in the 1720s, a decade which opened with financial scandals and the threat of corruption from top to bottom of the public world, not to mention the prospect of plague arriving from southern France, and a decade which finished with deficient harvests and

S. Wright (ed.), *Parish, Church and People: Local Studies in Lay Religion 1350–1750* (1988), 29–55.

[9] P. Slack, *The English Poor Law 1531–1782* (1990), 13; S. Reynolds, *Kingdoms and Communities in Western Europe 900–1300* (Oxford, 1984), 337–8. Cf. above, pp. 33–4.

[10] Above, p. 21; B. E. Supple, *Commercial Crisis and Change in England 1600–1642* (Cambridge, 1964); J. K. Horsefield, *British Monetary Experiments 1650–1710* (1960), chs. 5, 6.

widespread disease.[11] Even in the quieter reaches of the 1730s, we have only to look at the gin controversy to find again something like the moral panic of the 1690s, with the SPCK, hospital worthies, physicians, and informers joining forces against what Defoe called 'all the train of evils we are threatened with from pernicious Geneva'.[12] Disciples of an earlier godly Geneva would have fully understood and applauded.

If we are searching for circumstantial explanations for the multi-faceted welfare world of early Hanoverian England, we might also think the peculiar circumstances of London more obviously relevant than the general economic background. A metropolis of half a million people needed hospitals in Westminster as well as the City and Southwark, more than one pawnshop and dispensary, and several Societies for the Reformation of Manners, particularly in that inner ring of parishes round the old City where social problems congregated as thickly as social and religious reformers determined to tackle them. The whole arsenal of workhouses, charity schools, and reformation prosecutions had to be wheeled into action in the decaying parts of the West End from St James's Clerkenwell, Holborn, and St Giles in the Fields, down through Covent Garden and the Strand to St Margaret's Westminster.[13]

Even here, however, social circumstances did not make it inevitable that there should be that absence of a single metropolitan authority from which so much of the character of metropolitan welfare followed. Things might just possibly have been different if a different structure of government had been imposed, or perhaps one should say imposable, in the 1630s, for example, or the 1660s. Writing in praise of Greenwich Hospital in 1728, Nicholas Hawksmoor saw that there had been an alternative. Louis XIV had set an example in 'rectifying the irregular and ill management of the police of great cities'. If only London had been redesigned after the Great Fire, as Wren had wished, and if only legislation had restrained the growth of the suburbs 'or reduced them to the regularity of the new city', then London like Paris might have been reformed by a 'police architectonical'.[14] Once

---

[11] W. G. Hoskins, 'Harvest Fluctuations and English Economic History 1620–1759', *Agricultural History Review*, 16 (1968), 23; E. A. Wrigley and R. S. Schofield, *The Population History of England 1541–1871: A Reconstruction* (1981), 667; A. Gooder, 'The Population Crisis of 1727–30 in Warwickshire', *Midland History*, 1 (1971–2), 1–22.

[12] P. Clark, 'The "Mother Gin" Controversy in the Early Eighteenth Century', *Trans. Roy. Hist. Soc,* 5th ser., 38 (1988); 'Andrew Moreton' [Daniel Defoe], 'Augusta Triumphans', in *The Novels and Miscellaneous Works* (Oxford, 1841), xviii. 33.

[13] J. Landers, *Death and the Metropolis: Studies in the Demographic History of London 1670–1830* (Cambridge, 1993), 312–14; R. B. Shoemaker, *Prosecution and Punishment: Petty Crime and the Law in London and Rural Middlesex c. 1660–1725* (Cambridge, 1991), 289–300; C. Rose, 'Evangelical Philanthropy and Anglican Revival: The Charity Schools of Augustan London, 1648–1740', *London Journal*, 16 (1991), 36, 57–8.

[14] Nicholas Hawksmoor, *Remarks on the Founding and Carrying on the Buildings of the Royal Hospital at Greenwich* (1728), 6–8.

again, it was not a matter of inescapable economic circumstances but of policy and choice, and hence of cultural and, of course, political perceptions. Like Professor Hutton, we seem compelled to shift our attention from economics to ideology.

II

In doing so, we need to set England in its European context. As Hawksmoor's example reminds us, English perceptions had not been locked in an insular straitjacket since the fifteenth century. Previous chapters have shown them being reshaped, not least by winds of change blowing from continental Europe. The dictates of Christian charity remained fundamental, as an impulse for both voluntary and state activity from the fifteenth to the eighteenth century. But personal salvation had taken second place to social correction in the reforming aspirations of godly cities and some of the later religious societies, and they had been influenced by models manufactured abroad, from Geneva to Glaucha. Modes of analysis of the secular ills of a decaying body politic had changed even more; and educated physicians, from William Turner to William Petty and Bernard Mandeville, bringing to their diagnosis inputs from Bologna, Padua, or Leiden, had played a vital part in that.[15] Civic humanism, Reformed churches, and the absolutist rhetoric of the Bourbons had all had an impact. When Petty urged that 'domestic improvement' was specially 'to be commended', and when he compiled statistics to show whether 'the whole kingdom doth impoverish or improve', he was far from being intellectually isolationist.[16]

No more than in other countries were the consequences of these inputs necessarily favourable to the little platoons of parish vestries and voluntary associations. Some of them depended upon a strengthening of central executive power. The prime example, and a major innovation of our period, was quarantine against plague, imposed on both households and shipping, which fundamentally altered perceptions of public health, despite the retreat from some of its implications in the eighteenth century.[17] A comparable instance, to return to Hawksmoor, was provision for military veterans, a prime concern of any government with armies and navies to recruit and retain. Dr Hudson's work underlines how unlike other aspects of English social welfare that was. Organized centrally in its Tudor beginnings, then for nearly 100 years from 1593 imposed as a county and not a parish responsibility, in the eighteenth century it was again centrally organized by means of outpensions from Chelsea and the plentiful beds available at Greenwich. By the

---

[15] Cf. above, pp. 17–18.
[16] Bodl., MS Film 1955, Petty Papers, Box H. no. 60; MS Film 1952, Box C, no. 23.
[17] P. Slack, *The Impact of Plague in Tudor and Stuart England* (1985); above, pp. 144–5.

1740s nearly 10,000 men were being supported in this way.[18] Other achievements which we have seen drawing to a greater or lesser degree on foreign inspiration undeniably pointed in a different direction — as with the voluntary hospitals, or that host of improvements from street lighting to water supplies which, through a combination of private enterprise and public authorization, had transformed English cities between the reigns of Elizabeth I and George II. But there was a mixture of different kinds of provision for welfare, not exclusive reliance on public or private, central or local.

The same amalgam characterized other parts of Europe. The weight of its different components shifted between countries and often over time, but there was no stark contrast between an essentially voluntarist England and 'statist' approaches to welfare elsewhere. There were European extremes and a spectrum in between. At one end were the bastions of civic humanism in Italy and the United Provinces, the first relying heavily on confraternities, the second with subsidiary corporations and denominational groupings handling much of public welfare, neither of them having (or perhaps needing) organization on a uniformly parochial basis.[19] The imperial cities of Germany which lay geographically between them occupied much the same segment of the spectrum. As in Holland and Italy, their municipal élites might try on occasion to impose a centralized welfare system, but never with complete success. 'The sacrosanct tradition of voluntarism', which defeated the ambitions of Hamburg's Board of Health in 1715, always proved too strong.[20]

At the other extreme were the new bureaucratic states of the East, Russia and Prussia. The decrees of Peter and Catherine the Great, suppressing parish autonomy and imposing new welfare institutions, first through what was increasingly a state church and then via social welfare boards run by provincial governors, were for long little more than paper schemes.[21] The Hohenzollerns, however, were much more effective, and might seem to have sketched out in Prussia what could have been an alternative route for the Stuarts in England. Between 1713 and 1740 Frederick William I forged a powerful propaganda tool out of pietism and cameralism, the potentially

---

[18] G. Hudson, 'Ex-Servicemen, War Widows and the English County Pension Scheme 1593–1679', D.Phil. thesis, Univ. of Oxford, 1995; J. Innes, 'The Domestic Face of the Military-Fiscal State: Government and Society in Eighteenth-Century Britain', in L. Stone (ed.), *An Imperial State at War: Britain from 1689 to 1815* (1994), 111.

[19] B. Pullan, 'Charity and Poor Relief in Italian Cities', *Continuity and Change*, 3 (1988), 177–208; and for particular cities, B. Pullan, *Rich and Poor in Renaissance Venice* (Oxford, 1971), and J. Henderson, *Piety and Charity in Late Medieval Florence* (Oxford, 1994); J. I. Israel, *The Dutch Republic: Its Rise, Greatness and Fall 1477–1806* (Oxford, 1995), 354–60.

[20] M. Lindemann, *Patriots and Paupers: Hamburg, 1712–1830* (New York, 1990), 29–31. For the difficulties of boards of health trying to exercise authority in Italy, see C. M. Cipolla, *Public Health and the Medical Profession in the Renaissance* (Cambridge, 1976), ch. 1.

[21] A. Lindenmeyr, *Poverty is Not a Vice: Charity, Society and the State in Imperial Russia* (Princeton, NJ, 1996), 27–33.

divergent ideologies of religious reform and state regulation for the *gemeine Beste,* the common good. Reforming schools and workhouses and cutting the corporate privileges of guilds and companies down to size, he created a regime which was culturally as well as politically centralized.[22] His borrowings from August Francke make him look like the godly prince Samuel Ward of Ipswich hoped for, and he had the commitment to economic reform which William Petty would have welcomed in a royal patron.[23] Whether either of them would have appreciated the approximation to a 'command economy' finally erected by Frederick the Great is perhaps doubtful, but Charles I and James II might dearly have wished they had been able to travel down the same route.

It takes only a moment's reflection, however, to see that the circumstances which gave opportunities for state-building east of the Elbe were totally unlike those in England. Better comparators lie further west, where civic and corporate institutions were much more strongly rooted. The dukes of Savoy, for example, undoubtedly aimed at a 'police architectonical' of a Hawksmoor kind in the years around 1700, but they failed to impose a unified system of control on subsidiary charitable bodies, despite the fact that they had been partly responsible—in alliance with Andrea Guevarre—for their creation.[24] The problem was still greater for would-be absolute monarchs in France, whose well-publicized achievements Hawksmoor and the Stuarts so much admired. In practice their strategy had necessarily to be accommodation with other public and semi-public agencies. Colin Jones's studies of French charity and welfare in the seventeenth and eighteenth centuries lead him to the conclusion that 'the absolutist government in France . . . tended to support diversity and bolster existing privileges, balancing its own centralizing instincts with the conservation of local and corporative liberties'.[25]

That sounds very like the English situation described in previous chapters. Yet Professor Jones goes on to identify an important difference:

For all the trappings and rhetoric of absolute monarchy, and the occasional ringing declaration of intent, the French State during the Ancien Regime never achieved the kind of uniformity and community obligation in the relief of poverty that the English State achieved through the generalization of the parish-based rating system from the sixteenth century onwards.

[22] R. L. Gawthrop, *Pietism and the Making of Eighteenth-Century Prussia* (Cambridge, 1993), chs. 9, 11. For the Cameralist background, see M. Raeff, *The Well-Ordered Police State: Social and Institutional Change in the Germanies and Russia, 1600–1800* (New Haven, Conn., 1983), 41, 88–9, 121–5.

[23] Above, pp. 43, 92.

[24] S. Cavallo, *Charity and Power in Early Modern Italy: Benefactors and Their Motives in Turin, 1541–1789* (Cambridge, 1995), 86–94, 191–3. On Guevarre see also above, p. 136.

[25] C. Jones, *The Charitable Imperative: Hospitals and Nursing in Ancien Regime and Revolutionary France* (1989), 4.

From a French standpoint, therefore, it is possible to see the English government not as unusually circumscribed but as unusually powerful; and the
same lesson might be drawn if one adopted a more insular perspective and
looked at the four nations of the composite British state. From that point of
view, it is Ireland which is at a European extreme, unique in having no
nationwide system of public provision for the poor at all until 1838.[26]

With the Irish exception, however, a mixture of institutions, voluntary or
formally corporate, beneath a state umbrella of greater or lesser intrusive
effect, seems to have been characteristic of the organization of welfare in
western Europe, just as it had been characteristic of its general social and
political structure since the Middle Ages.[27] In the eighteenth century extra
ingredients were added, first and most quickly in England and Holland with
their new voluntary associations, but also in other countries where clubs and
societies as well as craft organizations increased in number and prominence.[28]
One result was debate about the consequences, about the virtues and vices
of particular kinds of association, and more generally about the boundaries
between private and public and how they should be defined and policed.[29] In
parts of Germany, including but not confined to Prussia, state supervision of
corporate bodies became a political ideal as well as practical policy, as it did
in France before and during the Revolution.[30] Guilds and corporations might
indeed be seen, by historians as well as contemporaries, and in England as
well as in Germany and France, as obstacles to rational economic reform and
development.[31] On the other side there was widespread admiration for the
purely voluntary charitable associations of England, and general appreciation that societies of all kinds might be bastions of free inquiry and civic

[26] Ibid.; J. Innes, 'What Would a "Four-Nations" Approach to the Study of Eighteenth-
Century British Social Policy Entail?' (unpublished paper, to which I am much indebted).

[27] On the latter, see Reynolds, *Kingdoms and Communities.*

[28] Israel, *Dutch Republic*, 1015; R. van Dülmen, *The Society of the Enlightenment: The
Rise of the Middle Class and Enlightenment Culture in Germany* (Cambridge, 1992), 10;
G. Rosser, 'Crafts, Guilds and the Negotiation of Work in the Medieval Town', *P&P*, 154
(1997), 6, n. 10; D. Garrioch, *Neighbourhood and Community in Paris, 1740–1790* (Cambridge, 1986), 173–80.

[29] D. Castiglione and L. Sharpe (eds.), *Shifting the Boundaries: Transformation of the
Languages of Public and Private in the Eighteenth Century* (Exeter, 1995).

[30] Oz-Salzberger, *Translating the Enlightenment*, 142–53; van Dülmen, *Society of the
Enlightenment*, 136; M. P. Fitzsimmons, 'The National Assembly and the Abolition of
Guilds in France', *Historical Journal*, 39 (1996), 133–54. Cf. Black, *Guilds and Civil Society*,
ch. 13.

[31] Fitzsimmons, 'National Assembly', 133–4; S. Ogilvie, 'Institutions and Economic
Development in Early Modern Central Europe', *Trans. Roy. Hist. Soc.*, 6th ser., 5 (1995),
221–50; Thomas Short, quoted above, p. 132; J. P. Cooper, 'Economic Regulation and the
Cloth Industry in Seventeenth-Century England', *Trans. Roy. Hist. Soc.*, 5th ser., 20 (1970),
95. For an example of Cooper's point that 'one aspect of the [1688] Revolution was the
triumph of local interest and the selfishness of corporations over economic reason', see the
opposition to naturalization proposals discussed in D. Statt, *Foreigners and Englishmen: The
Controversy over Immigration and Population, 1660–1760* (Newark, NJ, 1995), 96–7.

activism—or insubordination and subversion, depending on one's viewpoint. Whether they were objects of suspicion or approbation, there was no doubt about their importance.

There can be little doubt either about the distinctiveness of western Europe in this respect. The vitality and variety of its collective entities seem for centuries to have set it apart from other regions of the world. According to Toby Huff, for example, that was one reason why the rise of early modern science occurred in Europe and not in China or the Islamic world: in his view the early development of a theory of corporations in medieval Europe was crucial to cooperative scientific inquiry.[32] His argument bears some resemblance to that of E. L. Jones, who, again comparing Europe with China and Islamic countries, saw the whole 'European miracle' as a consequence of a number of competitive nation states, each providing a multitude of services for its citizens.[33] Since subsidiary and indeed competitive corporations were often the agents of Jones's 'service states', the two hypotheses about Europe's uniqueness can easily be yoked together. Whether in fact such radical consequences necessarily followed may, of course, be disputed. But for our purposes the worldwide comparison is salutary in setting England in its context: as one of a number of states whose history had by the eighteenth century given them a variety of corporate institutions and an unusual degree of civic consciousness as a result. Whatever arguments there may have been about the costs and benefits, they were all civil societies.

III

Against that background, any peculiarities there might have been in the English situation look like matters of detail rather than substance. There seems nothing very remarkable in the shifts of emphasis between central direction and local initiatives, between grand aspirations for reform and the pursuit of perfection in small communities, which have been discussed in this book. One might even ask whether the outcome—the varied mixture of voluntary, local, and public welfare provision in early Hanoverian England—was the result simply of political accident. It would be possible to argue that the closing off of some potential avenues of development was a consequence of political events: the defeat of monarchical absolutism in the 1640s or 1688, and of the advocates of comprehensive godly reform in 1660

[32] T. E. Huff, *The Rise of Early Modern Science: Islam, China and the West* (Cambridge 1993), ch. 4. Susan Reynolds stresses that the theory developed only slowly and far behind reality, but agrees on the importance of the collectivities themselves: *Kingdoms and Communities*, 36, 63–4. Cf. S. Reynolds, 'The History of the Idea of Incorporation or Legal Personality: A Case of Fallacious Teleology', in S. Reynolds, *Ideas and Solidarities of the Medieval Laity* (1995), ch. 6.

[33] E. L. Jones, *The European Miracle: Environments, Economies and Geopolitics in the History of Europe and Asia* (Cambridge, 1981), ch. 7 and pp. 237–8.

or after the 1690s. The flowering of associative and voluntary activity followed naturally.

Previous chapters have, I hope, shown that the story is more complicated than that. One can point to what one might call internal contradictions undermining each of the options I have looked at: the tendency of godly reform when confronted by reality to end in the enclosed and cloistered virtue of the gathered church or reformed hospital; the tension within early Stuart monarchy between the public rhetoric of power and the pursuit of profit which involved alliance with groups of adventurers; the inconsistency in the search by Hartlib and other projectors for powerful state patronage for a programme which rested not only on individual investigation and the nationwide free exchange of information but on collegiate discussion in societies of the like-minded; the unlikelihood, to put it no higher, of Parliament being able to produce a coherent programme when it represented and had to mediate between different group interests.

It would be a brave historian who argued with confidence that any one of these could have succeeded in imposing a purposeful, centralized, reforming agenda on the others. One might even suggest, remembering again the later fifteenth century and the European context, that the ultimate victors were inevitable from the beginning: that there was in 1500 already a deep-seated political culture which privileged local and corporate organizations, which easily overcame threats to it, and which, like a selfish gene, selected out from new stimuli those elements which enabled it to survive and thrive: corporations, civil parishes, trusts, voluntary societies.

There is much to be said for such a view. Yet it needs to be brought into harmony, finally, with an alternative and equally persuasive theme in English history and historiography: namely, the unusual strength of the central state. As early as the late Anglo-Saxon period, James Campbell finds a 'nation state', 'uniform and sophisticated' in its operation, supported by a system of public law scarcely threatened by other jurisdictions.[34] It was that which allowed later governments to command and impose uniformity, and to create, among other things, the system of parish poor rates which seemed to Colin Jones so remarkable when seen from the other side of the English Channel.

In the English case, therefore, we have an intriguing paradox: state and collectivities apparently flourishing together, neither diminished by the other. Far from being inevitably in conflict, or simply coexisting as they had to do in other countries, in England they gained from cooperation. Though there might be tensions between them, in practice they were mutually

---

[34] J. Campbell, 'The Late Anglo-Saxon State: A Maximum View', *Proceedings of the British Academy*, 87 (1995), 47; J. Campbell, 'Observations on English Government from the Tenth to the Twelfth Century', *Trans. Roy. Hist. Soc.*, 5th ser., 25 (1975), 54.

reliant. Campbell's early medieval state derived its authority from 'an extensive political nation . . . organised in an orderly hierarchy of vill, hundred and shire'; and one of the state's earliest activities was the maintenance of the public services of roads and bridges, where it necessarily depended upon these and other subsidiary bodies. They in their turn needed the sanction of the state if they were to have any continuing authority, as with the 'Commonalty of Rochester Bridge'—to cite a famous and long-lived example—which was legitimized by royal patents under Richard II and then by statute in 1576.[35] If local authorities were to force citizens to pave streets, they similarly required royal grants of pavage or, later on, enabling Acts of Parliament like those obtained by a number of towns between 1472 and 1487.[36] Many of the bodies empowered in these ways, including the custodians of Rochester Bridge, were in existence before they were officially recognized: it took time for the law to catch up with their presence and to define, for example, the notion of a corporation. But once it had done so, its authority was acknowledged and its constraints accepted along with the privileges it conferred. It is necessary to think of state power and community power in symbiosis, each dependent upon and supporting the other.

Even the Henrician and Edwardian dissolutions, the most powerful threat to the corporate fabric ever mounted in England, did not upset that reciprocal relationship for very long. Whatever the ambitions of the early Tudor monarchy, it was unable to dispense with corporations and little commonwealths. As we saw in Chapter 1, it needed them to run its houses of correction and to maintain hospitals and schools.[37] It equally needed the community of the parish to manage the poor law. Uniform poor rates might from one point of view demonstrate the power of the state: its ability to use local units for taxation purposes, as it had used the vill since at least 1334. But they showed also the strength of the parish as an institution, already in the 1520s capable of raising as much money for local purposes as the Crown was demanding from it in taxation.[38] Though intended as a residual last

[35] Campbell, 'Late Anglo-Saxon State', 52; J. Campbell, 'Was it Infancy in England? Some Questions of Comparison', in M. Jones and M. G. A. Vale (eds.), *England and her Neighbours 1066–1453: Essays in Honour of Pierre Chaplais* (1989), 1–18; N. Yates and J. M. Gibson (eds.), *Traffic and Politics: The Construction and Management of Rochester Bridge, AD 43–1993* (Woodbridge, Suffolk, 1994), 53, 130.

[36] *RP* vi. 49, 177, 179–80, 333, 391 (Gloucester, Canterbury, Taunton, Cirencester, Southampton, Winchester, and Bristol). For royal grants of pavage, see e.g. M. Carlin, *Medieval Southwark* (1996), 223–4.

[37] Above, pp. 26–7. The symbiosis between central and local government more generally in Tudor England is stressed in P. Williams, *The Tudor Regime* (Oxford, 1979), e.g. 463–6.

[38] C. Dyer, 'The English Medieval Village Community and Its Decline', *Journal of British Studies*, 33 (1994), 416; B. Kümin, *Shaping of a Community: The Rise and Reformation of the English Parish c.1400–1560* (Aldershot, Hants, 1996), 193; R. Smith, 'Charity, Self-Interest and Welfare: Reflections from Demographic and Family History', in M. Daunton (ed.) *Charity, Self-Interest and Welfare in the English Past* (1996), 32. The reasons for the shift of local responsibility from vill to parish in the later 15th and early 16th cs. have still to be properly investigated.

resort and not as the bureaucratic monster it ultimately became, the old poor law in effect furnishes the most striking example of state and community interacting creatively.

The advent of new forms of association in the later seventeenth and early eighteenth centuries did not change this state of affairs in any fundamental way. The law of charity and trusts, of corporations and companies, continued gradually to evolve, slowly responding to changing circumstances, but once formulated determining whether and how the collective bodies it recognized could hold and transfer property, borrow on its security, and limit their liabilities. The South Sea Bubble Act, for example, shaped behaviour in the 1720s as effectively as the Monopolies Act had 100 years before. For business companies it placed 'a premium upon the authority given by charter or Act of Parliament' to corporations, and thus encouraged resort to statute, but without inhibiting the birth and development of other kinds of voluntary organizations.[39] For several centuries England seems to have been able, more easily than other countries, to enjoy the benefits of both a flourishing corporate and voluntary sector and a powerful central authority and legal system, without the second smothering the first. It may be that that fine balance was what was peculiar, and peculiarly advantageous, in the English situation, in its culture as well as in its politics.

IV

What is certain, amid so much speculation, is that much had changed between the later fifteenth and early eighteenth centuries. Despite underlying continuities in assumptions and practices, definitions of public welfare had been stretched and articulated in new forms, and the agencies which delivered it had become more various and more self-consciously purposeful. Each of my episodes had contributed something to the outcome, so that there was a whole web of provision for public welfare, parts of it public and compulsory, parts of it not. Easily the most important part, however, and the backbone which gave substance to the whole, was indisputably public: the machinery which provided outdoor relief at the parish level, the inadvertent but increasingly indispensable creation of the Act of 43 Elizabeth.

Derided by successive generations of reformers as either too purposeless or too expensive, outdoor relief survived the Workhouse Test Act of 1723 and continued to grow. By 1750 poor rates were raising £690,000 a year, perhaps 1 per cent of the national income, sufficient to support nearly 8 per

---

[39] A. B. Dubois, *The English Business Company after the Bubble Act 1720–1800* (Cambridge, Mass., 1938), 435–6. Cf. J. Innes, 'The Local Acts of a National Parliament: Parliament's Role in Sanctioning Local Action', in D. Dean and C. Jones (eds.), *Parliament and Locality 1660–1939* (Edinburgh, 1998),36; and on limited liability, above, p. 130, n. 19. For increasing resort to parliamentary authority, see also P. Langford, *Public Life and the Propertied Englishman 1689–1798* (Oxford, 1991), 166–9.

cent of the population of England and Wales, most of them in their own homes. No other state could do that, though there were attempts in Scandinavian countries in the early eighteenth century to emulate it.[40] Equally, no other society could so easily have taken on board the notion that the poor had an entitlement to subsistence, an assumption which rested as much on the Elizabethan statutes as on the writings of John Locke until both were challenged by Malthus and a later school of political economy.[41]

Until then, a publicly funded system of relief was the foundation which allowed Englishmen to debate other means of regulating the poor almost as a luxury; and which permitted them to indulge their benevolence in ways which did not need to embrace the disadvantaged and the dispossessed with either the courage or the humility evident in some European versions of the new philanthropy of the Counter-Reformation. It was also a foundation which was by European standards astonishingly successful. In the early 1740s, England avoided the great subsistence and mortality crises which afflicted other countries, including Ireland;[42] and Professor Post's comparative study attributes that to 'the scale of welfare resources' exploitable by 'the rationalised social organisation' of the parish poor law. Prussia and Denmark were as fortunate as England, but hunger was mitigated there by an organized network of public granaries of the kind suggested in England from the time of James I to that of Davenant, but never implemented.[43]

To say that England did not need to be as *étatiste* and centralizing in its social policies in the eighteenth century as some other European countries is not to return to an interpretation based on economic circumstances. It is to say that the events of the sixteenth and seventeenth centuries which proved that centralizing social policies were politically impracticable had also left a residue of achievements which made them unnecessary.[44] The state could happily leave voluntary activity to fill the gaps and turn its attention elsewhere. Archbishop Temple might have said that eighteenth-century Britain

[40] Slack, *English Poor Law*, 30; R. Jütte, *Poverty and Deviance in Early Modern Europe* (Cambridge, 1994), 203.

[41] P. Slack, *Poverty and Policy in Tudor and Stuart England* (1988), 5–6, 192–4; T. A. Horne, *Property Rights and Poverty: Political Argument in Britain 1605–1834* (Chapel Hill, NC, 1990), 71–2, 167. On Locke, see also R. Ashcraft, 'Lockean Ideas, Poverty, and the Development of Liberal Political Theory', in J. Brewer and S. Staves (eds.), *Early Modern Conceptions of Property* (1995), 45–6.

[42] The Irish famine may have had a knock-on effect on England, aggravating epidemic disease and mortality there: J. Schellekins, 'Irish Famines and English Mortality in the Eighteenth Century', *Journal of Interdisciplinary History*, 27 (1996), 29–42.

[43] J. D. Post, *Food Shortage, Climatic Variability, and Epidemic Disease in Preindustrial Europe: The Mortality Peak in the Early 1740s* (Ithaca, NY, 1985), 174–201.

[44] Cf. oversight of local government more generally, where direct Crown involvement was arguably unnecessary after 1660 because it had become a routine judicial matter: negligence was identified and proceeded against under writs of *mandamus* and *certiorari*: J. Morrill, 'The Sensible Revolution', in J. I. Israel (ed.), *The Anglo-Dutch Moment: Essays on the Glorious Revolution and Its World Impact* (Cambridge, 1991), 102.

could afford to be a warfare state because eighteenth-century England was already, in attitude and practice, a welfare state.[45]

When the low-pressure regime of the late fifteenth century in some respects returned in the early eighteenth century, therefore, the machinery of public welfare had been ratcheted up by several notches. Parish vestries were running a flexible, if expensive, face-to-face relief system. A multitude of corporations, trusts, and voluntary associations was managing various kinds of service, including the hospitals and workhouses whose changing functions over two centuries we have surveyed. The mixture might not be fundamentally different in character from that of the later Middle Ages, but it was richer, better-resourced, with ends which were more closely defined and more effectively achieved.

One result, the product as much of continuity as of change, was a strengthening of the kind of civic consciousness which came from wide participation in the shaping and delivery of public welfare. Another was the creation of that Hanoverian society whose appetite and capacity for piecemeal betterment were universally admired, but whose resistance to radical reform from the centre economic and social projectors continued to lament. In short, it was a society which found improvement easier than reformation: an attribute, one might venture to suggest, which is common to all civil societies.

One reason for that is perhaps their consciousness of their particular and particularist histories. Christ's Hospital, Abingdon, has featured before in this book. Incorporated successor of a guild which had, among other things, built the great bridge across the Thames, it was itself one of the bridges across what might have been the great caesura of the English Reformation. In the 1620s, when Robert Burton was drawing up his prescription for a reformed and reforming nation, one of the hospital's governors, Francis Little, looked backwards: not to the past of the whole kingdom, though he knew something about it, having been MP in 1597, but to the past of his own little commonwealths: the municipality and hospital of Abingdon, with their charters, and the endowed school which both supported.[46] Seeing, as he well might, transience and change as well as continuity, he began to collect portraits of their benefactors and records of their deeds; and he urged his

---

[45] Prof. Pat Thane thinks comparison with a welfare state too sanguine, because the old poor law remained 'overwhelmingly residual in character': 'Old People and their Families in the English Past', in Daunton, *Charity, Self-Interest and Welfare*, 121. The extent to which it was residual is perhaps open to argument, but I am fortified in my adherence to the analogy by Prof. Stone's description of Napoleonic Britain as a 'warfare–welfare state': *Imperial State at War*, 21.

[46] G. Rosser, 'Solidarités et changement social: les fraternités urbaines anglaises à la fin du Moyen Âge', *Annales: Économies, Sociétés, Civilisations*, 48 (1993), 1140–1; P. W. Hasler, *The History of Parliament: The House of Commons 1558-1603* (3 vols., 1981), ii. 480.

successors as masters of the hospital to continue his work, as indeed they did.

Such memorials were reminders of how small improvements might surmount and subdue radical reformations. They also created corporate loyalties and civic identities. But in Little's view they did more than that. They gave some semblance of permanence to fragile human achievements. 'When all commonweals, cities and towns do end and perish,' he assured his readers, 'yet the histories thereof do remain and live.'[47]

[47] Francis Little, *A Monument of Christian Munificence,* ed. C. D. Cobham (Oxford, 1871), 94–5.

INDEX

Abbot, Robert 40
Abingdon (Berks.) 23, 26
    Christ's Hospital 25, 148, 165–6
    Holy Cross guild 148, 165
    school 22, 165
absolute power 53, 72, 92, 100, 128, 158–9,
    160–1
    see also command economy; political
        economy; royal prerogative
accountability 141–3, 149
Acle (Norf.) 38
Acts of Parliament, *see* statutes
Addenbrooke, John 137
agency 2, 12, 126
Agra 99
agricultural improvement 3, 69–70, 78, 80–
    1, 86
Aldrich, John 38 n., 39, 44
alehouses 43, 50, 60, 61, 62, 73
almshouses 25, 26, 110 n., 122, 131
    see also hospitals
Amsterdam 97
Andrew, D. 138
Andrewes, Thomas 85, 86
Andrews, Sir Matthew 110
Anglican societies 111, 117
    see also Reformation Societies; Society for
        Promoting Christian Knowledge;
        Society for the Propagation of the
        Gospel
apparel, excess in 34
    see also sumptuary laws
apprentices 54
    pauper 62, 66, 67
    see also children
Archer, I. W. 47
Armstrong, Clement 8, 14
army 65, 92
    see also maimed soldiers
Arnold, Sir Nicholas 23, 38 n.
Ashford (Kent) 110 n.
Aske's Hospital, Hoxton 120 n.
associated philanthropy 113, 153
    see also subscriptions
associative activity, *see* rights of association;
    voluntary associations
Atlantis, new 2
    see also Utopias

Atterbury, Francis 114
Aylesbury Men Case 117 n.

Baber, John 46
Bachelor, John 107 n., 111
Bacon, Francis 59–61, 69–72, 77, 80, 83, 84
    n., 88, 145
Bacon, Sir Nathaniel 42 n.
Bacon, Nicholas 26
balance of trade 93
Banbury (Oxon.) 35
Bankes, Sir John 69
Barnard, T. C. 93
Barnes, T. G. 57, 73
bastardy rates 51, 122 n.
Bath (Som.) 102 n., 132
Baxter, Richard 48, 52, 87
Beake, Robert 47 n.
Beale, John 87
Bedford, Earl of, *see* Russell, Francis
Bedford, Arthur 107 n., 113, 115 n.
Bedford Level 70
beer consumption 122 n.
beggars 8, 15, 16, 35, 44, 52, 77
Bell, Henry, junior 104, 105, 113, 115
Bell, Henry, senior 104
Bell, Robert 38, 104 n.
Bell, Thomas 18
Bellers, John 107, 108, 134 n., 137
Bentham, Jeremy 147
Bere, Thomas 110 n.
bien publique 6, 75
    see also public good
bills of mortality 93, 95, 100, 105, 135, 146,
    147
Black, A. 151 n.
Black Death 5, 153–4
    see also plague
Blith, Walter 81, 83
Board of Trade 102, 106, 109, 121 n.
    see also Council of Trade
boards of health 72, 157
Boghurst, William 99
Bologna 156
Bonner, Edmund, Bishop of London 19
bonum commune 6 n.
bonum publicum 1, 75
    see also public good